THE ANGLO-DUTCH WARS
OF THE SEVENTEENTH CENTURY

MODERN WARS IN PERSPECTIVE

General Editors: *H.M. Scott and B.W. Collins*

This ambitious new series offers wide-ranging studies of specific wars, and distinct phases of warfare, from the close of the Middle Ages to the present day. It aims to advance the current integration of military history into the academic mainstream. To that end, the books are not merely traditional campaign narratives, but examine the causes, course and consequences of major conflicts, in their full international political, diplomatic, social and ideological contexts.

ALREADY PUBLISHED

Mexico and the Spanish Conquest
Ross Hassig

The Anglo–Dutch Wars of the Seventeenth Century
J.R. Jones

The War of the Austrian Succession, 1740–1748
M.S. Anderson

The Wars of Frederick the Great
Dennis Showalter

The Wars of Napoleon
Charles J. Esdaile

The Spanish–American War: Conflict in the Caribbean
and the Pacific 1895–1902
Joseph Smith

The Wars of French Decolonization
Anthony Clayton

China at War, 1901–1949
Edward L. Dreyer

THE ANGLO-DUTCH WARS OF THE SEVENTEENTH CENTURY

J.R. Jones

LONGMAN
London and New York

Longman Group Limited,
Longman House, Burnt Mill,
Harlow, Essex CM20 2JE, England
and Associated Companies throughout the world.

Published in the United States of America
by Longman Publishing, New York

© Longman Group Limited 1996

First published 1996

ISBN 0 582 05631 4 CSD
ISBN 0 582 05630 6 PPR

British Library Cataloguing-in-Publication Data

A catalogue record for this book is
available from the British Library

Library of Congress Cataloging-in-Publication Data

Jones, J. R. (James Rees), 1925–
    The Anglo-Dutch wars of the seventeenth century / J.R. Jones.
        p.   cm. — (Modern wars in perspective)
    Includes bibliographical references and index.
    ISBN 0–582–05631–4 (CSR). — ISBN 0–582–05630–6 (pbk.)
        1. Anglo-Dutch War, 1652–1654. 2. Anglo-Dutch War, 1664–1667.
    3. Anglo-Dutch War, 1672–1674. 4. Great Britain—History, Naval–
    –Stuarts, 1603–1714. 5. Netherlands—History, Naval. I. Title.
    II. Series.
    DJ152.J66   1996
    949.2′04—dc20   95–36087
                                                                   CIP

Set by 5 in 10/12 pt Sabon
Produced by Longman Singapore Publishers (Pte) Ltd.
Printed in Singapore

CONTENTS

List of maps	vi
Abbreviations	vii
Chronological Table	ix
Preface	xi

THE CONTEXT OF THE ANGLO-DUTCH WARS

1	Introduction	3
2	The Marine Background	16
3	Materiel, Personnel and Administration	38
4	War and the Dutch State	64
5	War and the English State	82

THE COURSE OF THE ANGLO-DUTCH WARS

6	The First War, 1652–54	107
7	The Second War, 1665–67	145
8	The Third War, 1672–74	179
9	Conclusion	217

Select Bibliography	226
Maps	231
Index	235

LIST OF MAPS

1 Britain and its seas   232

2 The Battlegrounds   234

ABBREVIATIONS

BL	British Library
Cal.Cl.SP	F.J. Routledge (ed.), *Calendar of the Clarendon State Papers*, vol. v, (Oxford, 1970)
CSPD	*Calendar of State Papers, Domestic*
CSPVenetian	*Calendar of State Papers, Venetian*
Colenbrander	H.T. Colenbrander, *Bescheiden uit Vreemde Archieven omtrent de Groote Nederlandsche Zeeoorlogen* (The Hague, 1919)
DLC	P. de la Court, but attributed to John De Witt, *The True Interest of the Republic of Holland* (1746)
EIC	East India Company (English)
FDW	S.R. Gardiner and C.T. Atkinson (eds), *Letters and Papers Relating to the First Dutch War, 1652–1654* (1898–1930)
HMC	*Historical Manuscripts Commission*
MP	Member of Parliament
Mignet	L.M. Mignet, *Négociations relatives à la succession d'Espagne sous Louis XIV* (4 vols; Paris, 1835–42)
Pepys	R. Latham and W. Matthews (eds), *The Diary of Samuel Pepys* (1970–83)
PRO	Public Record Office
Thurloe	T. Birch (ed.), *A Collection of the State Papers of John Thurloe* (1742)
VOC	Verenigde Oostindische Compagnie (East India Company)
WIC	Westindische Compagnie
Wicquefort, *Histoire*	A. de Wicquefort, *Histoire des Provinces-Unies* (4 vols; Amsterdam, 1861–74)

The words ship and ships in the text invariably mean men-of-war; vessels are merchantmen.

Dates are Old Style when referring to internal affairs in Britain, New Style for those of the Dutch Republic and France; when ambiguities may arise both are given; years start on 1 January.

CHRONOLOGICAL TABLE

1651	March–June	St John-Strickland mission to the Hague
	October	Navigation Act
1652	May	Tromp–Blake clash off Dover
	June	War
	July	Tromp and Blake in northern waters, off Shetland
	August	De Ruyter and Ayscue action in the Channel
	Sept./October	Kentish Knock
	Nov./December	Tromp outward bound, Dungeness
1653	Feb./March	Tromp homeward bound, Channel Fight/Portland
	June	Gabbard/North Foreland
		Close blockade
	July/August	Terheid/Texel, Tromp killed
	November	Heavy Dutch losses in four-day gales
1654	April	Treaty of Westminster ratified
1664		Holmes, then De Ruyter, raid West African forts
	December	Allin attacks Smyrna convoy
1665	4/14 March	War declared
	June	Lowestoft
	July/August	Sandwich off Norway, Bergen attack
1666	January	French declaration of war
	June	Four Days Fight
	July	St James Day/Two Days Fight
1667	June	Dutch in the Medway
	July	Treaty of Breda
1670		Secret treaty of Dover
1672	13/23 March	Attack on Smyrna Fleet in Channel

	17/27 March	Charles II declares war
	28 May/7 June	Sole Bay, Sandwich killed
	13/23 June	French take Utrecht
	July	Arlington-Buckingham embassy to Louis
1673	January	Zas and Arton, Dutch agents, arrested
	28 May/7 June	First Schooneveld action
	4/14 June	Second Schooneveld action
	August	Kijkduin/Texel
	October	Louis XIV declares war against Spain
1674	February	Charles II signs a separate peace

PREFACE

This study originates in the course on seapower which I operated at the University of East Anglia from 1964 to 1990, and consequently I owe much to all those who took this course and participated actively in the discussions and the illuminating Anglo-Dutch wargames which formed a core element. Some of the main themes were presented in a paper given as part of a series – Sea Power, Past and Present – organized by Professor Paul Kennedy at Yale in 1986 and clarified in discussions which followed afterwards, and subsequently with my colleagues in Norwich. My other, very belated, acknowledgement of a debt is to those who served in the 21st Escort Group during the final campaign of 1944–45 against the U-boats which gave me a brief experience of naval warfare and of winter weather in the Western Approaches.

I am deeply grateful for the unremitting and vigilant help and advice of the series editor, Dr Hamish Scott, throughout the long period during which this book has been under way.

THE CONTEXT OF THE
ANGLO-DUTCH WARS

1 INTRODUCTION

It cannot be said that the three Anglo-Dutch Wars of the seventeenth century have left any real impression on the national consciousness of Britain, and they have attracted comparatively little historical attention outside the Netherlands. For later generations of strategic analysts, with the very important exception of Mahan, they appeared to contain little that was interesting or relevant. Moreover, although Mahan made much use of developments and incidents during the Anglo-Dutch Wars to substantiate or illustrate his principles and conclusions, it is remarkable that the admirals, naval writers, politicians and, above all, the ruler of Wilhelmine Germany resolutely failed to see the close resemblances between the position of the seventeenth-century Dutch Republic and their own, something that should have stood out from Mahan's discussion. In particular they ignored the basic fact that the geographic disadvantages of Imperial Germany were considerably greater than those of the Dutch, that they lacked 'ready access' to the oceans with the British Isles standing across the exits from the North Sea like an eagle with its wings outstretched – as a Dutch skipper described the position before the first Anglo-Dutch War even began. Nor did Tirpitz (or his critics) see that in 1673 De Ruyter achieved as much as any fleet in being of inferior strength could ever hope to achieve, a successful defensive campaign. Of course this failure was politically motivated; a study of the Rump's reaction to the Dutch decision to set out a massively expanded fleet in 1652 would have warned the Kaiser and Tirpitz that the enlarged High Seas Fleet would be seen in Whitehall as a provocative challenge that had to be met.[1]

In the British naval tradition, and for British historians, the wars against Bourbon, Revolutionary and Napoleonic France have

---

1 The place of publication is London unless otherwise stated. H.H. Herwig, *Luxury Fleet* (1980) especially chs iii–v; Herwig, 'The Failure of German Sea Power, 1914–1945: Mahan, Tirpitz and Raeder Reconsidered', *International History Review* (1988) 10, pp. 68–105.

obscured the earlier Dutch Wars, which lacked outstanding figures to compare with Hawke, St Vincent and Nelson. Seventeenth-century sea-battles appear to be little more than crude slugging matches, devoid of much strategic or tactical skill, and without significant technological developments. Consequently they have not been generally commemorated: only two twentieth-century battleships received the names of Dutch War admirals, and eleven of the seventy-eight Captain-class frigates of the Second World War. The Dutch Wars have also faded into relative obscurity because they did not fit into the historical pattern created by Britain's foreign policies and foreign wars over the succeeding three centuries. The prevailing principle of the preservation of a balance of power in Europe, and later in the world, resulted in Britain fighting against the predominant, the would-be hegemonistic power; first against Louis XIV, with the Dutch as allies, then against the first French Republic and Napoleon, Wilhelmine Germany and Hitler. By contrast the seventeenth-century Dutch Republic appears retrospectively to be a weaker power than either the Commonwealth or Charles II's England, and in the third war the latter went explicitly against the balance of power principle, allying with France because it was the stronger state. The three wars, then, can be seen as gratuitously aggressive and fought for ignoble objectives, for gross materialistic gain. Undoubtedly many of those who were concerned with their launch and direction had been influenced by the mercantilist notions generally current, with the belief that wealth was finite, that one nation could become wealthier only by depriving its rivals of their share of international trade, and that it was by state action that this should be achieved, by protective tariffs, prohibitions and subsidies and by naval warfare.

The Navigation Acts of 1651 and 1660 have always been seen as the centrepiece of British mercantilist policies, and many historians have seen them as direct causes of the Dutch Wars, and some as evidence of the increasing or even predominant influence of the mercantile bourgeoisie, organized in the chartered companies and backed by the City.[2] The pursuit of mercantilist policies to develop and expand overseas trade, primarily at the expense of the Dutch, has been seen as a crucial outcome of the so-called English Revolution of the 1640s with its changes in the distribution of influence and power within the state, changes which were in the Marxist interpretation to survive the Restoration so that Charles II had no choice but to con-

---

2 C. Hill, 'Soviet Interpretations of the English Interregnum', *Economic History Review* (1938–9) 8, pp. 162, 167.

tinue with these policies.[3] However, the wars that resulted, and which are seen as the reason why England replaced the Dutch Republic as the predominant commercial power, are taken as read, as merely the mechanics of an inevitable and scientific process of historical change: for Marxist historians the only area of naval history which deserves detailed examination is that of naval mutinies. At the other end of the political spectrum nationalist German historians and polemicists of the nineteenth century located mercantilist policies and the emergence of professional navies in the processes of 'state-building', the construction of strong central authority which enabled England to advance its interests and acquire an empire nearly two centuries before Germany found itself in a position to begin to do the same.[4] As the British Empire, the British economy, and the navy on which both ultimately depended for survival, all began to come under pressure, the arguments used by German writers to advocate expansion were adopted for essentially defensive purposes by the British partisans of Imperial Preference and Tariff Reform. They wanted not only to turn the Empire into a federal political entity underpinned by fiscal protection but also to construct an Imperial navy to which Australia and Canada would make major contributions. All these policies ran entirely counter to the prevailing ideology of pre-1914 Britain. Cobdenite Free Trade theses always emphasized the message that free trade meant international cooperation and interdependence, and therefore acted as a major force for peace. The navy's role, according to these concepts, was to preserve peace not to wage war. It had the mission of ensuring the freedom of the seas – which in the seventeenth century had been a Dutch principle (except of course in East Asian waters). In this idealized role the English navy acted only against those who disturbed or abused this freedom; it suppressed the slave trade, checked Chinese and Buginese pirates, made invaluable hydrographic surveys of all the oceans. Its roles could hardly be further removed from the use by seventeenth-century governments of their naval power in brutal wars of aggression against the Dutch. Those wars were immoral, economically senseless and best forgotten as part, even a formative part, of the corrupt old order which had now been replaced by liberal principles and practices.

Considering the continuing strength of the maritime tradition in the Netherlands it is surprising how much less historical attention was

---

3 C. Hill, *Century of Revolution* (1961), pp. 156, 159, 210, 215–16.
4 A.V. Judges, 'The Idea of a Mercantile State', in D.C. Coleman (ed.), *Revisions in Mercantilism* (1969), pp. 51–3.

given to naval history than in Britain. J.C. de Jonge's massive volumes seemed to be sufficient.[5] The general public certainly venerated the flag-officers who sacrificed themselves in ensuring national survival in the wars forced on the Dutch by English aggression, which were seen as the heroic aspect of the Dutch Golden Age. At times these wars were used for partisan political purposes by republicans, simply because they occurred during the Stadtholderless period and consequently their successes did not contribute to the glorification of the House of Orange. De Ruyter and De Witt served as an inspiration for the Patriots of 1787 and of the later Batavian Republic. Polemical manipulation of the wars has occurred only during periods when hostility flared against Britain, for example during the war of aggression against the Transvaal. The Dutch Nazis, the NSB, tried to use them to evoke enmity to Britain. Their party greeting '*hou zee*', came from the traditional seamen's call. Mussert, in his notorious Lunteren speech in 1940, depicted Germany as the Dutch people's friend against hostile Britain. De Ruyter even appeared on a recruiting poster for the Waffen SS, with the astonishing call to 'show yourself a true Netherlander' like him by enlisting for service on the Eastern front. With the disappearance in the last years of the twentieth century of the traditional certainties, and the consequential collapse of the pillars (*zuilen*) which formed the bases of Dutch society, respect for heroism has gone totally out of fashion. Socio-historical studies have uncovered the underside of life during the Golden Age, revealing for example the miserable conditions endured by seamen in both naval ships and merchant vessels, and the characteristics which Temple attributed to the Regents of his time – the application of reason to affairs of state and the pursuit of policies based on considerations of interest – are dismissed as elitist and hypocritical. However, such simplified and dismissive views should not be allowed to obscure the essential features of the three Anglo-Dutch Wars and their importance in the development of the two states and societies in which, to very varying extents, what we see as 'modern' characteristics began to predominate.[6]

---

5 J.C. de Jonge, *Geschiedenis van het Nederlandsche Zeewezen* (5 vols; Haarlem, 1858–62). But now see J.R. Bruijn, *The Dutch Navy of the Seventeenth and Eighteenth Centuries* (Columbia, SC, 1993); the standard *Algemene Geschiedenis der Nederlanden*, vol. vii (Utrecht, 1954) pays scant attention to the wars, pp. 129–31, 141–3, 147–50.

6 S. Schama, *Citizens* (1989), p. 250; G. Hirschfeld, *Nazi Rule and Dutch Collaboration* (Oxford, 1988), pp. 251 n.39, 261, 272.

The Dutch Republic was unique in early modern Europe because it was based on a recent rebellion against a legitimate sovereign, who was 'abjured': this enabled some of its English and all its French enemies to stigmatize it as a standing threat to all monarchies. It had a federal system of government, almost all its rulers were middle class, the magistrates of towns who after 1650 curbed and controlled the clergy, and were able consequently to ensure a degree of religious freedom.[7] However, it is misleading to make generalizations about the eight provinces which, for most purposes, have to be placed in different categories. In the landward provinces aristocrats and landed gentry retained influence, and wealth and population were draining away from the towns. Only in Holland, and to a lesser extent in Zeeland, was there a predominantly urban society dependent on trade and industry, one that was the first in Europe to achieve self-sustaining economic development. It was precisely these two provinces which were deeply involved in, and affected by, the naval wars against England. Similarly, on the other side of the North Sea, it was the second most highly developed region in Europe – London, the south-eastern counties and East Anglia – which were the most involved and affected: life in the western counties, Wales and Scotland was comparatively unmarked except for higher levels of taxation. Holland provided most ships to the Dutch navy, Amsterdam practically all the most effective, the 'great ships' which could be built only in Amsterdam and Zaandam yards. Similarly the entire English naval effort depended on yards and bases around the Thames estuary, from Harwich to Chatham.[8]

However, although Holland on the one side, London and the south-east on the other, provided the sinews of war in materiel, money and personnel, they were not responsible for the outbreak of any of the wars. The States of Holland made repeated attempts to get the States General to recognize the Long Parliament after the defeat of Charles I. The foreign policy of the Rump in the three years before the first war was determined by a small self-selected group of radicals who owed their positions of power at Westminster and in the City of London to coups which were backed by military force. There was consultation between the Commonwealth Council of State and the mercantile community through an advisory Council of Trade,

---

7 For the development and detail of Dutch government see J.I. Israel, *The Dutch Republic: Its Rise, Greatness and Fall 1477–1806* (Oxford, 1995).

8 For all materiel aspects of the respective navies see F. Fox, *Great Ships: The Battlefleet of Charles II* (Greenwich, 1980).

and after the Restoration ministers arranged for the chief trading companies to be invited to submit their views, and grievances against the Dutch, to a committee of the House of Commons (1664). But the crucial decisions to embark on wars, or on policies with a high risk of provoking a war, were taken by ministers and politicians who cannot be said to be acting under pressure, or in direct response to mercantile calls for action. The determinants of foreign policy, of decisions of war or peace, in England and the Dutch Republic were essentially dissimilar.

In England relations with foreign states had been a peripheral issue since at least the 1620s. Critical domestic political questions absorbed the attention of successive sets of rulers, with foreign policy a subsidiary matter. The Rump Parliament and Cromwell were primarily concerned with strengthening the security of the isolated and execrated Commonwealth; in this context relations with the Dutch were influenced by the close links between the Stuart and Orange families and by the fact that only the Dutch had a navy capable of covering a major intervention in the British Isles.[9] Concentration on domestic political issues of fundamental character continued after the Restoration. Charles II's ministers, far more than Charles himself, were responsible for initiating projects to increase the powers and enhance the authority of the Crown: aggressive foreign and mercantile policies were a means towards achieving this aim. The duke of York and his associates provoked the war of 1665 by ruthlessly bringing pressure to bear on the Dutch, combining expeditions sent to destroy their forts and trade in west Africa, and to take possession of New Netherland in America, with a campaign of diplomatic intimidation by Sir George Downing at the Hague that made systematic use of all available (and some invented) commercial grievances. The naval officers associated with James wanted an actual war in order to gain prize money and promotion, the junior ministers aimed at displacing their seniors in order to gain power and higher office for themselves. The publicly stated purpose of bringing pressure to bear on the Dutch, and then for declaring war upon them when they acted in self-defence – the redress of commercial grievances, the extortion of commercial concessions that would allow English trade to expand and profit (although how this would work out in practice was never satisfactorily explained) – was real, but essentially subsidiary to the private ambitions of its instigators. The king made

9 J.R. Powell, *The Navy in the English Civil War* (Hamden, CT, 1962), pp. 178–9, 1983; Israel, *Dutch Republic*, pp. 604–5.

a pretence of assenting with reluctance, but his support was ensured by promises that increases in trade would benefit royal revenues, for example by the institution of a general and perpetual excise such as the Court proposed in 1666.[10]

The war of 1672 represented a second and better planned attempt to achieve these ends. It was launched without any consultation of mercantile interests and with only an unconvincing pretence of benefiting English commercial interests. This war, which depended on the secret Dover treaty of alliance with France, and involved a considerable expansion of the standing army, was designed by its initiators – James and the so-called Cabal ministers – to annihilate the Dutch, extort a large indemnity to cover the costs of the war, and appropriate much of their trade by setting up William as a puppet ruler who would accept commercial disabilities in return for protection against the Dutch republicans. The profits of a short decisive war were expected to free the Crown from a degree of dependence on Parliament which no previous monarch had ever experienced – the necessity of summoning parliamentary sessions every year since 1660 was evidence of this – and from the more general dependence on the (increasingly conditional) cooperation of the 'political nation', that is freeholders and members of urban corporations. Trading rivalry with the Dutch was by no means dead but only those merchants and trading interests with particular causes of complaint against the Dutch favoured a third war. So, in contrast to the position in Holland where the interests of trade were paramount, its *salus populi* as Cromwell himself said, on the English side governmental concern for trade was an accompaniment of the first war, in the second the means of enlisting mercantile support, but in the third a largely fraudulent pretence.

By ignoring this difference, in particular by paying virtually no attention to the third war, Charles Wilson presented what was fundamentally a flawed thesis in his pioneering study, *Profit and Power* (1957 and 1978), giving an exaggerated estimate of the influence exerted on policy-makers by contemporary English mercantilist writers and the ideas which they propagated. In what is tantamount to a postscript added to his main discussion, in a footnote, Wilson conceded the important point that their versions of mercantilist theory and practice were significantly different from those that underlaid the systems established in continental monarchies. In these systems

---

10 P. Seaward, *The Cavalier Parliament and the Reconstruction of the Old Regime* (Cambridge, 1989), pp. 259–65.

all the initiatives were the work of sovereigns and their ministers, and the primary objective was to increase the power of the ruler. Wilson argues that the English versions of mercantilism saw the ruler, or the state, as the means by which the ultimate objective of increased wealth was to be achieved, and gave equal importance to private or corporate economic interests with governments in initiating and implementing policies directed against the Dutch and intended primarily to increase the wealth of the nation. The implication is that the enhancement of the power of the ruler was a secondary consideration. Such an interpretation could be reached only by ignoring the third war. Had Wilson examined the policies that led to what was blatantly a Court-inspired war of naked aggression he would have found that few members of the mercantile community favoured the war, and none were consulted about the policies which precipitated it.[11]

Wilson's excessive attention to mercantilist writings and his exaggeration of their influence led him to neglect what in this study I contend to be a central and crucial feature of all three wars, and indeed of the whole area of politics during the decades after 1648 – the constantly changing relationships between those who claimed, both in and out of Parliament, to represent the interests of the nation (including mercantile ones), and the persons and groups in government who actually formulated and executed policy decisions. And at no other time in the whole of English or British history has this essential context to decision-making been more fluid, and the changes more sweeping and conclusive. The Rump Members of Parliament (MPs) and their City of London associates who pressed for action against the Dutch in 1651–52 suddenly lost all their influence in April and May 1653. By the end of that year the belligerent Fifth Monarchy Men, who advocated continuing the war until the Dutch, as the symbols of worldliness, had been hammered into total submission, were abruptly propelled into the wilderness by Cromwell, and they found no Moses to guide them back. In the run-up to the second war, as the consequence of his own Machiavellian designs, Charles II was in a position to choose between completely different lines of policy being advanced by two utterly dissimilar and competitive groups of ministers and courtiers. Parliament in 1670–71 voted money for ships which junior ministers, kept unaware of Charles's real intentions, said were needed to give teeth to the Triple Alliance with the Dutch and

---

11 C. Wilson, *Profit and Power* (The Hague, 1978), pp. 153–4.

Sweden in order to check France; they were of course intended to fight the Dutch. Consequently it is a principal theme in this study that all policies towards the Dutch Republic have at all stages to be directly related to a political context that was constantly changing, at times abruptly and unpredictably. This is not to deny that mercantilist arguments about the need to use the power of the state to bring about a substantial alteration in the existing commercial and maritime balance between England and the Dutch Republic attracted considerable attention and support – particularly in vulgarized forms – but the reasons for taking action were far more complex.

Sir William Temple described 'Reason and Interest' as the two characteristic marks of Dutch government during the era of True Freedom, the Stadtholderless period of 1650–72. The Interest was that of Holland, as described in the book of Pieter de la Court, that of the merchants, financiers and entrepreneurs who constituted the Regent rulers of its towns with their associates, and who were all dependent directly or indirectly on foreign trade. The Reason was provided largely by the province's pensionary, who presided over its States and communicated its recommendations to the States General, Johan De Witt, who served from 1653 to 1672. It was to his leadership, statecraft and insight that the Republic owed its survival, above all in the years of catastrophic naval defeats (1653, 1665); it was only after 1668 as his domestic support began to fragment and his external problems became intractable that his confidence and judgement became suspect.[12]

While the thesis that the English fought these three wars with the prime objective of achieving the domination of Europe's trade needs substantial qualification, it is clear that the Dutch were fighting to protect and conserve the trade on which Holland and Zeeland entirely depended. From the Dutch perspective these wars were entirely defensive: survival was the aim, there was no way in which they could hope to gain from them, to 'win'. From 1650 onwards a succession of English actions appeared to be designed to inflict serious damage to their maritime trade; the 1651 proposals for a union of the two republics was seen as a cover for political domination, which would be used to the disadvantage of the Dutch. The seizure of Dutch vessels with cargoes from France in 1650–52 was seen as achieving by violent methods the objectives that the Navigation Act 1651 was to achieve by statutory means, the crippling of the Dutch entrepôt trade which

12 Sir William Temple, *Observations upon the United Provinces of the Netherlands* (Oxford, 1972), p. 65.

depended on colonial and French commodities. The second war was preceded by much more blatant pressure: another and more extensive Navigation Act, the seizure of New Netherland, the destruction of the Westindische Compagnie (WIC) forts in west Africa. And when De Witt ruled out appeasement and retaliated in kind the English began systematically to seize Dutch vessels, including an attack on a Smyrna convoy. Another such convoy was attacked in 1672 and English ministers earlier behaved in a transparently dishonest fashion in obstructing and finally sabotaging the negotiations that had been set up in 1668 between the English and Dutch as allies for the peaceful resolution of mercantile disputes.

English seizures of Dutch vessels in the Channel and North Sea in 1650–52, 1664–65 and 1672, that is before a state of war was declared, were justified by the English claim to sovereignty over the seas – at the maximum extending as far as Finisterre and the coasts of Norway but certainly including all the waters adjacent to the Dutch Republic itself through which their trade had to pass.[13] The Rump and Cromwell were as insistent on this claim as Charles I had been, and Shaftesbury in addressing Parliament in 1673 referred to Charles II having 'the Dominion and Property of his own seas'; one of the explicit aims of the third war was to extort a recognition that the Dutch must pay licence money for fishing in 'British waters'. Such recognition would be tantamount to accepting that all Dutch vessels (and indeed naval ships also) could cross these seas only by the grace and favour of the English Crown, something that could be withdrawn without redress. The English would be able to squeeze the life out of the Dutch Republic – just as, on a smaller scale, the Dutch stopped all direct trade with Antwerp by their mastery of the estuary of the Scheldt. From the Dutch perspective the English aim in all three wars was no less than the conquest of the seas, and the reduction of the Dutch to a state of total and helpless submission.

De Witt agreed with de la Court in believing that it was in the nature of monarchical governments to wish to be conquerors and therefore to initiate policies of aggression. On the other hand they believed that, because of its very different character, a true republic was bound to be concerned primarily with trade and prosperity, self-preservation and peace. Interestingly this extremely self-centred and self-regarding opinion was not shared by one Venetian observer, who commented that the Dutch were wrong in thinking that money and trade could supply the state with the means to defend itself,

13 See T.W. Fulton, *The Sovereignty of the Sea* (1911).

the sinews of war.[14] Applying Machiavellian principles he detected a major weakness in the fact that the merchants and financiers who constituted the Regent class did not, unlike the Venetian aristocracy, serve in the navy and army, although when De Witt sailed with the fleet as a naval commissioner, and would have commanded in battle had one occurred on that sortie, he was subject to near-universal criticisms that he was out of his element. Although very different in their personalities and outlook, both Downing and Temple believed that, because they were both based on Interest, both Dutch society and the Stadtholderless form of government were more vulnerable than traditional societies and monarchical forms of government. Without the leadership of the House of Orange, and with the landowning aristocracy having very limited influence, they had no natural leaders. If they could be subjected to intense pressure men would lose confidence in the future of the Dutch Republic as the best base for their business activities and would emigrate – as their grandfathers had done from the territories reclaimed by Spain – and towns in Holland would contract and decay like those in Brabant and Flanders. Louis XIV and his ministers went further in their contempt for a bourgeois ruling class who, in their judgement, lacked the personal sense of honour and native courage to conduct affairs of state, let alone wage war; they were corrupted by their concern for material wealth – an astonishing judgement from the creator of Versailles and the new men who were establishing new aristocratic dynasties equipped with bogus genealogies.[15]

The third war differed in all essentials from the first and second. It was a planned war of aggression, not a result of miscalculations on both sides and of processes of escalation, as the first and second had been. It was fought in company with an ally, France, indeed a predominant ally whose army's invasion of the Dutch Republic came within a very narrow margin of achieving total victory. The campaign at sea by a combined Anglo-French fleet achieved very little. This was partly because an effective strategy was not worked out, and partly for the elementary reason that appalling weather hampered operations, but its failure exposed the limitations of seapower as

---

14 *Calendar of State Papers, Venetian* (henceforth *CSPVenetian*), *1671–72*, p. 291; H.H. Rowen, *The Ambassador Prepares for War* (The Hague, 1957), p. 152.

15 C.G. Picavet, *La Diplomatie française au temps de Louis XIV* (Paris, 1930), p. 159; N. Japikse, *De Verwikkelingen tussen de Republiek en Engeland* (The Hague, 1900), app. pp. liii–liv; A. de Wicquefort, *Histoire des Provinces-Unies, 1648–1676* (1861–74) (henceforth Wicquefort, *Histoire*), vol. iv, p. 435.

an instrument of conquest – even when directed against such a vulnerable target as the panic-stricken Dutch Republic (or what was left of it) in the summer of 1672.

Charles, James and the Cabal ministers required a decisive outcome of the war at sea if they were to achieve their essentially political objectives. Their aim was to convert the Dutch Republic into a client state or dependency ruled by William III as hereditary prince. He would require constant support to defend his position against his republican or Louvestein enemies, and would therefore have an identity of interest with England in limiting the wealth and influence of the mercantile elite, the Regents, who ruled during the Stadtholderless period, and consequently would accept commercial restrictions on Dutch trade. However, this political strategy contained fatal fallacies. Although William offered in early 1672 to obtain the redress of English commercial grievances in a last effort to dissuade Charles from declaring war, he made it clear to the English ambassadors who visited him in July, when Dutch fortunes of war were at their nadir, that he would never accept the role of an English client and betray the Republic as Charles expected him to.[16] Secondly, Colbert, the French minister who was responsible for finance and trade, formulated precise and specific plans for the transfer of a large proportion of Dutch trade to the companies into which he was marshalling French merchants. In the memorandum which he submitted to Louis there is no mention of the likelihood that his English allies would also be expecting to make economic gains. There is, however, no evidence of similar planning by English governmental agencies, such as the Council of Trade: it seems to have been assumed without further thought that victory would enable English merchants and trading companies to displace their Dutch competitors.[17]

Although Colbert planned to ensure that a dictated peace treaty brought France substantial economic advantages this is not to say that Louis was waging an explicitly economic war. His own objectives were diplomatic, concerned with making it certain that he would be able to obtain his dynastic 'rights' in relation to the succession to the Spanish Crown. By annexing Maastricht and the Generality lands in the south of the Dutch Republic he would virtually encircle

16 N. Japikse (ed.), *Correspondentie van Willem III en van Hans Willem Bentinck* (The Hague, 1932), vol. ii, pt I, pp. 40–1; H.T. Colenbrander, *Bescheiden uit Vreemde Archieven omtrent de Groote Nederlandsche Zeeoorlogen* (The Hague, 1919) (henceforth Colenbrander), vol. ii, p. 155.

17 Colenbrander, vol. ii, pp. 153–4.

the Spanish Netherlands, his prime objective among all the territories of Spain. More generally the defeat of the Dutch would mean the elimination of the only state with the financial resources to subsidize allies, and so form combinations of states to check and contain France. And with France as a neighbour, no Dutch government would dare to try to obstruct French policies, even if they affected Dutch interests.

The war and the alliance between the two monarchs also fitted into a long-term English political strategy, one concerned with domestic politics. The objectives of Charles, James and the Cabal ministers, but above all of James who provided with Clifford the driving force behind these policies, was to use a victorious war and the French alliance to obtain substantially greater power and authority for the Crown. The undertaking which Charles gave in the Dover treaty, and which he never fulfilled, to make a public declaration of his conversion to catholicism, would symbolize royal independence from reliance on his subjects. Louis agreed to provide him with military assistance if the declaration provoked rebellion. It is impossible to judge how serious Charles was in making this proposal, but James was in deadly earnest, as he showed by resigning his office of lord high admiral in 1673 rather than dissimulate by taking the Test and the anglican sacrament. For Charles the war and the French alliance represented a gamble from which he withdrew when both his navy and the French army failed to force the Dutch to submit. James, on the other hand, was the partisan of a permanent alliance with France, making a demonstration of his francophile sympathies by contracting a second marriage to Mary of Modena, a French protégée, in November 1673, that is at the very time that Parliament and the public were becoming violently hostile to both France and catholicism. It was not until after his accession and his break with the Tories and the Church of England that he was able to renew the attempt to realize the policies of 1670–73. But even before the war ended in 1674, when William was still technically an enemy prince, suggestions were being made for his marriage to James's elder daughter Mary. The period of political instability that followed the third war, and was a direct result of the suspicions and tensions which it provoked, did not end until 1688, when James found himself unable to fight a fourth Anglo-Dutch War because the English would not rally to him against William.

2 THE MARINE BACKGROUND

THE PHYSICAL ENVIRONMENT

All the major engagements of the Anglo-Dutch Wars were fought in a very limited area, the North Sea south of latitude 54°30', that is from the southern edge of the Dogger Bank to the Straits of Dover, and, mainly in the first war, in the Channel. This is in sharp contrast with the wars against Bourbon, Revolutionary and Napoleonic France, during which fighting ranged across the Atlantic and in the Mediterranean, Caribbean, Indian Ocean and Baltic. There are resemblances between the strategic position of the Dutch Republic in these wars with that of Imperial Germany in 1914–18, with the British Isles overshadowing their naval bases and commercial ports, like an eagle's wings over its prey, but there is an essential difference: the Dutch unlike the Germans tried to maintain a regular flow of their trade during wartime. Their vessels had to pass through the same narrow seas in which naval operations were taking place, as did the high proportion of English vessels based on London and the Thames trading with distant countries, and also the vital coal trade from the Tyne, whose cessation would have made Londoners shiver, starve and turn rebellious. Consequently it is the physical characteristics of the southern North Sea and the Channel – their winds, tides, shoals, havens, sea-gates and traffic – that provide the physical context for these wars, one which placed major constraints on all strategic and tactical decisions and moves.[1]

---

1 S.R. Gardiner and C.T. Atkinson (eds), *Letters and Papers Relating to the First Dutch War, 1652–1654* (1898–1930) (henceforth *FDW*), vol. i, pp. 31–2, 100–2. Those who directed the wars were generally ignorant of the basic facts of geography and hydrography: Clarendon did not know (until 1667) where Sheerness was; De Witt thought that the English fleet could be bottled up in the Thames estuary by two blockships. Edward Hyde, *The Life of Edward, Earl of Clarendon, being a Continuation of the History of the Great Rebellion* (Oxford, 1827), vol. iii, p. 194; T. Birch (ed.), *A Collection of the State Papers of John Thurloe* (1792) (henceforth Thurloe), vol. i, p. 557.

The most distinctive feature of this main theatre of operations was the constant close proximity of the fleets and their bases to each other. The fact that these were close-range wars cancelled out the many administrative and logistical weaknesses that had to be eradicated during the later oceanic wars of Britain against France and Spain. The short distances within a compact theatre made possible a rhythm of intensive naval warfare not to be equalled until the titanic series of battles between the United States and Japanese navies in 1942–45 – the Coral Sea, Midway, the fighting around Guadalcanal and the Philippines. Six engagements were fought in 1652–53, five in 1665–67 and four in 1672–73: compare with these the two (Vigo and Malaga) of 1702–13, and the two major battles of 1914–18.[2] But even in this compact area it was still easy for both fleets to sail expressly to meet and fight the other and to be frustrated by the physical characteristics of these narrow seas. Persistent gales, contrary winds, poor visibility, misleading or quickly outdated information, the dangers imposed by shoals, navigational uncertainties and inaccuracy, all combined on many occasions to baffle even the most belligerent commanders (like James and Rupert), and to disrupt all strategical planning.

Weather

A fundamental point that influenced everything connected with the Dutch wars is the fact that they occurred during the Little Ice Age of the seventeenth century, when the path of the high-altitude jet stream was considerably further south than in the twentieth, and was of greater strength. The sub-polar low-pressure belt moved further south, truncating movement northwards of anticyclones from the area of the Azores. The results were a higher incidence of severe depressions in areas from 50° to 60° north, with far more frequent severe gales than in the twentieth century, and shorter summers and growing seasons. Winds from the east and north-east were more frequent than they have been in recent times. Winter polar ice moved south; in 1670 and again in the 1690s it almost surrounded Iceland. High pressure stationary in winter over Scandinavia produced winter flows of Arctic air from the east which were often prolonged into May.[3] These aided the Dutch. Prevailing easterlies enabled them to

---

2 In logistical and administrative terms the cycle of battle–refitting–sortie–battle in 1653, 1666 and 1673 is comparable with that of Bomber Command in 1942–45.

3 H.H. Lamb, *Climate, History and the Modern World* (1982), pp. 201, 208, 233n.; Lamb, *Climate Present, Past and Future* (1977), pp. 452–3, 466–7, 490.

get their divisions to sea from the Texel, Maas and Scheldt, and to cross the North Sea in attempts to surprise the English before their ships from Portsmouth or the French from Brest in 1672 and 1673 could link up with the main fleet based on the Thames.

The Dutch were fortunate that in none of the war years were their sea-gates blocked by ice, as most of their merchant sailings had to be made during winter. However, the climatic downturn did lead to difficulties and losses. After the near-disaster of February 1653 the Channel could not be used, so Dutch merchant shipping had to be routed 'the long way round', north-about the British Isles, through latitudes where winter gales were almost continuous and bad weather was frequently encountered in most summers. In 1652 several returning vessels were driven on to the Shetlands. In November 1653 after bringing a convoy home from Norway, Witte de With was ordered by the States General, who ignored his desperate warnings, to keep his fleet outside the Texel for another sortie: a four-day gale of exceptional severity followed which caused losses of ships and men that were as great as those suffered in any of the heavy defeats of the first war.[4]

Prolonged bad weather frequently disrupted operational plans, and in 1672 affected the outcome of the war. The collapse of the Dutch landward defences – partly caused by a long winter and spring drought that lowered the level of the Rhine so that it could be forded – necessitated the landing of guns and soldiers from the fleet. This compelled De Ruyter to keep his weakened fleet behind the shoals, ready to sortie only if the allies attempted a landing. But the allies achieved nothing despite having unchallenged naval supremacy from June until September. This was almost entirely due to continuously appalling weather. Gales made it impossible to blockade the Texel or maintain station on the Dogger – the best position for intercepting homeward-bound vessels. They made it impossible to lie offshore at anchor. Councils of war could not be convened because rough seas made it unsafe for captains to be rowed to the flagship in longboats. Dismasted ships had to be sent back to dockyards. The number of sick grew. Well might an English officer complain that the Dutch must have enlisted Laplanders, outlandish nomads whom myth credited with the magic power to raise storms.[5]

---

4 *FDW*, vol. i, pp. 389–91, 400–6; vol. vi, pp. 154–6, 161–4, 175.

5 *Calendar of State Papers, Domestic* (henceforth *CSPD*) *1672 (May–September)*, pp. 5, 206, 213, 343, 413, 425, 625; *Historical Manuscripts Commission* (henceforth *HMC*) *15th Report, app. 1*, vol. iii, pp. 8–9; R.C. Anderson (ed.), *Journals and Narratives of the Third Dutch War* (1946), pp. 110–11, 115–17, 124, 126, 143.

Tides

Neither side could do more than ride out gales, but the Dutch frequently displayed superior seamanship in utilizing the tides. One Dutch captain being overhauled in light winds by superior English ships escaped by waiting until the tide was running strongly, then suddenly took in his sails and anchored; his English pursuers were carried past by the tide and could not beat back against it. On the last day of the Channel Fight in 1653 Blake stood off and anchored, confident that he had Tromp's remaining ships trapped against the French coast south of Gris Nez, but the latter used the tide to get through the Dover Straits and seek safety among the Flanders Banks. In terms of seamanship the Dutch achieved an even more spectacular success when they used an outgoing tide to take the captured *Royal Charles* down the narrow Medway and out to sea. Rupert showed equal skill and daring when he used an ebbing spring tide to take the whole fleet through shoal waters that were at other times impassable, and forced the Dutch fleet that was blockading the main channel of the Thames to withdraw.[6]

Shoals[7]

The North Sea is generally very shallow. Only a few parts of the area of operations have more than 120 feet of water, most have about 80 feet. This made anchoring in the open sea feasible with mostly good holding ground – mud, sand and shingle. Its numerous shoals greatly influenced naval operations and posed dangers to all deep-draught ships. Shaped by tidal streams, many shoals which at low water were covered by insufficient water seamed the entrances to the Thames. Those in the estuary itself – the Gunfleet Sand, Sunk, Barrow – have parts that dry out at low tide and set up identifying breakers at most other times. Much more dangerous were those like the Kentish Knock, the Gabbards and the Galloper, well out of sight of land and lying from south to north across a theoretically direct line between the exit from the Thames and the Dutch coast. Charts gave only approximate positions, which in any case shifted. Strong tidal streams made captains uncertain of their own exact position when relying on dead reckoning, and there were no other ways of estimating longitude. In wartime rudimentary navigational aids

---

6 Colenbrander, vol. i, p. 429; *FDW*, vol. iv, p. 110; Anderson, *Journals and Narratives*, pp. 81, 93, 112, 123.

7 See Map 2.

– poles or spars stuck in the sand – were often removed or not replaced after being dislodged by storms. Consequently the largest ships were often at risk: during the Four Days Fight three English ships ran aground on the Galloper and one (the *Royal Prince*) became a total loss. In 1672 a pilot took James's flagship over the Kentish Knock, with only inches of water under the keel. The English did not have the advantage of superior local knowledge of these waters since before the Navigation Acts more Dutch than English vessels used these Thames channels.[8]

Shoals on the English side created hazards. Those on the other side of the North Sea, skilfully exploited by the Dutch, proved to be a most important factor in enabling the Republic to survive, indeed one of three or four essential reasons why they were able to avoid total defeat at sea. The southernmost shoals lie in closely packed layers off the Flanders coast to which they at first, from the west, run parallel: inshore the Snouw, Breedt and Smal Banks, the Dyck, Ratel, and then ten to fifteen miles offshore the Ruytingen and Bergues. The Dutch took full advantage of two of their features, gaps running north to south between the shoals, with sufficient water for their ships to escape through when being pursued by English ships, whose captains lacked the confidence to follow. Behind the shoals there are channels running west to east (the direction taken by a rising tide), allowing a fleet to reach the safe anchorage of the Wielings without having to come out into the open sea. So these shoals provided an accessible safe refuge for the Dutch in case any engagement in the seas south of the Kentish Knock went against them. Blake and Monck compared this Dutch practice to Highlanders taking to the Scottish mountains to escape pursuit.[9]

Dutch commanders had intimate knowledge of these shoals and waters going back to their long blockades of the Dunkirk privateers before 1648. Dutch ship designs also made their captains and pilots more confident in using shoal waters. Because of the shallow approaches to their main ports (only twelve feet on the Pampus, off Amsterdam) their ships were broader in beam with far less fine or sharp lines than their English opponents. This made it possible for them to have shallower draughts, and they could lie on the bottom

8 Colenbrander, vol. i, p. 335; Anderson, *Journals and Narratives*, p. 105; *CSPD 1672 (May–September)*, pp. 87–8.

9 *FDW*, vol. v, pp. 82, 84; *HMC 15th Report, app.* 1, vol. iii, p. 9; Spragge, commenting that English charts misplaced these shoals by several miles, forecast that no 'entire' victory could be won until they were accurately surveyed.

(mud or sand) without damaging their hulls, and without heeling over so far as to displace guns, stores or ballast.[10]

In 1673 De Ruyter's use of the less extensive shoals to the north of the Wielings – the Bol van Heyst, Bol van Knokke and Droogte van Schooneveld – enabled him to organize and undertake what remains the most effective naval campaign ever waged by the commander of an inferior fleet against a vastly superior enemy force. From his secure anchorage in the Wielings, where minor damage could be repaired and supplies taken on from nearby Vlissingen, he sortied through the channel between these shoals and the shallow Raan Bank to the east. He then anchored on the edge of the Schooneveld, termed by the English his 'hole', from where he kept them under distant observation: if they sailed towards him with a westerly he could use the same wind to retire into a channel where they dared not follow, and he could also rely on using it to minimize losses if an action went against him. The more bovine English officers compared the Dutch to foxes or badgers and slated their conduct as cowardly, but De Ruyter knew, like Jellicoe at Jutland in 1916, that he could lose the war in an afternoon. As another tactic to reduce such a danger he delayed his challenges to the allies to the afternoon, so as to shorten the duration of any engagement and to strike at the allies before they could deploy their entire fleet. This prudence and his skill produced two tactically indecisive actions that in an overall strategic sense proved to be decisive. With the allied fleet unable to force a decision and with time and resources running out, and Parliament refusing to vote more money, Charles II had to drop out of the war.[11]

Further north the sea-gates to the Maas and Texel did not enjoy similar offshore protection from shoals. The Texel entrances were narrow, and difficult to use at certain states of the wind. With only one ship able to enter at a time English commanders considered a direct attack too risky, but Dutch ships seeking refuge there were also at risk. After Lowestoft and the St James Day Fight, many fleeing Dutch ships had to wait outside before the tide allowed them to enter, provoking English claims that a relentless pursuit would have infallibly led to their destruction. Similarly the Dutch ran risks when their fleet had to sortie in the face of the enemy, in 1653 to link up with ships sailing from the Wielings before Tromp's last fight. Dutch seamen somewhat fatalistically accepted these limitations, but De Witt shamed them by going out personally

---

10 See below, pp. 205–7; *FDW*, vol. v, p. 311.
11 *CSPD 1673*, pp. 300, 308–10, 338.

to sound a passage formerly regarded as impassable for large ships. Merchant vessels also made regular use of the Terschelling sea-gate, between that island and Vlieland with an extensive anchorage behind: it was here that Holmes destroyed 150 unguarded vessels in 1666. Further east the Ems estuary afforded a refuge for VOC (Verenigde Oostindische Compagnie – East India Company) and other valuable vessels, which used a route down the eastern North Sea from Norway during periods of English naval supremacy, as in 1665 and 1672.[12]

Harbours and roads[13]

A mark of the increasing professionalism of officers on both sides was the common practice of making and recording exact observations of the approaches to havens and anchorages. Those on the English side of the sea were very advantageously situated. Chatham, the main naval base and yard, lay up a winding and difficult tidal river, but the fleet anchorage at the Nore (off Sheerness) was close by, and could readily receive men and supplies from London and the depots along the lower Thames. From the Nore, used as the assembly point, the fleet could move in all but northerlies to the forward operational anchorages off the Essex coast and Sole Bay in Suffolk. The latter was well placed for supplies from Harwich, Ipswich and Yarmouth: it was accessible for scouts from the Dutch coast with intelligence of enemy movements, and the fleet could get to sea in all but constant easterlies. The Downs, the anchorage between the Kent coast and the Goodwin Sands, provided another secure and strategically well-sited haven. From there, using tides if winds were unfavourable, the fleet could observe and block the Dover Straits, move into the Channel or sail into the southern North Sea. The availability of these anchorages or roads enabled the fleet to remain at sea continuously after leaving its bases in the spring, and they were close to the yards to which the more seriously damaged ships had to be sent for repairs. During the wars Harwich was developed as a base, but with rather limited facilities. Portsmouth assumed greater importance in 1666 (when the French were enemies) and 1672–73 (when they became allies). Plymouth was used as an assembly port for London-bound EIC (East India

---

12 J.K. Oudendijk, *Johan de Witt en de Zeemacht* (Amsterdam, 1944), p. 128 plate depicting De Witt sounding; R.C. Anderson (ed.), *The Journal of Edward Montagu, first Earl of Sandwich* (1929), pp. 205–6.
13 See Map 2.

Company) and other valuable vessels, who would later be escorted up Channel.[14]

The English fleet had no bases or anchorages where supplies could be obtained north of Harwich and Sole Bay: this is another indication of how nearly all the action was concentrated in the southern North Sea. If driven north by bad weather the fleet could shelter in the lee of Flamborough Head, but when it sailed north on rare offensive missions (Blake 1652, Sandwich 1665) it was operating at the limit of logistical practicalities. Sandwich's force returned from the Bergen operation with virtually no food left, large sick lists from malnutrition, and lame ships.[15] In contrast it is difficult to see how any Dutch trade could have been continued in any of the wars without constant use of ports and anchorages in southern Norway. They provided assembly points for all homeward-bound vessels, not only those sailing north-about the British Isles but also those from the Baltic, Archangel and the Greenland and Spitzbergen fisheries. There they could wait for escort on the last and most dangerous stage of their return voyages. It was south of the Dogger that Sandwich captured two VOC vessels in 1665, and that another sailed (by night) into the middle of the allied fleet in 1673. The Dutch also used Spanish ports (particularly Cadiz) as remoter assembly points but these had the disadvantage that they were watched by English ships based on Tangier. Allin attacked but failed to take the Dutch convoy from Izmir (Smyrna) at the start of the second war close to Cadiz, and the very last engagement of the wars was a frigate action off Cadiz in 1674. However Tangier, unlike Gibraltar in later wars, did not enable the English to institute a permanent and effective guard on the Straits.[16]

Intelligence

Despite the short distances involved in campaigning in the southern North Sea, commanders at sea rarely received intelligence about enemy movements and plans in time to make use of it. Most of their information came from skippers of neutral vessels – Swedish and Hanseatic – crossing the area of operations on their way to or

14 Almost all the vessels returning from the Mediterranean, America, Africa and Asia were at this time based on the Thames and discharged their cargoes there.

15 Anderson, *Journal of Sandwich*, pp. 260–1; Colenbrander, vol. i, p. 259.

16 A.W. Tedder, *The Navy of the Restoration* (Cambridge, 1916), p. 98; F. Fox, *Great Ships: The Battlefleet of Charles II* (Greenwich, 1980), p. 55; the harbours used by the Dutch were Bergen and Flekkefjord, north of the Naze.

from the Channel. Some of this was unreliable, particularly about the exact positions of enemy sightings: most skippers navigated by dead reckoning. The most accurate intelligence concerned ship movements through the Dover Straits. In the first two wars the Dutch through Glarges, their agent at Calais, could match the English observers at Dover; using French fishermen he also reported on English use of the anchorages in the Downs. His reports reached the Hague within a day, but if the Dutch fleet had put to sea there would be indefinite delays before they could be acted on.[17]

By contrast governments received a wealth of political and background intelligence. The packet ship between Harwich and Helvoetsluis continued to cross throughout all three wars, conveying passengers, letters and, for surprisingly long periods, diplomatic couriers. The four Dutch commissioners sent in the summer of 1653 to see if a settlement could be negotiated sent back to the Hague reports on the damage suffered by the English fleet in engagements, with estimates of how long it would be before the fleet could return to sea. Similarly Downing, who remained at the Hague for months after war was declared in March 1665, bribed one of the States General's navy deputies who supplied him with information about Dutch naval preparations and strategic intentions as well as details of political developments. His paid agents met officers and seamen off the fleet, pumping them for information about battle damage and the likely time repairs would take. During the first war secretary of state John Thurloe received similar information from several correspondents, including Aitzema the historian.[18]

Only on one occasion does it seem clear that intelligence contributed in a major way to achieving a victory. In June 1653 the English learnt of Tromp's plan to sortie from the Wielings and draw off the English so that the Texel ships could come out. Afterwards critics alleged that his defeat could have been avoided if the Harwich packet had been stopped from sailing. The English defeat in the Four Days Fight (1666) was certainly attributable to intelligence – bad intelligence uncritically accepted and acted on by the Council. It persistently credited wildly inaccurate reports about the approach

---

17 *FDW*, vol. ii, pp. 61, 189, 236; vol. iii, pp. 162, 165–7, 237; vol. v, p. 231; Thurloe, vol. i, p. 389.

18 *FDW*, vol. v, pp. 408–10; vol. vi, pp. 31, 229; Oudendijk, *Johan de Witt en de Zeemacht*, pp. 96, 100 and note 4.

of the French fleet to link up with the Dutch. It sent Rupert down Channel, leaving Monck with an inferior fleet to face the Dutch.[19]

Information received from renegades and traitors was usually unreliable, and the importance of the role which they played in operations was exaggerated. Men like Howard and Bampfield, as double agents, took money from both sides. Captain Heemskerk received the credit for piloting Holmes's raiding force through the Terschelling sea-gate and received the honour of a Charles II knighthood. But Holmes actually relied on an English master who had served in Dutch vessels, and on a Danish helmsman.[20] Similarly although in popular (English) legend English seamen who had defected to fight for Dutch dollars were credited with having made possible the raid on the Medway, the Dutch themselves rightly gave the credit to their own captains and pilots. Lieutenant colonel Doleman, who had helped mediate peace in 1653–54, did command the Dutch landing force that attacked Landguard fort in 1667, but his attack failed. However, belief in a danger from traitors was common in both countries, and reflected their bitter political divisions. But although Royalist exiles hailed the Dutch victory at Dungeness (1652) as hopefully the beginning of the downfall of the Commonwealth, and Orangists hoped to turn defeat into a restoration of the Stadtholderate, neither party (nor the English republicans after 1660) significantly influenced the course of the first and second wars.[21]

WAR AND TRADE

Trade rivalries inevitably spilled over into local hostilities in all the regions of the world where the Dutch and English engaged in competition. However, naval successes in distant seas did not, and could not, affect the outcome of these wars, in marked contrast to the situation in the eighteenth-century wars against France and Spain, when blockades of enemy bases in Europe gave Britain the local superiority needed for conquests in America and the Caribbean. But conflicts outside Europe contributed significantly to the poisoning of Anglo-Dutch relations, and the use of violence by the rival trading

19 The inquiry into the 1666 failure of intelligence turned into a political hunt for scapegoats; see below, pp. 95–6, 170.

20 R. Ollard, *Man of War: Sir Robert Holmes and the Restoration Navy* (1969), pp. 151, 158.

21 Thurloe, vol. i, p. 260; G. Penn, *Memorials of Sir William Penn* (1833), vol. i, p. 466; Wicquefort, *Histoire*, vol. iii, p. 314.

companies – backed by their respective governments – in west Africa precipitated the second war.

The Baltic

In the seventeenth century the Baltic was of central, not peripheral, importance in European trade and international politics. The bulk trade with countries around it, known to the Dutch as their 'mother trade', formed the basis of their entrepôt economy, although exports of grain (largely through Danzig) declined after 1648. The involvement of Denmark, which controlled its entrances, on the Dutch side in the first and second wars meant that it remained open to the Dutch, but was closed for the English. This caused serious difficulties for the latter, who could obtain naval stores on a reduced scale only via Hamburg, and the capture of a Hamburg convoy gave the Dutch their only major success in 1665. Limited quantities of timber, of variable quality, were obtained from Scotland and New England, but the cost and uncertainty of delivery dates contributed to the fatal decision not to set out a fleet in 1667. The wars did affect Dutch trade with northern and eastern Europe. Disruption of their fisheries reduced the quantity of their staple export, herring in brine; the navy's need for seamen reduced the number of summertime sailings (and ice prevented access to eastern ports in winter, when the fleet was laid up); insurance premiums went up, and Swedish and Hanseatic vessels took over much of the carrying trade. The preferential toll which Denmark had had to concede by treaty in 1645, with collection and banking of the receipts placed under Dutch control, which would have given them a massive and permanent advantage over the English, had to be cancelled. Economic dependence and the need for protection against Sweden tied the Danes to the Dutch, but the English attempt in 1665 to capitalize on the resentment which this satellite position created failed only because of the mischances which wrecked the attempt to seize VOC and other vessels in Bergen. But had this joint piratical scheme succeeded Denmark would have become, probably temporarily, the ally of England.[22]

---

22 C.E. Hill, *The Danish Sound Dues and the Command of the Baltic* (Durham, NC, 1926), p. 121; J.T. Rutt (ed.), *The Parliamentary Diary of Thomas Burton* (1828), vol. iii, p. 438; Thurloe, vol. i, pp. 258, 287.

Trade and the guerre de course *in the North Sea and Channel*

This was the focal area through which all Dutch and nearly all English trade had to pass and were at their most vulnerable. The Dutch had experienced heavy losses in the 1630s and 1640s to the Dunkirkers waging a *guerre de course* in the service of Spain, and English trade had suffered far more than is realized during the civil wars from royalist privateers.[23] Initially the Dutch saw themselves as facing a major threat from the English fleet. In 1652 Blake sailed north to attack the fishing fleet and intercept vessels returning north-about; Tromp was sent to protect them. In November he escorted a vast outward-bound convoy down Channel, defeating Blake's attempted interception off Dungeness, but in February 1653 when using the same route to return he suffered unacceptably high losses of vessels and escorts. The near-disaster validated his view that it was impossible for the fleet to provide escort protection for convoys and at the same time fight the English fleet.[24] This experience forced a reappraisal of strategy and the adoption of new methods to safeguard trade during the second war, changes that were entirely attributable to the leadership of Johan De Witt. In the dire crisis that followed the defeat off Lowestoft (June 1665) he ignored representations for special treatment from all mercantile pressure groups, including the VOC, in imposing an embargo on outward sailings during the summer campaigning seasons. This meant that the fleet could concentrate exclusively on finding and fighting the English fleet, and that it would be adequately manned. Homeward-bound vessels from distant places were given routing instructions by consuls in Spain and, in the first two wars, France to whom information could be sent overland. 'Advice' ships were sent into the Western Approaches to meet and instruct vessels sailing direct across the ocean. All vessels from the west were to make for Norwegian ports and wait there until escorts home could be provided at the end of the summer. Alternatively if the English fleet was not likely to be out, as in 1667 after the Chatham attack, the last stage of the return route down the North Sea was likely to be comparatively risk-free: in 1666 after the Four Days Fight over-confidence led many skippers to make the attempt, only to run into the English fleet off the Dutch coast. In times of great

23 J.R. Bruijn, *The Dutch Navy of the Seventeenth and Eighteenth Centuries* (Columbia, SC, 1993), pp. 25–8; P. de la Court, but attributed to John De Witt, *The True Interest of the Republic of Holland* (1746) (henceforth DLC), pp. 157–93; J.R. Powell, *The Navy in the English Civil War* (Hamden, CT, 1962), pp. 186–7.

24 *FDW*, vols iii and iv have extended and detailed material on Tromp's outward and homeward bound convoy operations.

and obvious danger – 1665 and 1672 – even convoys had to use the longer, evasive route along the eastern fringe of the North Sea down to Heligoland and then west to the Dollart.[25]

These governmental restrictions on commercial sailings meant that the capital invested in vessels and cargoes produced no return for at least half of each year of war, and state revenues suffered from the reduction in receipts from 'convoy and licence' (customs) dues. Merchants were also desperately anxious for the safe arrival of vessels from south-western Europe and the western hemisphere with cargoes of commodities for re-export to eastern and central Europe, fearing that any lengthy interruption would lead to Amsterdam's decline as an entrepôt. But the first and third wars lasted for only two campaigns, and in the third and last year of the second war (1667) the Dutch were close to renewing a flow of trade like that of peacetime. Furthermore the Dutch economy generally, and a high percentage of individual merchants and entrepreneurs, had sufficient capital reserves to survive. In one respect embargoes, and the reduced tempo of trade that they produced, resulted in reactive developments that actually increased the effectiveness of Dutch naval power and also helped to sustain the economy. Many entrepreneurs who found themselves unable to invest their capital with any realistic hope of making quick returns switched to putting their money into capers (privateers), particularly in Zeeland where most merchants had limited financial reserves, and in Amsterdam where there was a great deal of capital with limited opportunities for investment. As in France after 1793 there was a direct correlation between downturns in economic activity and booms in privateering. Some capers needed only modest investment. Craft of up to fifty tons, with fifty or more in their crew and only six to ten guns, infested the approaches to English ports, and especially the Thames estuary, where they could attack and retire across shoal water, sometimes with the aid of oars. Larger privateers infested the Western Approaches taking valuable English and French vessels returning from the West Indies, Virginia and the Newfoundland banks, and ambushed those sailing to and from the Mediterranean and Africa off the Spanish and Portuguese coasts. The English could convoy outward-bound vessels through the most dangerous areas, but return convoys could be given only less than adequate protection of one or two ships, because colonial governors in most cases wished to retain ships for their own local defence. Oceanic rendez-vous could not be organized because there was no

25 *FDW*, vol. iii, p. 349.

way of determining longitude, and convoys usually became dispersed by the weather and the variable sailing qualities of the vessels forming them. Moreover captains often followed secret instructions from their employers to sail or 'romp' ahead, and by reaching port first obtain higher prices for their cargoes.[26]

Many historians have tended to ignore, or greatly to underestimate, the impact made by Dutch privateering during the three wars. The historiographical context for dismissive conclusions, or for not asking the question at all, is the long-lived influence of the great American historian, A.T. Mahan. As the propagandist for building a large United States battle fleet, Mahan had to demolish the popular belief that, as in the war of 1812, the appropriate role for the United States navy was commerce raiding, the *guerre de course*. Mahan propounded the thesis that this could never have decisive results; instead the navy should prepare for one or more titanic battles like Trafalgar, and the Japanese victory at Tsushima seemed to prove him right. Failing to foresee the development of U-boat warfare, admiralties and historians concentrated on battleships and fleet warfare. But if Dutch privateering is placed in the political context of the three wars it can be seen to have had a decisive influence. The mercantilists in the Rump, James's navalist and Court interest in the years before 1665 and 1672, the authors of pamphlets calling for action against Dutch competitors, all claimed that these wars would bring national, corporate and individual gains, that through an increase of the English share of international trade brought about by the use of force the wealth of the nation would be promoted. Dutch privateering successes in the second and even more in the third war contradicted these claims, and did considerable damage to the economy.[27]

In the war of 1652–54 English privateers wreaked havoc and the fleet also took many prizes; by contrast it was only in the last months that the Dutch achieved any significant successes. The English lost between 300 and 400 vessels, the Dutch far more, probably well over 1,250; the fact that some of the English vessels were more valuable than the *fluyts* which formed the bulk of the English prizes taken from the Dutch does not seem to have affected the balance between relative losses significantly. The English instigators of the second war confidently predicted an even more favourable ratio, but the number of prizes taken by each side seems to have been approximately equal,

---

26 Colenbrander, vol. i, pp. 161, 167; *CSPD 1672 (May–September)*, p. 190.
27 A.T. Mahan, *The Influence of Sea Power upon History* (1890), pp. 8, 131–8.

and since the English merchant fleet was much smaller its losses were proportionately far greater. In the third war the Dutch had much the better of the war against trade and shipping. Embargoes kept their vessels in harbour during the summers. This resulted in a doubling of the number of privateers sent out, compared with the previous wars. They infested coastal waters around the British Isles. Larger privateers operated with great success in the Western Approaches taking many valuable vessels from the Mediterranean and West Indies: they had the advantage of using Spanish ports as bases and for the sale of prizes, remitting the profits home to bolster the hard-pressed economy.[28]

Marine losses undermined business confidence in England during the war of 1672–74. Merchants and entrepreneurs had been systematically canvassed to give advance support to action against the Dutch in 1664, but no attempt at consultation was made before the third war, and in 1673 they became extremely anxious about the prospect of Charles having to follow Louis's lead in declaring war against Spain. This would certainly have plunged the economy into a severe depression. By the autumn of 1673 experience had disproved the earlier, crude mercantilist notions that wars of commercial aggression could be made to produce both short- and long-term profits and national prosperity.

The same crude mercantilist notions led to misuse of the fleet in both the second and third wars, when it was diverted after major naval victories to go commerce raiding. The cost of these operations greatly exceeded the likely profits the main fleet could hope to achieve, but personal hopes of financial gain led admirals and captains to advocate the continuation of this fallacious strategy. There were also too many in the government, especially the commissioners and sub-commissioners of prizes, who had a direct personal interest, to accept that the *guerre de course* waged by the fleet could never serve the national interest.[29]

Trade and relations with France

The exchange of bulk commodities from the Baltic region with French wine, brandy, silk, fine textiles, and the import of French salt for

---

28 Bruijn, *Dutch Navy*, p. 90; 'Dutch Privateering during the Second and Third Anglo-Dutch Wars', *Acta Historiae Neerlandicae* xi (The Hague, 1979), pp. 79–93.

29 Anderson, *Journal of Sandwich*, pp. 277–82; Ollard, *Man of War*, pp. 148–58; *CSPD 1672*, p. 634; *CSPD 1672–73*, p. 17; *CSPVenetian 1671–72*, pp. 304–5.

preserving herrings, formed the basis of the Dutch entrepôt trade. By 1650 they enjoyed a virtual monopoly. English trade had been virtually destroyed by an unofficial war which developed after 1649 between the French Court, sponsors of the exiled Stuarts, and the regicide Commonwealth. All the conditions existed then, political and economic, for a full-scale war, and for the 'export' of the English Revolution to France, a move that some historians of the Rump think that its leaders 'ought' to have made. The Fronde rebellions coincided with the French prohibitions of trade with England, but neither the Rump nor Cromwell wanted a breach with France. They declined an offer from the city of Bordeaux, before it rebelled, of exclusive trading rights. They rejected repeated approaches by the diplomatic representative of the frondeur leader Condé for an alliance against the Stuarts and their French patrons, disregarding his bait of trading privileges at the expense of the Dutch.[30]

With the re-establishment of French royal authority all trade matters became a part of state policy. After 1661 Louis XIV changed the terms of trade by authorizing Colbert's protectionist policies, which were also intended to reduce reliance on Dutch and English merchants and vessels to export French commodities. This led to a *petite guerre* of economic discrimination which continued even when either the Dutch or the English were allied to France. In 1666–67, knowing that the Dutch desperately needed his diplomatic and naval assistance Louis intensified his tariff policies, although it was his Dutch allies who were most seriously affected. Then in 1670–72, after the reversal of alliances, he evaded with ease English attempts to conclude a commercial treaty that would involve concessions on his part, because he knew that Charles needed French subsidies. The strength of his military and diplomatic position made him indifferent to the resentment of mercantile interests. When the Dutch sued for peace in 1672 he demanded that they dismantle all the protectionist barriers which they had imposed in retaliation for his measures: as a result of his victories they were to become economic as well as political dependants.[31]

---

30 Thurloe, vol. i, pp. 216, 224–5, 240, 245, 250; *CSP Venetian 1651–52*, p. 82; J.J. Jusserand, *Recueil des instructions données aux ambassadeurs et ministres de France*, vol. xxiv, Angleterre i (Paris, 1929) pp. 86, 101, 106, 150.

31 E. Frémy, 'Causes économiques de la guerre d'Hollande', *Revue d'Histoire Diplomatique* (1914) 18–19, pp. 523, 530–1, 537, 540–1; Wicquefort, *Histoire*, vol. iv, p. 434.

Spain and the Mediterranean

In the competition for what was termed the lucrative Straits trade, or *Straartvaart*, the English and Dutch alternated in distinct phases as the more successful. These alternations were due to political changes rather than to changes in competitive efficiency. During the twelve-year truce of 1609–21 the Dutch supplanted the English in the Levant, but when their war with Spain resumed the sustained and systematic enforcement of the ban on Dutch ships by the *Almirantazgo* wiped their trade out: it was the effectiveness of this ban that made Dutch merchants regard the English Navigation Acts with such foreboding. It gave the English a dominant share of trade between Spain and northern Europe and a valuable entrepôt trade with Flanders. But when the ban was relaxed, from 1647, the English position collapsed, the Dutch recovered their former dominance and this gave them naval supremacy in the Mediterranean in 1652–54. They had instituted a system of convoys to protect their vessels: the Commonwealth was about to imitate this practice when the war broke out, but decided to retain the ships in home waters. Van Galen's squadron was opposed by inadequately manned converted merchant vessels whose commanders, Appleton and Badiley, disagreed over tactics, and were hampered by the unsympathetic attitude of the Grand Duke of Tuscany. After a heavy defeat off Livorno the surviving ships withdrew to England. Cromwell's war against Spain postponed the recovery of English trade until after 1660, when the Dutch share of Mediterranean trade went into a long-term decline, accelerated by Sandwich's 1668 treaty with Spain which gave English merchants privileges that the Dutch had acquired in 1646–48.[32]

East Asia

Although the VOC's trade with south and east Asia formed only a small part of the Dutch trading economy, its achievements (and early dividends) were spectacular and provoked envy mingled with hostility in other countries. But by the 1650s by fair competitive efficiency, and the use of what the English regarded as total lack of scruple, the VOC built what an English secretary of state called a 'sea-monarchy' that strengthened an already dominating position during the three wars.

---

[32] J. Corbett, *England in the Mediterranean* (1917), vol. i, pp. 212–32; Fox, *Great Ships*, p. 55; J.I. Israel, *Empires and Entrepôts* (1990), pp. 144–6, 148, 150–1, 154–5, 190–1, 204–5, 209–10.

The EIC (and the French) did not possess the resources in Asia to make headway against it. As Downing saw, it was only by exerting pressure at home, by compelling the States General to coerce the Heeren XVII, the directors of the VOC, that any redress of claims for compensation could be obtained.[33]

The dominance of the VOC was based on their success in operating the 'country trade', the exchange of commodities between Japan, the Indonesian archipelago, Ceylon, India and Iran. Batavia (Jakarta) acted as the entrepôt, as Amsterdam did in Europe, and as the centre of governmental and commercial direction for the forts and trading posts whose number was being extended throughout the period. The country trade required and supported a large number of well-armed vessels, and of employees whose whole working lives were spent in Asia.[34] These gave the VOC a permanent and decisive advantage over its English and French rivals, who had to send out expeditions from Europe that were subject to appalling wastages from disease. In the third war the VOC fitted out twenty-six armed vessels from its local resources to oppose a French expeditionary force of nine ships under de la Haye, which carried 3,000 men. It reduced this force, which soon became weakened and demoralized by disease and desertion, by a series of blockades.[35] A separate EIC fleet of ten armed vessels was defeated in a set-piece battle south of Masulipatam, in the Bay of Bengal, while further east the VOC took most of the EIC vessels trading in the south China Sea, including those that were trying to break into its Japanese monopoly. The EIC had suffered many losses of vessels in the previous two wars, but the VOC had been deterred by the Moghul emperor from attacking the EIC's trading posts in India, although it did expel the English from their last foothold in Ceylon.[36]

By contrast in Indonesia the VOC was moving into a new, imperial phase of expansion. From the late 1650s it followed a systematic policy of reducing sultans who ruled coastal cities to political dependence. They were then compelled to agree to trade only with the VOC. The other tactic used to exclude the EIC

---

33 H. Furber, *Rival Empires of Trade in the Orient, 1600–1800* (Minneapolis, MN, 1976), p. 50 uses the term Dutch 'Thalassocracy'.

34 Ibid., pp. 36, 39, 50, 77; K. Glamann, *Dutch–Asiatic Trade, 1620–1740* (Copenhagen, 1958), especially pp. 3–6.

35 C.R. Boxer, 'The Third Dutch War in the East', *Mariners' Mirror* (1930) xvi, pp. 343–8, 361; Furber, *Rival Empires of Trade*, p. 111.

36 Boxer, 'Third Dutch War', pp. 352, 354–6, 358; W.W. Hunter, *A History of British India* (1900), p. 191.

was to declare war on a sultan and declare a blockade of his possessions: subsequently any EIC vessel trading with them was seized and confiscated as lawful prize by a court in Batavia. By this gambit English trade with Bantam and (before its capture) Macassar was seriously disrupted, leading to complaints that the Dutch aimed at establishing a *mare clausum*, closed seas. The tactics used by the VOC to tighten and extend its dominance poisoned Anglo-Dutch relations, producing claims which were pressed by English diplomats for over twenty years, but without success. In the 1650s the EIC claimed £2.5 million for damages suffered since 1611; the VOC responded with equally exaggerated counter-claims for £3 million. In the 1654 peace treaty the VOC was to pay £85,000, with £3,615 to dependants of EIC servants murdered in the so-called massacre of 1623, when the VOC eliminated the trading post at Amboyna.[37]

Neither this treaty, nor another signed in September 1662, settled all outstanding issues and the continuation of the VOC's expansionist policies created new ones. By the 1654 treaty Pulo Run in the Banda islands should have been returned, giving the EIC a chance to share in the spice trade of the Moluccas. But an expedition sent all the way from England to take possession was refused leave to land. The VOC took Macassar. The second war did not validate Downing's thesis that the VOC could be damaged at the European end of its trading system. The attack on its return fleet in Bergen failed, although two of its vessels were taken later off the Dogger. By 1667 the VOC 'actions' (share prices) recovered to their pre-war levels. In the third war the return fleet of 1671–72 – the richest of the century with fourteen vessels – reached the Ems after narrowly escaping interception off Heligoland. Despite this VOC actions slumped in value by more than half, but this was due to the panic loss of confidence caused by the French invasion. Once the survival of the state became assured they returned to just below their 1667 level, and this despite the disaster that overcame the 1672–73 return fleet. A Dutch expedition from the Cape captured St Helena, the staging point used by the EIC's return ships, which it was planned to ambush. However, an English task force arrived, recaptured the island and ambushed the VOC fleet and took three out of its six vessels; another was captured later a few miles off the Texel.[38]

---

37 Furber, *Rival Empires of Trade*, pp. 39, 48–9, 57, 84–6.
38 Furber, *Rival Empires of Trade*, pp. 43, 75, 85–6; T.H. Lister, *The Life and Administration of Edward, first Earl of Clarendon*, vol. iii, (1838), pp. 249–50, 256–8; the location of Pulo Run is 129° East, 4° 30′ South.

West Africa and the western hemisphere

The WIC, which seemed likely only during brief periods to emulate the success of the VOC, can be seen as representing the principles and practices of the past century which were becoming obsolete. It was founded in 1621, the year that the twelve-year truce expired, to wage economic and piratical war against Spain: it resembled the even less successful English Providence Island company with which many of the opposition to Charles I were associated, and the Western Design that inspired Cromwell's offensive in the Caribbean.[39] Ideologically inspired it was also expected to make profits, and these seemed assured when valuable sugar-producing areas of Brazil were taken, together with Angola in central Africa to supply the slave labour. But the cost of making and retaining conquests depended on high prices for sugar, and when these collapsed with expanded production in Barbados and other islands, from the late 1650s, the company approached bankruptcy. Angola had been recovered by the Portuguese in 1648, and the first Anglo-Dutch War prevented supplies and reinforcements being sent to save the last strongholds in Brazil. The WIC had to acquiesce in the loss of New Netherland, taken by an English expedition in 1664, months before the second war was declared, to close a loophole through which neighbouring English colonists in Maryland and Virginia could export tobacco in defiance of the Navigation Acts.[40]

These losses made the WIC hold on tenaciously to its west African forts in order to retain a major share in the massively expanding slave trade to the western hemisphere. In the mid-1650s the new war provoked by Cromwell's aggression, together with the continuing wars against France and Portugal, meant that Spanish colonists could obtain new slaves from no other source than the WIC, which no longer posed a threat to Spanish possessions. Consequently the WIC was permitted from 1662, as a sub-contractor for the *asiento*, to re-export slaves from Curaçao in Dutch vessels. English aggression in West Africa threatened its ability to continue this profitable trade, while the rival English Company, which included Court participants, was after the quick profits which the trade promised. Both received state support in their struggle. Charles loaned royal ships to the

---

39 K.G. Davies, *The North Atlantic World in the Seventeenth Century* (Minneapolis, MN, 1974), pp. 46–8, 123–4, 129–30.

40 Colenbrander, vol. i, pp. 134, 137; D.G. Shomette and R.D. Haslach, *Raid on America: The Dutch Naval Campaign of 1672–1674* (Columbia, SC, 1988), pp. 16–18.

African Company for Holmes's raid; De Witt ordered De Ruyter with a squadron of naval ships to carry out the counter-attack (1664–65). The results were mutually destructive. They gave the French an opportunity to enter the trade. The English Company had to be liquidated in 1670, to be reconstructed in 1672.[41]

In the West Indies and North America the Anglo-Dutch Wars first demonstrated basic strategic facts that were to determine the outcome of the eighteenth-century colonial campaigns. The local balance of forces could be radically altered at any time by the arrival of ships and troops from Europe and, second, the plantations and the wealth which they produced were very vulnerable. The Dutch concentrated on destructive raids. De Ruyter in 1665 set the pattern of sweeping through the West Indies, and then on his return voyage taking prizes off the north American coast and Newfoundland.[42] The other two major attacks were organized by the province of Zeeland, not the States General. Although Crijnssen captured Surinam in 1667 and Evertsen the youngest reoccupied New York in 1673, the primary Dutch objectives were prizes, not territories. The latter, particularly, did immense damage to the Virginia tobacco and Newfoundland fishery fleets.[43]

In operational terms the Anglo-French War of 1666–67 was a prototype of the next century's colonial wars. The French colonists were more belligerent and more effectively organized by their governors than the more settled English. They took St Kitts, Antigua and Montserrat, abducting their slave populations. But the English government showed itself more concerned with its colonies and the wealth that they generated than the French. Despite the exhaustion of resources at home it sent two formidable expeditions which transformed the strategic situation in the Caribbean, defeating French naval forces twice, retaking Antigua, Montserrat and Surinam, and capturing French Cayenne. These successes were achieved in the last stages of the war in Europe, or even after peace had been signed at Breda. Louis XIV was unaware of them when he revealed his valuation of colonies. Although aware of their potential wealth he was ready to give back all his colonial conquests in order to obtain

---

41 K.G. Davies, *The Royal African Company* (1960), pp. 21–2, 41–5, 64–6, 327; Davies, *North Atlantic World*, pp. 46–8, 115–17, 124–5, 129–30.

42 British Library (henceforth BL), Egerton MSS, 2543 f. 123.

43 Shomette and Haslach, *Raid on America*, esp. pp. 129–51, 162–96, 197–205; J.C.M. Warnsinck, *Abraham Crynssen der Verovering van Suriname* (Amsterdam, 1936).

English acquiescence for his territorial advances into the Spanish Netherlands, which for him greatly exceeded in value and importance the sugar-producing islands. In the peace of 1667 all colonial conquests except Surinam and New Netherland were returned to their former owners; in 1674 the Dutch returned New York.[44]

---

44 Wicquefort, *Histoire*, vol. iii, pp. 316–17.

3   MATERIEL, PERSONNEL AND ADMINISTRATION

The Anglo-Dutch Wars, the earliest in the sequence of oceanic sailing-ship wars that continued up to 1815, established certain new patterns in the practices and methods used in naval warfare. These followed particularly from important developments in materiel and personnel which the English navy introduced, and which the Dutch imitated when they realized that their survival depended on their doing so. Concentrated campaigns of frequent, large-scale engagements between the main fleets saw the 'great ship' emerge as the decisive weapon, which had important consequences. In earlier naval campaigns, outside the Mediterranean, fleets contained some purpose-built warships, but most units were hired and converted merchant vessels. The performance of 'great ships', also termed 'first rates' or 'capital ships', in the Anglo-Dutch Wars exposed the narrow limitations of converted merchant vessels with their puny armaments and lightly constructed, vulnerable hulls. The second and third wars saw an increase in the size and the number of guns carried by first rates, and also proportionately by second, third and fourth rates. This general tendency, with the Dutch quickly following the English practice, required professional career officers and senior ratings and put an end to the dual system by which a ship's master (usually a former merchant skipper) was responsible for seamanship and navigation, while the captain controlled the ship in battle. By the time of the third war captains, officers and most senior ratings were dedicated to the service in both combatant navies; only the seamen were transferred from the merchant service – in the English case mostly by impressment.[1]

Fleets of purpose-built warships made other new or greatly expanded demands. They needed extensive refitting between battles, refits and maintenance between campaigns (and between wars). They

1 M.S. Anderson, *War and Society in Europe of the Old Regime* (Leicester, 1988), p. 27; later equivalents of the term 'great ship' are 'capital ship' or 'ship of the line'.

required more complex equipment, and much greater logistical and administrative back-up, than did contemporary armies. The efficiency with which naval dockyards, naval architects and the Ordnance office carried out their work, and their direction and supervision by administrators, could therefore be crucial. More generally naval warfare, to a greater extent than military operations, depended on mental qualities which our world attuned to constant and rapid change takes for granted, but which were much less required and common in the seventeenth century – the capacity to adapt to changing conditions, a flexibility of response in unexpected circumstances, a readiness to analyse the causes of failure, to revise or discard traditional practices if they no longer appeared to be working and not to shirk from experiments and innovations. Even though the wars did not produce any radically new technological developments – the Dutch project of a revolutionary mechanical ram and the English invention of an incendiary shell both failed – the techniques of naval warfare were transformed and systematized with, significantly, the English navy the clear leader for all but the last year of the third war.

In 1652 the Dutch were universally regarded as the leading naval power so that their defeats in 1652–53 came as an unexpected shock to both domestic and foreign observers who either ignored, or were unaware of, two developments before hostilities began. At the end of 1651 the States General resolved that a monster fleet of 150 ships should be set out the next year. The objective was to deter or rather intimidate the English from stopping and searching Dutch vessels for contraband, but the effect was to expose the reality of Dutch naval weakness. It proved to be impossible to set out as many as 150 ships and many of those that were commissioned turned out to be too small and weakly armed to impress; it was seen as a paper fleet.[2] The five provincial admiralties possessed only seventy-nine ships, many of them old or unseaworthy, and several were weakly armed converted merchant vessels. Tromp's fleet in the first months of the war had only one ship, his flagship the *Brederode*, with more than fifty guns; one-third had between thirty-one and forty, two-thirds between twenty and thirty. By contrast the English could set out five with over fifty guns, and half their capital ships had forty or more; this disparity in armaments soon made itself felt at the Kentish Knock, and even at Dungeness when a few English great

2 Thurloe, vol. i, p. 158.

ships held off a much larger number of Tromp's.[3] The Dutch did not profit from experience. In October 1652 they discussed a programme of new construction, but the complacency induced by their very modest success off Dungeness led to a decision being postponed until the near-disaster of the Channel Fight in February 1653 made a decision necessary. In authorizing the construction of thirty new ships the States General made one innovation, and confirmed an earlier decision, that were both to have important long-term effects. First, the programme was to be financed out of the common funds disposed of by the States General, and not by the five admiralties, which did not have the money to cover the cost, and the new ships were to be retained in service after the war ended. This decision marked the real genesis of a professional Dutch navy: astonishingly after peace was made with Spain in 1648 the best ships, including Tromp's then flagship, the *Aemilia*, were sold off.[4] Second, the States General followed an earlier recommendation that the new ships should be built on a design based on the *Aemilia*, a ship built in 1632 and whose main armament had never exceeded forty guns, and explicitly rejected an alternative design for ships resembling the English great ships which had been doing so much damage. This decision went against Tromp's own stated demand for ships with heavier and more guns, but the decision was not wilful or blind, even though it proved to be disastrous. Ships based on the design of the *Aemilia* were faster and handled better than the larger English ships whereas to build ships with similar armaments to those carried by these English ships would require the widening of their beam, affecting their sailing qualities. Political considerations also contributed to this conservatism in design. The decision meant a reduction in the importance of the admiralties, and the other four were jealously aware that the idea had originated with the Amsterdam admiralty, which alone possessed the facilities to build ships comparable in size with the English.[5]

In practical terms, so far as the war of 1652–54 was concerned, the question of which design to follow proved to be irrelevant. The

3 *FDW*, vol. iii, pp. 116–20; vol. iv, pp. 313–16, 336, 355, 366–7; Wicquefort, *Histoire*, vol. ii, p. 121; J.R. Bruijn, *The Dutch Navy of the Seventeenth and Eighteenth Centuries* (Columbia, SC, 1993), p. 71.

4 Bruijn, *Dutch Navy*, pp. 62–3, 73–4.

5 Colenbrander, vol. i, pp. 146, 496; Thurloe, vol. i, p. 539; *FDW*, vol. iii, pp. 152–4; vol. iv, p. 380; M. Baumber, *General-at-Sea: Robert Blake and the Seventeenth-Century Revolution in Naval Warfare* (1989), p. 117; Bruijn, *Dutch Navy*, p. 73.

postponement of the decision to start building new ships until the spring of 1653 meant that none of them was completed in time to participate in the war. Increasing shortages of money and materials slowed construction, and yards had to concentrate work on the speedy repairing of battle-damaged ships in time to be ready for the next engagement. By contrast the Commonwealth had made a decision in March 1649 to initiate a naval construction programme of ships that in accordance with pre-civil war naval doctrine were to be large and heavily armed; it could almost be said that this decision, made at a time when no one was thinking of a war against the Dutch, actually predetermined the outcome of the battles of 1652–53. It was also a great advantage that the pre-war construction of great ships left the English yards free to undertake the repair of battle damage, and at the same time construct 'frigates' in time to take part in the war. These were not ships of the same type as the classic eighteenth-century frigates which acted as scouts for the fleet and were used against privateers. The frigates built in 1652–53 were third and fourth rates, designed to take their place in the line with the first and second rates. They carried armaments comparable to those of all but a very few Dutch ships. They were economical to build in terms both of labour and materials, the latter an important consideration as the Baltic was closed to English trade.[6]

The most important reason for the failure of the States General to realize that not only their existing ships but also those they were voting to build were under-gunned, and so would be unable to stand up to the English fleet, was that to imitate English designs and build ships comparable in size and armament meant discarding all previous Dutch naval doctrine. Unlike the English, the Dutch did not rely entirely on gunnery, and this was reflected not only in the smaller number carried by their ships, but also in the lighter shot that their guns fired. The regular armament of the larger English ships comprised eighteen and twenty-four pounders, and there were some thirty-two pounders, but only a few Dutch ships had eighteen pounders. Their lighter main armament was aimed mainly at bringing down the enemy's masts, rigging and sails in order to disable ships which could then be boarded and taken, or set ablaze by fireships. Contingents of soldiers were carried who with their muskets and light ordnance (Falcons and Falconets firing two and one pound shot) were to disable enemy personnel on the upper deck and then

---

6 F. Fox, *Great Ships: The Battlefleet of Charles II* (Greenwich, 1980), pp. 52–9, 175; *CSPD 1651–52*, p. 493; *FDW*, vol. iv, p. 66.

board. But in the battles of 1652 and 1653 the sheer weight of English broadside fire kept Dutch ships at a distance, unable to close except at prohibitive cost in casualties among the soldiers, and the greater penetrative power of the English guns resulted in their being badly holed and taking on water; at the Gabbard Tromp's flagship the *Brederode* was repeatedly holed on the waterline and took in so much water that the pumps only just managed to keep her afloat.[7]

For the States General to change its policy and imitate the English naval doctrine of relying on superior gunnery would involve discarding as obsolete virtually all their existing ships, and recognizing as an illusion the assumption that when war broke out the fleet could be materially strengthened by converting merchant vessels. All battle tactics would also have to be changed. A similar problem faced every admiralty and government when the *Dreadnought* was completed in 1906, the all big-gun ship that rendered obsolete all existing battleships, which became known very significantly as pre-Dreadnoughts. Twentieth-century policy-makers reacted quickly and positively: they were attuned to a world of rapid technological changes, where in a decade submarines, radio and turbines were introduced. But the members of the States General in the 1650s lived in a more static world. They were sons and grandsons of the men responsible for the astonishing development of the Dutch economy and the successful war against Spain, a generation who had settled comfortably into prosperity, satisfied with the proven methods that had brought success. Unfortunately for the Dutch Republic the results of their mistaken judgement in ordering ships that could not withstand the English were still to be felt when the second war began in 1665. A significant proportion of ships in Obdam's fleet consisted of the inadequately armed ships ordered in 1653, and in an additional programme authorized in January 1654, and these ships were semi-obsolete from the time they were completed.[8]

In the last months of 1653 the inadequacies of Dutch ships generated defeatism. As in the last desperate year of Nazi Germany stories were circulated of 'wonder weapons' that would totally alter the situation. An imaginary blunderbuss-like cannon firing incendiary shells was said to have destroyed several great ships. Round-the-clock working was actually instituted in Rotterdam to build a revolutionary

---

7 *FDW*, vol. v, pp. 24, 194; Thurloe, vol. i, p. 271; Colenbrander, vol. i, p. 166; *CSPVenetian 1664–65*, p. 146.

8 F.T. Jane, *Jane's Fighting Ships 1914* (1968), p. 41; Thurloe, vol. i, pp. 539–40, 594, 629; Fox, *Great Ships*, p. 175.

mechanical ship designed by a French mathematician. Resembling a galley in its dimensions (seventy-six feet by seven) it was to have two keels, two rudders and a mechanism which the inventor claimed would give it a speed of fifteen miles per hour with which to ram enemy ships, and an unlimited range. Great secrecy was maintained at the construction site, with screens erected to keep out the curious crowds, and the inventor (who smoked over forty pipes of tobacco a day) keeping himself aloof. But this ship was never tested, or probably even completed, and soon the project for this 'mad ship' attracted general derision, but the fact that it was taken seriously for a time revealed the helplessness of the Dutch situation.[9]

Both navies deployed converted merchant vessels in the first and second wars, but seldom in the third, while on the English side they played an important role only at Dungeness in 1652. Apart from their light armament – although often carrying up to forty guns, all but a few of these were smaller than twelve pounders – and lightly built hulls, their chief weakness lay in the lack of professional discipline in their officers and crews. At Dungeness, when half Blake's fleet consisted of converted merchant vessels hastily assembled to meet an unexpected Dutch sortie, most of them conspicuously failed to support their admiral: to avoid a repetition it was ordered that in future this type of ship should not constitute more than 20 per cent of any fleet, that all with fewer than twenty-eight guns should be discarded and that all captains and officers should be appointed by the state, rather than the former master and mates being taken over with the ship. Safeguarding the owner's interests would be the task left to a 'ship's husband'. After Dungeness English admirals saw little use for these ships in battle, relegating them generally to convoy escort work, but Sandwich in 1665 put them in the rear division, where they would not get in the way but could be used against crippled enemy ships if the Dutch were forced to retire. It was not until the third war that the Dutch realized that converted vessels (except for those provided by the VOC) did not add strength to the fleet in battle.[10]

Both navies put captured enemy ships into service, but these proved to be less useful than prizes taken in the later French wars. The English placed little value on captured Dutch ships, selling off most of them in 1660 and 1667–68 in order to reduce navy debt.

9 *FDW*, vol. v, p. 412; Thurloe, vol. i, pp. 521 2, 595, 629.

10 *FDW*, vol. iii, pp. 167–8; vol. v, p. 257; G. Penn, *Memorials of Sir William Penn* (1833), vol. i, p. 427.

Others were sunk as blockships in the Thames and Medway in 1667 or retained as hulks. The Dutch took fewer but extremely prestigious prizes: *the* prestige ship of the Commonwealth navy, the *Naseby*, renamed in 1660 the *Royal Charles*, was towed away from the Medway and included in the Dutch fleet in 1672. But she had too deep a draught to be compatible with De Ruyter's strategy of using the offshore shoals in 1673 and so was broken up.[11]

Small prizes were often used as fireships, expendable ships filled with inflammable materials and barrels of gunpowder and 'fireworks' to project them on to an enemy and set him ablaze. This was the most hazardous of all forms of service at sea, comparable to forming part of the 'forlorn hope' in an army assault. Even when approaching crippled ships, the crew came under musket fire; they knew that a single cannon shot could ignite their own lethal cargo, and the boat on which they relied to escape could be sunk or taken by an enemy longboat. Whereas young army officers often headed a forlorn hope in order to distinguish themselves, taking the instant death or quick promotion gamble, fireships did not attract a naval elite. Their officers and crews were usually as dubious as the seaworthiness of the ships they manned, the very reverse of glory-seekers. Consequently the vast majority of fireships were prematurely ignited and once their crews abandoned them they lost way, drifted off target or could be fended off by longboats. Experience during the wars showed that fireships were of limited effectiveness against undamaged ships: for example two attacks by a number against the Dutch in the very confined waters of the lower Thames in 1667, although an improved type of slow-burning fuse had been fitted, ended in complete failure – which led to some of the captains being shot for cowardice. They were effective in finishing off cripples in the immediate aftermath of battles, but when the Dutch were pursued to their own coast the remaining fireships could not keep up with the fleet. On the other hand they were used with great success by Holmes the previous year against a congested mass of merchant vessels in the Vlie anchorage.[12]

Dutch naval administration was based on the same basis of particularism and provincial autonomy as its political institutions. It comprised five admiralty colleges: Rotterdam (the senior), Amsterdam

11 Colenbrander, vol. i, pp. 331, 337; *FDW*, vol. iii, p. 379; J.R. Tanner (ed.), *Pepys's Naval Minutes* (1926), p. 353; Fox, *Great Ships*, p. 69.

12 J.R. Powell and E.K. Timings (eds), *The Rupert and Monck Letter Book, 1666* (1969), pp. 126–7; *FDW*, vol. v, p. 47; R. Latham and W. Matthews (eds), *The Diary of Samuel Pepys* (1970–83) (henceforth Pepys), vol. viii, pp. 259–60, 354, 357–8.

(which had the most resources), and the North Quarter in Holland, Harlingen in Friesland and Middelburg in Zeeland. Each college contained representatives from the others to act – nominally at least – as checks on the local majority. The colleges maintained bureaucrats to collect their permanent income from their region: uniform taxes on imports and exports, on ships' tonnage and (imposed in 1652) a levy on the value of incoming and outgoing goods (the *veilgeld*). Theoretically equitable, this system had weaknesses. The Amsterdam admiralty usually had funds, Rotterdam managed to stay solvent, but the other three often had difficulties in setting out all their ships by the stipulated date: in 1672 their delays caused the abandonment of the original strategy to strike at the English fleet before it could link up with the French. There was no uniformity in ships or armaments; ships provided by the three less affluent admiralties were smaller. Problems arose about repairs and refitting when Holland admiralties' ships were stationed in the Wielings, and Zeeland ships in the Texel. With each admiralty responsible for dockyards, ship construction, stores, recruitment and appointments, there was an unavoidable tendency to promote local interests, and particularly those linked to admiralty college members. They were also responsible for discipline, and charges that well-connected individuals were shielded from the consequences of malpractices and cowardice produced vituperative recriminations between the provinces, especially when operations were going badly.[13]

Although the admiralty system had these defects it represented the only way of balancing all interests. Frederick Henry as admiral general had tried in 1639 to establish a superior admiralty consisting of one delegate from each of the five, but Amsterdam had wrecked this proposal that would (and was intended to) reduce its influence. Frederick Henry and William II were primarily concerned with the army, not the navy, but De Witt was able without too much difficulty to make the system work. His office of pensionary of Holland had no institutional connection with either naval administration or strategy, but through sheer personal energy and determination he provided the central direction and clear strategic thought that was damagingly absent in the first months of the first war. His ability to take much-needed initiatives and ensure practical cooperation between the entities concerned with naval affairs stemmed from his function as reporter to the States of Holland of its *zeecommissie*,

13 Bruijn, *Dutch Navy*, pp. 5–11; H.H. Rowen, *John de Witt: Grand Pensionary of Holland* (Princeton, NJ, 1978), pp. 80–1; *FDW*, vol. v, pp. 394–6.

its committee on naval affairs, and his acting as spokesman for the States at meetings of the States General. De Witt's recommendations were usually accepted, but this achievement depended on an almost unbearable burden of work which De Witt imposed on himself in order to anticipate and remove obstructions and difficulties beforehand. He maintained a constant correspondence with the three Holland admiralties, and kept in close touch with the other two, but this administrative leadership would have been impossible without the close working relationship which he possessed with David and Job de Wildt, the father and son who served the key Amsterdam admiralty as secretary and under-secretary throughout De Witt's time as pensionary.[14]

This connection was particularly valuable because nearly all the main developments concerning ships, armaments and personnel were initiated by the Amsterdam admiralty. After the first war it built new and extensive dockyards, magazines and storehouses on the Haven, away from the city centre. It put up the proposal which was passed through the States and the States General by De Witt for the building of new ships (1653), and most of them were built at Amsterdam or its satellite yards at Zaandam. Although still smaller than the English great ships, these new ships required more officers to handle and fight them; consequently the professionalization of the Dutch naval officer corps extended to the provision of lieutenants and midshipmen. This expansion of the number of officers, and the emergence of a career structure, strengthened the connections with the Regent class. Although former merchant seamen were still the predominant element in the officer corps during the three wars, this period saw the beginning of the process of 'aristocratization' as younger sons and relations of Regents began to take naval commissions.[15]

The Dutch had fewer problems than the English in manning their wartime fleet as they had a much larger pool of seamen on which to draw. Indeed at the very beginning, in 1652, the inept politicians thought that they could man the fleet and maintain something approaching peacetime levels of trade, but when bigger ships came into service in the second war it became necessary to impose embargoes prohibiting outward sailings, so that economic necessity would compel seamen to enlist in naval ships. These embargoes provoked opposition from influential trading interests, but De Witt proved to

14 Bruijn, *Dutch Navy*, pp. 39, 76–80; J.K. Oudendijk, *Johan de Witt en de Zeemacht* (Amsterdam, 1944), pp. 32–3, 37, 95, 120.
15 Bruijn, *Dutch Navy*, pp. 79–80, 112–24.

be impervious to their protests, rejecting proposals for special deals by, for example, the Muscovy and Greenland (whaling) merchants, under which their ships would be allowed to sail during the summer campaigning season (the only time of the year in which their northern voyages were possible) in return for providing token quotas of seamen – although admittedly the hardiest and most useful of all. In this, as in other matters, De Witt put the public interest before even the most influential private interests: nothing could be further from the Marxist and Marxisant view that he was the instrument or tool of an aggressive Dutch bourgeoisie. However, De Witt had a chillingly utilitarian attitude to the recruitment of ordinary seamen whom he treated as a necessary but expendable and consumable commodity like sails, cordage and planks. There was in peacetime an excess of seamen, particularly on the Amsterdam labour market, which was reflected in low wages, and in wartime the local admiralty exploited the lack of employment to pay even lower rates. Nevertheless both these sets of rates were still higher than those that could be obtained in Baltic and northern countries, so that large numbers of Germans, Norwegians, Scotsmen and Balts were available for service in the fleet. Englishmen who served in Dutch merchant vessels in peacetime frequently transferred to the Dutch navy, many as senior ratings. This heterogeneous body of seamen served and fought for money. Low as the rates were, they were at least paid in cash, unlike the English, who had to wait for wages in 1653, and in 1666 had eventually to accept tickets in lieu of non-existent money, that is IOUs that depended on the honour and credit of Charles II, which no free and sane person would trust.[16] But De Witt consistently resisted pressures to increase seamen's wages, even in crisis situations: otherwise, he said, 'the state is at the mercy of Jan Hagel', that is of the rabble. In 1653 wages had had to be raised to eighteen guilders a month to offset the deterrent effect of heavy battle casualties. In 1665 his resistance proved effective: wages rose only from twelve to fifteen. But after his death in 1673, when seamen were urgently needed to replace the normal contingents of soldiers, who had to be landed to shore up the landward defences of Holland, they rose again to seventeen.[17]

Without De Witt's determined leadership it is difficult to see how the Dutch Republic could have survived the defeats of 1653 and 1665. By unremitting labour and resourcefulness he provided the

---

16 Ibid., p. 129; F.J. Routledge (ed.), *Calendar of the Clarendon State Papers*, vol. v (Oxford, 1970) (henceforth *Cal.Cl.SP*) p. 440.

17 Bruijn, *Dutch Navy*, pp. 129–31, 136–8.

coordination of governmental agencies and the unified policy which was necessary. As much as William III in the even graver crisis of 1672, De Witt was the saviour of the Dutch Republic; without him the great sea commanders, on whom historical attention was for long concentrated almost exclusively, could not have kept the English at bay. Although most of the leading naval officers had Orangist sympathies, and frequently engaged in vicious personal vendettas and recriminations, De Witt knew that national survival depended on them. Like the antique heroes of the Roman Republic they sacrificed their lives for what Tromp called 'our dear fatherland': he was killed in 1653, eight out of sixteen flag-officers died in the second war, five in the third. De Witt did all that he could to reward those who displayed courage, even in defeat. Flag-officers received gold chains, captains lesser ornaments. Big cash rewards were offered to captains who destroyed enemy flagships, and improved prize money arrangements were made. Dead heroes were given splendid memorials: the superb baroque tomb of Tromp in the Oude Kerk in Delft greatly impressed Pepys, who thought that English officers too would be inspired to heroic deeds if they could be sure of a similar monument. On a more mundane level De Witt promised captains, who had the responsibility for provisioning their crews and often had to wait for long periods before being reimbursed by their admiralty, that he would ensure prompt repayments. The corollary of this care and attention to leading officers can be found in the dire warnings issued of draconian punishment for captains who failed to do their duty, which led after shameful defections from beaten fleets to exemplary sentences being executed, to encourage all others.[18]

On the Dutch side it was the catastrophic situation created by repeated defeats in 1653 that necessitated De Witt's taking control over administration generally and directing operations at sea. A much lesser crisis, the defeat off Dungeness in November 1652, impelled the English government to make important changes to their naval organization and administration. From the inauguration of the Commonwealth in January 1649 the Rump Parliament and its council of state knew that the survival of the regime depended as much on the loyalty and efficiency of the navy as on its incomparable army. They had experienced the dangerous crisis created by the mutiny of most of the fleet during the summer of 1648, after which the officer corps had to be purged, army officers brought in to naval commands, and godliness became a leading qualification for naval commissions

---

18 Ibid., pp. 50–3, 121–2; Tanner, *Pepys's Naval Minutes*, p. 94.

and promotions: the pay of officers had also been increased. The seas had to be cleared of royalist privateers, an undeclared war waged against France. Foreign intervention in the form of aid for the Irish and Scots had to be prevented. Although there was no reason at the time to fear a full-scale war against the Dutch, the Rump initiated an ambitious programme of naval construction with an emphasis on great ships, and these were to prove the decisive factor in the first war.[19] It also established a simple but effective system of administration. The admiralty committee of the Council of State, consisting of politicians headed by Sir Henry Vane, coopted 'regulators' who were mostly London merchants and shipowners to investigate and report on questions concerning ships, personnel and dockyards. At Chatham they uncovered corrupt practices, including bizarre behaviour by the master mast-maker, who had embezzled timber to build not only his furniture but also coffins for himself and his wife. This partnership with radically minded members of the mercantile community extended to legislation. In 1650 two Convoy Acts reflected the importance of reviving trade and the need for expert advice: one set up a committee of merchants to advise on the provision of convoys, the other appropriated 15 per cent of receipts from customs for escorts. In August the Council of Trade was established. But the logical consequence of the partnership was the Navigation Act of November 1651, not a Dutch war. So far was the admiralty committee from thinking such a war to be desirable or inevitable that in January 1652 it recommended, and the Rump approved, the sending of a trade protection fleet to the Mediterranean to check French privateering.[20]

The Dungeness defeat provoked an important administrative change. In December 1652 the admiralty committee was replaced by admiralty commissioners directly responsible to the Rump, six in number – four politicians, two London merchants, with Robert Blackborne as their efficient secretary. One pressing reason for the change concerned the appointment of sea-officers: the committee, like the Dutch admiralties, had appointed men whose main qualification was their connection with its members, and MPs generally, and many of these political appointees had shown

19 Bruijn, *Dutch Navy*, pp. 69–70; B. Capp, *Cromwell's Navy* (Oxford, 1989), pp. 42–72.

20 Capp, *Cromwell's Navy*, p. 80; *Commons Journals*, vol. vii, p. 69; *CSPD 1651–52*, pp. 127–8; C.H. Firth and R.S. Rait, *Acts and Ordinances of the Interregnum* (1911), vol. ii, pp. 444, 495.

cowardice or incompetence in the battle. Recommendations from flag-officers had been ignored; in future any of them available were to be consulted.[21]

The commissioners instituted reforms of an absolutely fundamental importance, a remarkable achievement in the middle of a crisis which posed innumerable and formidable problems of getting ships ready for sea and combat, manning and victualling them, procuring guns, powder and shot at short notice, and all in mid-winter when usually operations were at a standstill and logistical preparations for the next campaign just beginning. Both the main reforms proved to be durable. The Articles of War formed the basis for the maintenance of naval discipline for over two centuries. The scales of pay now promulgated were to continue until the mutinies of 1797 with only minor modifications: until this time rates of pay were (as Blake pointed out) substantially lower than those in the Dutch Navy. However, the efficiency of this naval administration should not be exaggerated, as Oppenheim tended to do.[22] Serious deficiencies hampered operations. Ships had to remain in port because of victualling problems. Local authorities were totally unable to cope with large numbers of wounded, sick and prisoners; commissioners were not appointed to take charge until as late as September 1653. In the autumns of 1652 and 1653 serious disorders occurred when money was not available to pay off crews. Pressing provoked resentment, particularly because many of the press gangs consisted of soldiers, not naval personnel, and relations between soldiers and seamen on shipboard became envenomed. But overall the administration did function much more effectively than in the second war because the financial position never deteriorated to the point of near-bankruptcy reached at the end of 1666, even though the war in its later stages was being financed largely out of capital, from the proceeds of the confiscation of royal and church property. But tax revenues were more buoyant than in the second war, when the plague disrupted the economy, and could be increased to meet the current needs of expenditure: in December 1652 the monthly assessment and charges on delinquents' (royalists') estates were increased. The yield from customs went up, whereas the Dutch revenue from the same source slumped, and this despite a sharp increase in rates. But although

---

21 *Commons Journals*, vol. vii, pp. 225, 228; M. Oppenheim, *A History of the Administration of the Royal Navy 1509–1660* (1896), pp. 306, 347–51.

22 Oppenheim, *History of the Administration of the Royal Navy*, pp. 311–14; *FDW*, vol. iii, p. 14.

limited profits could be made from the war itself – over £200,000 was raised by the sale of prizes – expenditure on it, on top of the cost of maintaining the army which actually exceeded the amount spent on the navy, could be supported only by the accumulation of debt which outgrew the regime's ability to service it.[23]

The restored monarchy inherited a large and potentially powerful fleet of fifteen great ships and twenty-five others capable of fighting in the line. At first a fleet of this size was a financial embarrassment; it had been maintained at this level to fight Spain, but the disbandment of the politically unreliable army took first priority. Most of these ships could not be paid off until 1661, a delay that substantially increased the already massive debt of approximately £1.3 million. The condition of many of the ships had deteriorated. The depleted stocks of timber, cordage, sails, masts and boats could be replenished only by the same businessmen to whom most of the debt was owing, which made wholesale or partial repudiation of debts contracted by the usurped administrations impracticable. These financial constraints put a brake on the aggressive policies which James and his associates began to formulate. It was not until the end of 1663 that naval credit recovered and suppliers of goods and services regained full confidence in the administration. But even then responsible officials such as William Coventry and Samuel Pepys were disturbed by what they rightly considered to be an extremely premature surge of aggressiveness – the expeditions sent to take New Amsterdam and to raid WIC forts in west Africa – because of the probability that these would precipitate a new general war against the Dutch.[24]

Financial constraints meant that only two second rates were completed before the second war broke out in 1665 – the *Royal Oak* and *Royal Katherine* – and only one second rate, five third rates and five smaller ships could be completed while the war was in progress.[25] This lack of building contrasted sharply with Dutch wartime construction of forty second, third and fourth rates, only a few of which were replacements for ships lost in the Lowestoft defeat. The Dutch programme amounted to little short of the construction of an entirely new fleet. Lowestoft showed up the inadequacies of even the most heavily armed ships already in service, so that the

---

23 Oppenheim, *History of the Administration of the Royal Navy*, pp. 317–18, 324–6, 368–9; M. Ashley, *Financial and Commercial Policy in the Cromwellian Protectorate* (1962), pp. 42n., 47.

24 Pepys, vol. iv, p. 389.

25 Fox, *Great Ships*, pp. 73–82.

new ships had to be as heavily armed as their opponents if they were to challenge a new engagement with any hope of success. Consequently ten of the new ships carried eighty guns, another twelve had seventy, and the guns themselves were heavier: for the first time some thirty-six pounders were installed, and all these great ships had twenty-four pounders in their lowest tier of guns, with eighteen pounders in the middle tier. The effects were felt in the Four Days Fight of 1666 when the English suffered their heaviest losses in all the three wars.[26] In following the English example of placing reliance on gunnery the Dutch also rather belatedly imitated the English practice of fighting in line; these changes, together with De Ruyter's effective leadership, meant that at last the Dutch were able to hold their own in set-piece engagements. However, these changes also provoked an escalation of naval armaments. The English had to replace the heavy losses which they suffered in the Four Days Fight and in the Medway; of the three first rates built since 1649 they lost two and five of the eight second rates. Their replacements marked a significant increase in size and guns; seven first rates had between ninety-four and a hundred guns, including a few forty-two pounders, and four third rates carried between sixty-four and seventy. This time it was the Dutch who took a naval holiday: ironically the only major warships built in Dutch yards between 1667 and 1672 were for the French navy and were to be used against their builders in 1672–78. In addition the French constructed at Brest and Toulon four enormous first rates, the largest warships ever built up to this time, carrying up to 120 guns in three tiers. But like the earlier Danish monster ships they were failures and spent most of their lives laid up in reserve. The large English first rates also failed to make a decisive impact in the third war, because their size and deep draught prevented them operating in the shallow waters off the Dutch coast where De Ruyter deployed his fleet in his classic defensive campaign of 1673.[27]

Enumeration of the number of guns carried, and of the weight of the shot which they fired, does not automatically indicate superiority in battle. There is evidence that by the time of the third war the Dutch could maintain a higher rate of fire than their opponents. More guns required larger ships' companies, and with no additional spaces available for storage, big ships ran out of water, beer and pro-

---

26 Ibid., pp. 116–17; Thurloe, vol. i, pp. 539–40; Bruijn, *Dutch Navy*, p. 78; Tanner, *Pepys's Naval Minutes*, pp. 241–2; Oudendijk, *Johan de Witt en de Zeemacht*, p. 180.

27 Fox, *Great Ships*, pp. 95–110, 117, 121–3.

visions quickly. Accommodation between decks became even more congested; sickness rates could be higher as a result. The weight of the ordnance carried by the biggest ships affected their sailing qualities and could make them unstable; the ratio of the weight of the guns carried to the ship's tonnage was 1:8 or 1:9, and a forty-two pounder with its carriage weighed three tons or more. This made it imperative for naval architects to position the lowest tier of the heaviest guns very close to the waterline, within five or even four feet. These guns could not be used in even moderate seas. In ships heeling to a stiff wind the lowest tier would be under water on the lee side, while those on the windward side would be pointing skywards. The biggest guns, the forty-two pounders, required a very large charge of powder which produced a massive recoil: this stressed and, unless care was taken, would break the ropes that secured their carriages, and loose cannon would create havoc and terror on gundecks. Moreover the manufacture of these massive cannon strained the extreme limits of contemporary metallurgical technology; production was limited in quantity and the product often proved unreliable, particularly under the conditions of these wars when there were frequent engagements (three in 1653, two – but one of four continuous days – in 1666, three in 1673) in which cannonades were fired for up to twelve hours. Cannon frequently misfired, split or burst. In 1666 all twenty-two of the forty-two pounders manufactured for the new *Loyal London* burst during proof test-firing. Failures also marked two creditable English attempts at applying the new scientific methods to naval technology. Members of the Royal Society were consulted in designing the hull of the *Royal Katherine* in an endeavour to reduce water resistance, but the result was an unstable ship that had to be 'girdled', that is have her beam widened. Second, in 1673 the test-firing of a new invention, a hollow shot filled with explosives designed to have an incendiary effect, was a failure in front of an audience comprising Charles, James and Rupert.[28]

As a result of the Rump's 1649 purge of some two-thirds of its officers the navy was politically reliable in the first war, giving the lie to royalist predictions that part at least would defect to the Dutch. A similar purge could not be attempted in 1660–61, because there were insufficient experienced Cavalier officers available even for a peacetime service. However, a scheme was introduced in 1661 to commission the younger sons of the landowning nobility and gentry,

---

[28] Ibid., pp. 20–1, 73–6, 129; Tanner, *Pepys's Naval Minutes*, p. 241.

and a new generation of what were termed 'gentlemen commanders' emerged alongside the captains and lieutenants who had served the Commonwealth. It was inevitable that when the second war went wrong, recriminations should develop between these two very different types of sea-officers, the gentlemen commanders and the 'tarpaulins', between older men who had triumphed in 1652–54 and the brash younger men who owed their commands to family connections and political loyalties. Historically the gentlemen, depicted as inexperienced, dissolute (though it is difficult to see why this should be relevant) and recklessly aggressive, have had a bad press, not least because Pepys (hardly a model of rectitude) disapproved of them. However, their advance has to be put into the context of a more general process of aristocratization, which similarly affected the church, as the governing class eagerly used every patronage opportunity to place relations and clients in governmental offices: the same processes were working in the Dutch Republic and France.[29]

The Commonwealth had employed tarpaulins, men bred from boyhood to the sea, because very few men of gentry stock were willing to serve at sea. Having learned their trade in merchant vessels they tended to be older than most post-Restoration officers, but some had to be removed after Dungeness for lack of pugnacity, to be replaced by lieutenants promoted for their proven fighting qualities. Tarpaulins were far less politically conscious and active than contemporary army officers; the frequent political changes – the dissolution of the Rump, the end of the Nominated Parliament, the creation of the Protectorate – had few repercussions. Again in 1659–60 Sandwich and Lawson met with little active dissent when they initiated moves that brought the Restoration nearer. Few officers refused to take the oaths to the king, although some who did were still regarded as unreliable and received no further appointment, while some twenty captains were not recommissioned until 1665 when the war made their services indispensable. Among masters and senior ratings, with fewer Cavaliers to challenge for places, there was greater continuity in personnel.[30]

Uncertainties about retaining or obtaining commissions enhanced the importance of having a powerful patron. Monck, whom even Charles hesitated before double-crossing or antagonizing, was the most influential among those with a Commonwealth past because

---

29 Capp, *Cromwell's Navy*, pp. 155–201; J.D. Davies, *Gentlemen and Tarpaulins: The Officers and Men of the Restoration Navy* (Oxford, 1991), pp. 130–2.

30 Ibid., pp. 28–30, 35, 129, 132, 134–6.

of his general role in 1660: Sandwich, Penn and Lawson also acted as patrons for former Commonwealth officers, Rupert for former royalist officers, but, as lord admiral, James had the final say. Fortunately for the navy James followed the advice of his secretary William Coventry in resisting Cavalier demands for the progressive elimination of all officers who had served the Commonwealth. A Bill introduced in the Commons in 1663, to confine all civil, military and naval offices to men who had not served the Long Parliament or Commonwealth, would have had disastrous consequences had it passed. A few leaders, Monck and possibly Sandwich, could have been excepted by name, but their dependants would have been ousted since the object of the Bill was not to give the restored monarchy greater security, as was pretended, but to empty offices so as to fill them with relations and clients of Cavalier peers and MPs. Had it passed it is difficult to see how a Dutch war could have been fought; in the fleet in 1665 out of one hundred and seven captains only ten were former royalist officers, with thirteen younger gentlemen commanders.[31] But after Coventry was replaced in 1667 as James's secretary by Matthew Wren, the proportions began to change, so that by 1672 former Cavaliers and gentlemen commanders held as many commissions as captains as the ex-Commonwealth men and tarpaulins: in James's own division all captains were Cavaliers and gentlemen commanders. One result of the increase in their number was a marked rise in factional in-fighting.[32] Gentlemen commanders were more aggressive than tarpaulins in competing for appointments and promotion as well as in combat, ruthlessly denigrating rivals, badgering their patrons, and using their connections at Court. In 1666 captains were energetically enlisted into the rival Rupert and Monck factions by their recruiting agents, Holmes and Jeremaiah Smith. Holmes tried to destroy Smith's reputation by fabricating charges of cowardice: a duel resulted – Pepys expressed his disappointment when he learned that Holmes had not been killed, as at first reported. In 1672 James kept control, but his successor in command, Rupert, fully involved himself in playing the factional game, shamelessly pushing his own protégés (especially his former page, Sir William Reeves). In retaliation Sir Edward Spragge, who enjoyed James's favour, criticized Rupert's leadership as incompetent. The officers of a faction-ridden fleet were united only by their biting criticisms of French naval behaviour, based on their belief that most

---

31 Ibid., p. 23; Pepys, vol. iv, pp. 125, 136, 196.
32 Davies, *Gentlemen and Tarpaulins*, pp. 35, 161.

French captains had, under orders, allowed the English to do the fighting and suffer losses while they stood off at a safe distance. Ominously by the end of the 1673 campaign, after a pamphlet – *An Exact Relation of the Several Engagements and Actions of His Majesty's Fleet* – made public Rupert's partisan version of events, it became probable that the factional divisions within the fleet would become linked with rival ministers in the council, and hostile groups in the Commons, including those that wanted an end to the war.[33]

Factional in-fighting also damaged the naval administration in the second and third wars. Members of the Navy Board were connected to varying degrees with the leading ministers, among whom there was more enmity than harmonious cooperation. The administrative structure of a Treasurer, Comptroller, Surveyor, Clerk of the Acts and three commissioners represented a return to pre-civil war practice when the navy had been smaller and naval business less complex. The instructions which governed, or were supposed to govern, the Board's operations also went back to Charles I's reign, with minor modifications.[34] From Pepys's *Diary* we can see that antagonistic personalities could express themselves, with adverse effects on the conduct of business, because their areas of responsibility were excessively large and in places ill-defined. In emergencies the system could be bypassed. Coventry and Pepys had on critical occasions to act like French *intendants*, collecting information from dockyards and officials to make reports directly to James and extract orders from him. But the system was not in itself defective: the virtual collapse of the navy in the winter of 1666–67 was first and foremost due to lack of ready money and the failure of governmental credit, and to the divisions within a heterogeneous ministry which shirked making difficult but inescapable decisions. It was ministerial failures to put the public interest before their own, their lack of application to their duties, that Pepys deplored. Of course both he and Coventry did not neglect advancing their own affairs, but it cannot be said that self-interest actually led them to evade their responsibilities or neglect their work. Coventry did withdraw from all naval business because of his disgust with ministerial negligence, but he was to return to office as a member of the new Treasury commission which set out to

33 Ibid., pp. 146–58, 162–3, 170; Pepys, vol. vii, pp. 314–15, 333, 348; R. Ollard, *Man of War: Sir Robert Holmes and the Restoration Navy* (1969), pp. 136–7, 141–2, 164; R.C. Anderson (ed.), *The Journal of Edward Montagu, first Earl of Sandwich* (1929), p. 234.

34 Pepys, vol. x, pp. 291–8.

reorganize royal finances: his decision amounted to a recognition that without improved management of credit and expenditure any devoted and painstaking attention to naval business was unlikely to repay the effort involved.[35]

Lack of ready money and the exhaustion of naval credit created appalling difficulties in the autumn of 1665 which, at that time of year, particularly affected the paying-off of ships coming in as the campaign ended. Most seamen from the fleet were discharged with tickets in lieu of money wages. These could be exchanged for cash only at public houses and with money-lenders, and then only at extortionately large discounts. The prevalence of plague in communities along the Thames meant that the skippers of merchant vessels, and the captains of ships being kept in service during the winter, would not recruit seamen from infected areas, and under no circumstances would they take men from hospital who had earlier been discharged from the fleet as sick or wounded. Nor were there any casual jobs available in a capital that was deserted by all who could afford to flee and live elsewhere. Seamen were well aware that their prospects were dire and unsurprisingly their disaffection led to disorders. The officers issuing tickets had to be given armed protection. Sporadic rioting occurred. But there was no possibility of their disaffection sparking off serious trouble in London in 1665, because all life in the City and its riverside suburbs was paralysed by the plague, and in 1666 because of the confusion caused by the Great Fire.[36]

The flight from London of all men of wealth in 1665 – bankers, goldsmiths and merchants – and the paralysis of trade and industry caused by the war as well as the plague made it difficult to raise money through loans or advances on taxes which Parliament voted. Without ready money the Navy Board was driven to a succession of hand-to-mouth expedients, most of which meant higher costs in the long run. Constant and quite forceful complaints to James and Charles achieved nothing. When Pepys presented the navy's financial accounts to the cabinet council – they were not presented to the Treasury until after its reform and reconstitution in 1667 – his audience comprised the greatest men in the kingdom: Charles, James, Rupert, Clarendon, the treasurer Southampton, Monck, secretary Morrice with Carteret (treasurer of the navy) and Coventry. After a presentation of the state of the navy Rupert, sensitive to any

---

35 In practice no major decision could be taken unless James was sufficiently interested to concern himself in the matter.

36 Pepys, vol. vi, pp. 210–11, 255, 288, 319.

implied criticism, lost his temper justifying his care of the fleet, but the rest stayed silent. None had any ideas of what could be done. Pepys reported that £100,000 was needed urgently; Charles could offer £5,000–6,000 (7 October 1666).[37] This bankruptcy of ideas was as important as the financial bankruptcy. It opened the way for innovatory moves by the Commons so that, instead of increasing the effective powers of the Crown, as some of the enthusiasts for the war had promised, the critical state of royal finances tempted the Commons into trying to go beyond its legislative role to take a direct part in the processes of government. First, the Commons demanded that it should conduct an audit of the royal accounts of expenditure which would require officials to give evidence on oath; this was prevented when Crown lawyers asserted that Parliament did not have the power to impose oaths. Second, after doing its own work, it was a sub-committee of the Commons committee of ways and means, not the Navy Board, which established the formula on which all naval estimates were to be based for the rest of the century: £4 monthly per man in service, £1 10s. for wages, the same sum for materials and £1 for victualling. Third and most ominously, the Commons, by a crude comparison of the sums they had voted, and the estimates presented by the Navy Board of money expended, came to the conclusion that nearly £2,400,000 (out of a total of £5,590,000) was not accounted for.[38]

Pepys described his failure to get a positive response from the cabinet council as an 'omen of ruin' for the navy, but both he and his colleagues knew that it could also lead to their own personal ruin. They ran the risk of being sacrificed as scapegoats to satisfy an angry Commons and public. Consequently although beset by problems for which they had no solution – particularly the paying off of increasingly mutinous seamen, and the relief of 'poor creditors' of the Crown who were themselves desperate to pay their own creditors – naval officials increasingly concentrated on preparing their cases against possible charges. For example, Coventry insisted that James must be told frankly and fully how bad the affairs of the navy had become, 'as a guard to ourselves hereafter when things shall come to be worse'. The threat of a partisan Commons investigation drove the key officials to a damage-limitation exercise; long before the council, which did not make the decision until February 1667, they realized that the main fleet could not be set out to sea in the summer of 1667.[39]

37 Ibid., vol. vii, pp. 296–7, 307, 311–13, 331.
38 Ibid., vol. vii, p. 308; *Commons Journals*, vol. viii, p. 634.
39 Pepys, vol. vii, pp. 331–2, 334, 351.

Lack of money exacerbated every administrative and logistical problem in 1665–67: this showed that money really was the source of naval power, and that lack of finance led directly to disaster. In 1672–73 financial problems of such a magnitude did not recur, but serious weaknesses in manning, and the provision of services and supplies to the fleet, did significantly reduce its effectiveness. In the context of the development of the science of naval warfare it was these weaknesses that continued to make seapower a comparatively blunt and unreliable instrument of policy. In the eighteenth century the navy was able to maintain close blockades of the main French and Spanish bases for months or even years. This called for a high level of routine organization and logistical support that was far beyond the capacity of the admiralties on either side during the Dutch Wars. After the Gabbard in 1653, Monck's victorious fleet blockaded the enemy coast for a month, but this was about the limit of an improvised watch. The critical restriction was the effect of a prolonged time at sea, with reducing rations, on the health of the ships' companies. In 1653 soldiers were sent to sea in the fleet just before the battle with inadequate clothing for bad weather conditions, and without bedding; the unsurprising result was a high incidence of sickness which necessitated the return of the ships to the English coast.[40] Defective drink was a major cause of serious sickness in all three wars. A fleet manned by about 16,000 men required about 500 tuns of water a week, but water deteriorated rapidly because of the dubious sources from which it was drawn and by infections from dirty barrels; Spragge in 1673 suggested that springs and conduits should be dedicated for naval use.[41] Whereas in the case of bad or putrid provisions, such as meat, fish and cheese, a seaman could cut out the worst bits and (not being a fastidious eater) consume the less tainted remainder, whole barrels of water could become infected so that all who drank it would suffer the ill consequences – usually a form of dysentery whose consequences in congested ships provided with few heads can hardly be imagined. Beer was less susceptible to contamination, but much of it was of poor original quality. In addition all forms of drink were adversely affected by defective casks and barrels. The English victuallers in 1673, presumably in order to maximize their profits, used barrels without iron hoops to bind them securely. These barrels could not withstand the effects of being moved about when ships rolled and pitched, so that those containing beer

40 Thurloe, vol. i, p. 327.
41 *HMC 15th Report, app. pt 1*, vol. iii, p. 9.

and water were staved in, and those containing fish leaked the brine in which they were preserved and had to be dumped. Consequently the fleet had to return prematurely from the Dutch coast: in characteristic fury Rupert wanted to have the victuallers responsible brought in custody to the fleet and compelled to remain to share the dangers and diet of the seamen.[42] In 1665 many coopers died from plague and survivors dispersed themselves away from London. The lack of skilled labour and a shortage of staves led to many ships receiving inadequate provisions; a Hamburg convoy was delayed for months waiting for escorts, and Sandwich's fleet returned from Norway with everyone on very short rations and a large sick list.[43] But on other occasions the fleet was kept well supplied. In 1672 Narborough recorded an orderly process of victualling with the kinds of food that would actually prevent the scurvy which during these wars debilitated seamen – cabbages, carrots and turnips – as well as thirty tuns of vinegar with which to clean the gun decks on which the seamen lived.[44]

The comparatively undeveloped state of naval logistics and administration made it impossible for either fleet to maintain the prolonged blockades that became a matter of routine in the eighteenth-century wars against France. Short-duration blockades were imposed, invariably after battles, and this in itself put the blockaders at a disadvantage. They had to keep the sea, repairing damage as best they could while sending the most heavily damaged ships home. By contrast the defeated fleet – Blake's after Dungeness, Tromp's after the Gabbard in 1653, Obdam's in 1665 – sought safety in ports and sheltered anchorages where major repairs were easier to accomplish. The frequent battles during these wars saw enormous expenditure of powder and shot, and the blockaders needed to rebuild their stocks; after the Gabbard the fleet had only sixteen shots per gun left and needed 6,000–7,000 barrels of powder, towards which frigates could bring only about 1,000 for transfer at sea (weather permitting).[45] The blockading fleet also needed replacements for casualties and the sick because the enemy was likely to attempt a sortie within a matter of weeks, whereas in the next century blockaded French and Spanish fleets normally remained within their

42 *CSPD 1673*, pp. 261–2, 384–5, 398; *FDW*, vol. iii, p. 384.
43 *CSPD 1665–6*, p. 59; Pepys, vol. vi, pp. 296, 300.
44 R.C. Anderson (ed.), *Journals and Narratives of the Third Dutch War* (1946), pp. 66–7, 69, 109, 148.
45 *FDW*, vol. v, pp. 194–5.

bases for months or years on end. With blockades lasting so long the admiralty's organization necessarily became highly developed; ships blockading Brest retired in rotation to Torbay for provisioning, and the Portsmouth dockyard evolved a programme for refitting ships in turn. The seventeenth-century blockades were too short and occasional for this need to be appreciated, and it is doubtful if the administration could have provided such a regular service. Another big difference was that English ships blockading the Dutch coast, or Dutch in the Thames estuary, could remain at anchor for most of the time; this reduced wear and tear on the ships (and their crews), but it involved risks. The English were always aware of the danger of being driven on to a lee shore; the fleet had frequently to get under way in a hurry, abandoning anchors which had to be replaced. Longboats, which were too heavy to be hauled up out of the water, were another item of expensive equipment which bad weather could quickly turn into consumables. In operational terms they were more important at this time than in the French wars. The absence of efficient signalling systems meant that they were used by flag-officers to transmit orders. They towed crippled ships away from the main action and were used to keep fireships at a distance. Occasionally they were employed to land soldiers: in 1667 by the Dutch to take Sheerness on Sheppey, and in the unsuccessful attack on Landguard fort, the main defence of Harwich. The English used them for the landing on Terschelling in 1666. A shortage of longboats in 1673 helped to frustrate the poorly planned project to land an army on the Dutch coast. The deep-draught colliers could not get close inshore, consequently the soldiers would need to be ferried ashore in longboats.[46]

Although navies were still a rather blunt instrument of power, the Dutch wars show that naval warfare was more complex and logistically demanding than contemporary military campaigns. Armies could largely live off the countries in which they were fighting, and the new device of 'contributions' – formal agreements extorted from enemy or neutral territories to provide food, fodder and services – made it no longer necessary for army movements to be dictated by the need to find and ravage areas in which supplies existed. Navies had to be kept regularly supplied from home bases: fleets contained as many mouths to be fed as Norwich or Haarlem. They also carried incomparably more heavy weaponry than even the largest armies. A single great ship in 1672 carried more guns than any field army and more powder and shot were expended in a single major battle than

46 W.G. Perrin (ed.), *The Naval Miscellany*, vol. iii, (1928), p. 13.

any European army consumed in a campaign. The loss of a great ship, such as the *Royal James* at Sole Bay, involved the loss of more guns (eighty-two) than any army lost during the European war of 1672–78. As a Dutch commentator bewailed, naval warfare could be horrendously expensive: the cost of building a fortress and a great ship was similar, but whereas the former should last for a millennium the latter could be destroyed in an hour. Armies often suffered appalling human casualties, but only major and prolonged sieges made the same kind of demands for heavy equipment and logistical support services as were routine in naval campaigns.[47]

The effectiveness of navies depended on the efficiency of their dockyards, and the care which administrators took in keeping them well stocked with an extensive variety of materials. They had to make good battle damage as soon as possible. Winters were spent in cleaning foul hulls, caulking to prevent leaks, replacing masts, spars and rigging, mending sails. Vast quantities of timber, cordage and pitch were needed, whose prices soared once hostilities began. One of the hidden weaknesses of the English navy in 1665–67 lay in the low level to which stocks of essential materials had been allowed to fall, despite the encouragement of aggressive policies by James which had made war likely. The Dutch navy came increasingly to rely on the facilities maintained by the Amsterdam admiralty, and particularly its extensive storehouses. Chatham was the principal English dockyard; in wartime it worked in combination with the yards and victualling depots on the lower Thames. It was easily the largest industrial unit in the country; in 1665 it employed over 800 shipwrights, joiners, caulkers and labourers, and there were another 600 men working at Deptford and Woolwich. In 1672–73 more than 2,000 men worked in the dockyards. Units of this size and internal complexity – with ropeyards, foundries, building slips, lofts for sails and storehouses for timber, masts (which had to be kept in water), cordage, guns and small arms – required skilled management and constant supervision. In both England and the Dutch Republic the efficient performance of wartime tasks depended crucially on a reliable cash-flow to the yards, but delays and shortages of money often impaired work. At certain critical times, in Holland in the late summer of 1653, in England in the autumn of 1666, an almost total lack of ready money with which to pay wages and purchase materials led to a virtual standstill in the navy yards. Flag officers and captains subjected the officials in the dockyards to constant and often unfair criticism for delays

47 Thurloe, vol. i, p. 462.

in effecting repair work and supplying equipment but, unlike the regular routine demands with which the EIC and VOC yards had to cope, most of the work with which the navy yards had to deal came in unpredictable and irregular bursts.[48]

The administration of the Chatham yard provoked deep and general criticism after the Dutch attack up the Medway in 1667. The workforce failed to help shift ships under refit further up the river. Many workers, unpaid for weeks, took advantage of the confusion to make off with pieces of timber, tools and other objects which they could sell. The commissioner, Peter Pett, who had been in office since 1648 (and his father before him from 1630 to 1647), became the universal scapegoat for the disaster. Coventry and Pepys loathed him. James expressed his instinctive distrust for Pett by saying that he could never trust him because he lifted up the whites of his eyes as he spoke, a characteristic James associated with the cant dissembling of the Puritan rulers of the Interregnum. Pett was undoubtedly guilty of making large profits out of his office, to which he had a quasi-proprietorial attitude, but the ministerial and parliamentary attacks so over-stated his responsibility, and were being so blatantly exploited to cover other persons, that Andrew Marvell made a mockery of the charges in his satiric poem 'Last Instructions to a Painter'. The threatened impeachment was not pressed. However, it seems that after his removal the yard functioned more efficiently in 1672–73, but money was not in such short supply then as it had been in 1665–67.[49]

---

48 D.C. Coleman, 'Naval Dockyards under the Later Stuarts', *Economic History Review* (1953–4) 2nd series vi, pp. 135–48; Fox, *Great Ships*, pp. 11–13; *CSPD 1651–52*, pp. 127–8, 362–3; Pepys, vol. iv, pp. 256, 258, 260.

49 Pepys, vol. viii, p. 231; on the Medway fiasco see P.G. Rogers, *The Dutch in the Medway* (1970).

4 WAR AND THE DUTCH STATE

One of the characteristics of the Anglo-Dutch Wars that made them unique in the context of the seventeenth century was that governments in both countries had to rely on the cooperation of representative institutions. One consequence that followed was that public opinion and private interests could not be neglected. In constitutional theory kings of England had exclusive prerogative powers of peace and war, and in the Dutch Republic only a small number of members of the urban oligarchies (and fewer nobles) participated in decision-making in the States General. But in practice governments in both countries found it necessary to manage opinion with a stream of propaganda 'relations', but critical and alarmist accounts also appeared, especially in the Dutch cities. At times of defeats and crisis Orangist pamphlets tried to incense the population against its government, and to stir up greater hostility to Holland in the other provinces. However, there were limits to the ability of either governments or polemical journalists to mislead their publics for long. Each capital was close to the focal areas in the North Sea where actions were concentrated; for example during the Four Days Fight the noise of massed gunfire (as with the Somme barrages of 1916) could be heard in Hyde Park. After the Texel fight in 1653 members of the States General by walking down to Scheveningen could see the English fleet parading its victory close inshore, refuting claims of Dutch success. Objective indicators of the success of operations existed in the variations in the 'actions' (stock) of the VOC and in maritime insurance premiums; errors in these areas cost money.[1]

The constitution of the Dutch Republic worked to its disadvantage during the wars against England. Its founding Union of Utrecht (1579) provided for little more than an alliance between the prov-

---

1 J.I. Israel, *The Dutch Republic: Its Rise, Greatness and Fall 1477–1806* (Oxford, 1995), p. 848, table 39; Pepys, vol. vii, pp. 140–1; Thurloe, vol. i, p. 438.

inces, necessary if Philip II was to be resisted. Throughout the two centuries it existed, sovereignty remained in each of the constituent provinces, in their representative bodies (their States) each of which was constituted differently. Seven provinces sent deputies to the States General with binding instructions on how they should vote. Each province in rotation supplied the president, which prevented the office becoming one of importance. Each deputation had one vote; in theory there was no weighting for population, or the proportion a province contributed in revenue, although in practice little could be decided against Holland's opposition. But Holland could not necessarily get the decisions that its interests required since unanimity was formally required on all important matters.

In times of crisis the States General displayed several serious weaknesses. First, if new issues arose the deputies did not have the power to make immediate decisions: delays must occur while they sought new instructions from their 'principals', the provincial States (which had to be convened). Second, nothing reported to, or decided by, the States General could be kept secret – to the obvious advantage of the English. And in practice jealousy of Holland's predominant influence led other provinces – Zeeland particularly, and Gelderland used as an Orangist pawn – to obstruct business. However, the power that the constitution gave the provinces to protect their rights ruled out any change. Even in 1672 – the year of catastrophe – William purged the governing bodies of the towns but respected the constitution, although he made a tentative attempt to take over the sovereignty of Gelderland in 1675.[2]

The absence in the constitution of any provision for an executive arm of government for the Republic, a reaction against Philip II's centralizing policies, also led to serious governmental weaknesses during the wars, and particularly in 1652–53. The Stadtholderate was a provincial not a federal office: in theory there could have been seven different Stadtholders, and during the second half of the seventeenth century a cadet branch of the House of Orange officiated in Friesland and Groningen. William II had wanted to make the office hereditary, but legally Stadtholders remained servants of the sovereign provincial States, which paid their salaries, and constitutionally it was entirely proper for the States of Holland to decide not to replace him when he died in November 1650, and to suppress the office by the Perpetual Edict of April 1667. Consequently the first and second wars occurred

---

2 Israel, *Dutch Republic*, pp. 815–18; Wicquefort, *Histoire*, vol. iv, pp. 548–9.

during the first Stadtholderless period, the era of the so-called True Freedom.

It was, then, a new form of executive authority, one that was entirely untried, that the Dutch Republic relied on during the first war. English victories provoked scathing criticisms of the incompetence of the Regent oligarchs responsible for the conduct of the war. In 1653 (and again in 1665) Orangists exploited mass, almost instinctive, demands for the restoration of the offices of leadership which the House of Orange held from the 1580s – the captain and admiral generalships – although William was too young and William Frederick, the Stadtholder of Friesland and Groningen, was not an inspiring figure.

Attacks on the conduct of war by Regent oligarchs were motivated by panic and by political partisanship, but they also reflected the contemporary and near universal belief that the direction of wars was exclusively a matter for aristocrats and members of royal families. D'Estrades, a French diplomat generally sympathetic to the Dutch, commented scornfully (and mistakenly) on De Witt's leadership 'that a Dordrecht lawyer does not dispose of the strength of mind that one will find in a man of birth'. Another French diplomat dismissed the possibility of mere 'merchants' acting effectively as leaders; they lacked the necessary sense of honour, their ambitions were for wealth not glory.[3]

These contemptuous strictures had some foundation. Every deputy who attended the States General, acting under tight instructions, adopted a particularist attitude towards the affairs of the Republic. They were there to promote and defend the interests of their province and their town, and this could result in the adoption of short-sighted policies that only served particular interests, or the blocking or obstruction of necessary decisions. On the other hand the Regent oligarchs from the mid-1630s came to believe that Frederick Henry and William II were subordinating all other interests to those of the House of Orange, were perpetuating war against Spain in order to further their ambition of establishing a hereditary dynasty.[4]

In the relatively poor and less urbanized landward provinces – Gelderland, Overijssel and Utrecht – there were no interests of suf-

---

3 Colenbrander, vol. i, pp. 218–19; Wicquefort, *Histoire*, vol. iv, p. 158n., this view of the Dutch Republic as a contradiction of European norms encouraged aggression, 'qui se fait brébis [a black sheep] le loup le mange'.

4 DLC, pp. 89, 161, 184, 209.

ficient strength capable of indefinitely withstanding outside pressures from either the House of Orange or the Regent party which ruled Holland, where every aspect of life was dominated by considerations of trade and industry. Although many of its leaders no longer actively participated in trade as merchants, they were still heavily involved as financiers and investors, and all knew that the tasks of governing and protecting their own interests would become impossibly difficult if the trade and industry on which the towns depended should be severely damaged. The governing elite in Holland was totally imbued with the principle that interest must be the guide of public policy as much as of everyday decisions by individuals. This concept, formulated by Pieter de la Court in his *Het Interest van Holland* (published in 1662), and to which De Witt himself contributed, represented the political philosophy of the True Freedom, the constitution of the Stadtholderless period of 1650–72.[5]

True Freedom meant, basically and negatively, the disappearance of a ruling family with interests of its own, many of which had proved to be inimical to the interests of the province: the dynastic link with the Stuarts, the preference for the army and its foreign officers over the needs of the navy, the maintenance of an expensive quasi-royal Court.[6] Positively the True Freedom meant practical and active freedoms – to earn a livelihood without restrictions by guilds, city authorities, the state or the clergy, to hold property (especially money) with security from appropriation, to have justice without discrimination on grounds of privileged status or religion. The dependence of all urban classes in Holland on trade, and the fact that decisions by the Regents were bound to affect the lives of the ordinary people among whom they lived, led Sir William Temple to the facile conclusion that Regents had no motive to distort public policies in order to serve their own particular interests, or act corruptly.[7]

Apologists for the True Freedom claimed that the exemplar for

5 Israel, *Dutch Republic*, pp. 759–60; G.J. Renier, *The Dutch Nation* (1944), pp. 124–30, 135, 137; DLC, pp. 68–71.

6 Israel, *Dutch Republic*, pp. 700–13; P. Geyl, *Orange and Stuart* (1969), pp. 5–10, 77–82; Thurloe, vol. i, p. 365.

7 Sir W. Temple, *Observations upon the United Provinces of the Netherlands* (ed. Sir G. Clark, Oxford, 1972), pp. 71–2, 83; Wicquefort, *Histoire* vol. iv, pp. 353–4; D.J. Roorda, 'The Ruling Classes in Holland in the Seventeenth Century', in J.S. Bromley and E.H. Kossmann (eds), *Britain and the Netherlands*, vol. ii (Groningen, 1964), pp. 109–32.

the magistrates of Holland was the early Roman Republic.[8] But as in the later Roman Republic, wealth and a taste for luxury dissolved the earlier simplicities of life. By the 1650s society in Holland was primarily concerned with money making and continued to be so even in wartime crises: in 1653 an English resident observed that even though the fleet had been battered in a series of defeats no merchant, tradesman, artisan or labourer would provide goods and services or work beyond 'the measure of the money which is given'. With tax revenues declining and state credit suffering the power of the state could collapse.[9] There was resistance to the idea of a national interest justifying the overriding of private rights and commercial freedom. In November 1664, with war clearly approaching, the States General placed an embargo on the export of masts in order to build up stocks, but this had to be rescinded as an illegal restraint on trade.[10] Some Amsterdam merchants used their freedom to export gunpowder to Hamburg, knowing from the high price offered that it would be re-exported to England.[11] Seamen who had signed on for a voyage to Java tried to set fire to their VOC vessel, to prevent it being converted into a warship in which they would be compelled to fight; they were hanged.[12] Shipbuilders used unseasoned timber because the war had forced up prices, and to use superior materials would erode their profit margins. When the need to concentrate naval resources in the narrow seas in 1652–53 led to the loss of the last surviving Dutch positions in Brazil, the WIC thought that peace with England would release powerful forces to retake them. Having worked out the costings of such an enterprise Holland refused: the fall in the price of sugar, due to the expansion of production in the West Indies, made reconquest an uneconomic proposition.[13]

The primacy of considerations based on money and profits in shaping Dutch policies served as the basic assumption for the diplomatic strategy followed by Sir George Downing in 1663–65. He thought that if unremitting pressure was maintained on the Dutch they would, for fear of provoking a new war that would depress

---

8 The Batavian rebellion against corrupt Roman governors, and led by Claudius Civilis, formed the basis for this identification, commemorated in Rembrandt's largest but now mutilated painting: A. van Schendel, *Rembrandt 1669–1969* (Amsterdam, 1969), pp. 98–103.

9 Thurloe, vol. i, pp. 330, 411.

10 Colenbrander, vol. i, p. 142.

11 Thurloe, vol. i, p. 529.

12 Ibid., vol. i, p. 523.

13 Wicquefort, *Histoire*, vol. iii, pp. 66–8.

their trade and profits, eventually and reluctantly concede English demands. For example he told members of the States General that the cost of paying the reparations which he was demanding was far less than that of setting out ships to deter English reprisals. Many of Downing's contacts were ready to respond as he wished, especially when he gave them the impression that their own particular interests would not suffer.[14]

This was the danger than De Witt had to overcome, that private and particularist interests would obliterate any awareness of the public interest, and that consequently in a crisis everyone would concentrate on looking after their own, that there would ensue a general *sauve qui peut*, the cry when a ship was sinking. Two extraordinary instances of such self-interest, of insularity in a literal sense, illustrate this danger. De Witt's friend de la Court suggested in his book that the interest of Holland could best be served, best because cheap and a form of self-help, by digging a vast canal to make the province an island. At the other extreme in terms of importance, a delegation appeared in London in February 1653 from the small and poor island of Ameland on the northern edge of the Wadden Zee, to ask the Rump to treat it as a neutral, claiming that it had been neutral throughout the Eighty Years War. Its justification, that the inhabitants' livelihood depended entirely on fishing, applied to only a slightly lesser extent to the fishing towns of the North Quarter, but there it produced a different reaction, an Orangist demand for the intensification of the war.[15]

More insidiously De Witt was hampered by the assumption that even in wartime commercial considerations should remain paramount. The VOC resisted the conversion of its vessels into warships, and tried to link the loans it was asked for with permission to undertake the usual outward sailings. Owners engaged in the Greenland and Spitzbergen whale fisheries and the Archangel trade exerted pressure for permission to send full crews – the hardiest of all Dutch seamen – on long summertime voyages which would deprive the navy of their services during the campaigning season. As with another state and economy committed to *laissez-faire* principles and practices – Asquithian England in 1914–15 – most merchants and entrepreneurs seemed to think that war could be waged on the basis of the economically intelligible, but politically and militarily

14 *CSPVenetian 1664–66*, p. 37 (21 August 1664).
15 DLC, pp. 291–4; Thurloe, vol. ii, p. 92.

suicidal, policy of 'business as usual'. De Witt knew that this was impossible.[16]

The most extreme instances of private interest being put before the public occurred during the desperate days of 1672. The Assembly of Gelderland and the States of Overijssel capitulated to the invading bishop of Münster, recognizing him as their sovereign in return for his confirmation of their particular privileges and toleration of the protestant religion.[17] The latter prevented troops in Kampen from offering resistance. At Utrecht the magistrates refused to allow William to enter the city and defend it, because this would require demolition of the suburbs to create a defensive fire-zone.[18] The most negative behaviour came (not unexpectedly) from the most despised and powerless section of the community – the boors or peasants. They tried first to prevent, and then to sabotage, the flooding of the polders on the eastern fringes of Holland, the only way in which the otherwise irresistible French invasion could be stopped. Eager to restart cultivation the boors tried to divert, or draw off the water, 'ignorantly' failing to see that it was really in their interest, in common with all Hollanders, rich and poor, urban and rural, to keep the French at bay.[19]

The Regent party similarly regarded ignorance in an inveterate form as the reason why the urban masses tended to be influenced by Orangist agitators and propaganda. According to de la Court, ignorance prevented ordinary people from knowing what actually constituted their own interest. It prevented them from using their freedom to exploit their natural abilities to improve their condition, regardless of whether a realistic chance for them to do so existed. Ignorance also made those at the bottom of the social and economic scales dangerous, and in the smaller-scale merchants, and tradesmen and artisans who were excluded from all influential urban offices they had potential leaders.[20]

Living at close quarters with the less well off and poor, the Regents were always aware of their vulnerability, which of course increased in wartime when the disruption of trade, and consequentially lower levels of employment, coincided with higher food prices. In the textile and fishing towns, where these pressures were greatest

---

16 Colenbrander, vol. i, pp. 157, 168–9, 173, 175–6; Thurloe, vol. i, p. 329.
17 Wicquefort, *Histoire*, vol. iv, pp. 361, 412–14, 422–5, 548–9.
18 Ibid., vol. iv, pp. 332, 415, 422–5.
19 S.B. Baxter, *William III* (1966), pp. 72–3.
20 DLC, pp. 317, 318–19.

in times of depression, the Regent party retained control only by behaving more flexibly, yielding in form by making representations to the States of Holland which echoed popular demands. But in such places – Haarlem, Leiden, Enkhuizen and Hoorn – the True Freedom could survive only by 'bridling' the people. Everything depended on the dependability of the provincial militia. As one observer commented in 1653, its dependability had nothing to do with loyalty or ideology. If the States paid the soldiers fully and regularly they would obey orders, but if their pay fell into arrears a total alteration of the government would follow.[21]

De Witt personally endured almost insufferable pressures, especially during periods when the war was going badly. At the Hague in August 1653 the fiscal stopped a boys' festival parade which was being turned into an Orangist demonstration. He took away their trumpet. On the pretext of demanding its return a crowd assembled after nightfall, wrecked the fiscal's house, then turned against the home of 'that rogue, the Prince-betrayer' De Witt, and would have demolished it but for the chance arrival of some soldiers. They ended by assaulting the lodgings maintained for Amsterdam deputies to the States General and the houses of Hagenaar officials. In all this the city militia were noticeable by their absence; the disturbances had erupted in a matter of hours and out of a trivial dispute.[22] In the later years of the True Freedom security received close attention, and the militia and even the army were seen by the Regents as being as much internal police as defenders of the Republic against external enemies. The army's lamentable performance against the bishop of Münster's forces in 1665, and the French in 1672, was a direct consequence. Higher officers had been appointed because they were politically sound, junior commissions were filled to satisfy political and local patronage groups.[23]

During the period of the True Freedom most of the clergy used their influence over the urban populations to promote Orangist principles. In theory clerics in their consistories depended on the governing bodies of the towns for appointment and salaries, but control over the most outspoken often proved difficult in practice. In 1651 inflammatory sermons against the emissaries of the regi-

---

21 Wicquefort, *Histoire*, vol.i, pp. 216–17; Thurloe, vol. i, pp. 329, 459; Temple, *Observations*, p. 71; Roorda, 'Ruling Classes in Holland', pp. 118–19.

22 Thurloe, vol. i, pp. 382, 391; Wicquefort, *Histoire*, vol. i, p. 216.

23 Wicquefort, *Histoire*, vol. iv, pp. 401, 403; N. Japikse, *De Verwikkelingen tussen de Republiek en Engeland* (The Hague, 1900), p. xxi.

cide Commonwealth stirred up so much popular hostility to the St John-Strickland mission that its work became almost impossible. Each successive regime in England was depicted as provoking God's anger – the Rump, Barebones, Cromwell – and these denunciations made the negotiation of peace more difficult. In 1665–67 despite Charles II's repression of the English and Scottish presbyterians, many of the clergy of the Reformed Church laid responsibility for the war and defeats on De Witt and the Regents, and called for an immediate Orangist restoration.[24]

The Dutch Republic fought the first and second wars without a captain or admiral general, and, with a Stadtholder only in Groningen and Friesland, it could be said to have been without a formal executive. In practice of course the necessary leadership was provided by Johan De Witt, whose office of pensionary of the province of Holland gave him the opportunity to lead its States and make use of its influence in the States General. The train of events in 1651–53 under De Witt's predecessor Pauw, when negotiations with St John and Strickland were mishandled, the Commonwealth provoked by an unrealistic decision to set out a large fleet of mostly feeble ships, Tromp given ambiguous instructions which produced the clash that precipitated war, and a faulty strategy that brought defeat, all validate the impression that De Witt's leadership was the crucial factor that enabled the Dutch Republic's survival.[25]

Yet De Witt's leadership was always vulnerable because he was rightly identified with the interests of Holland: on the statue of him which stands on the spot where he was killed is Temple's obituary verdict – he was a 'complete Hollander'. Indeed by collaborating with de la Court in his *Het Interest van Holland* (first published in 1662), he laid himself open to charges that the States of Holland regarded itself entitled to initiate and pursue policies that served its interests – without regard to the opinions of the other provinces – because it contributed most of the Republic's revenues and almost all the loans. During the first war De Witt had to repulse constant Orangist calls for a single captain and admiral general in place of an ineffective Regent leadership: 'we want a chief: we have too many masters when we need only one'.[26]

24 Temple, *Observations*, pp. 104–5; Colenbrander, vol. i, p. 158; Wicquefort, *Histoire*, vol. i, p. 158; vol. ii, 196, 217; Roorda, 'Ruling Classes in Holland', p. 122; Israel, *Dutch Republic*, pp. 637–76.

25 Thurloe, vol. i, pp. 185, 382; H.H. Rowen, *John de Witt: Grand Pensionary of Holland* (Princeton, NJ, 1978), p. 57.

26 Thurloe, vol. i, p. 299; DLC, pp. 316, 371.

The crushing naval defeats of June and July 1653 faced both Dutch factions with critical decisions. As well as demanding a captain general the Orangists asserted that the unfavourable situation could be retrieved by concluding an alliance with France, inviting Charles II to the Hague and championing his cause. Aid should be sent to the royalists in the Highlands and risings instigated in England and Ireland. In return appeals by Charles and Rupert to officers and seamen in the Commonwealth navy to defect with their ships would help restore a balance of forces at sea. For the Regent party this was a formula for endless war, and a French alliance would lead to war with Spain, and the annihilation of what survived of Dutch trade. But although they favoured an early peace with England, the commissioners sent during the summer of 1653 to undertake preliminary discussions found that Cromwell seemed to be persisting in the demands for a union or coalition which had proved to be the sticking point in the 1651 negotiations with St John and Strickland. The States General would never agree to the subordination which all Dutchmen thought this would mean, 'slavery' akin to that under Philip II in the Orangist view.[27]

Two of the four commissioners sent to London by the States General, Beverningk and Nieuwport, were Hollanders. Both provoked deep Orangist distrust, charges that they had secret instructions from Holland as well as formal ones from the States General. In the event it was through informal discussions with these two commissioners that Cromwell saw a way forward towards peace. He realized that De Witt, who from July 1653 was effectively head of the administration, identified trade as the vital interest for Holland, its *salus populi* as Cromwell agreed. When the States of Holland checkmated Orangist demands for an alliance with Charles II by resolving that no foreign potentate (meaning, but not identifying, Charles) should be permitted to enter the province, the conditions for a trade-off came into existence. The States of Holland and the Commonwealth had in common an interest in excluding the House of Orange from office, and its partisans from power and office which would include control of the Dutch fleet.[28]

However, while the Barebones Parliament existed, little progress was made. Those whom an English correspondent called the 'Louvestein heeren' found themselves increasingly entrapped. The English Council of State persisted with unacceptable demands for

27 Wicquefort, *Histoire*, vol. ii, pp. 218–19; Geyl, *Orange and Stuart*, pp. 72–3.
28 Thurloe, vol. i, pp. 438–9, 601.

union or coalition, to which the Dutch responded with limited offers of a 'strict and near alliance', an 'intrinsical union' as close as was ever made between two *sovereign* states: the word sovereign set a limit to conserve the independence of the Dutch Republic. Detailed proposals for mutual consultations between the two governments, and a Dutch guarantee of assistance against all aggression by land or sea, fell far short of the security requirements of the Commonwealth. They consciously excluded promising assistance against internal subversion or rebellion; by contrast in 1709 when they had more faith in the durability of British regimes the Dutch agreed to uphold the Hanoverian succession, and sent troops to defend it in 1715.[29]

In 1653–54 the States General would never have passed any measure excluding the House of Orange from office in the Republic. All that the 1654 peace treaty demanded was that holders of office must take an oath to respect and obey the treaty, and this included an article prohibiting assistance to royalist opponents of the Commonwealth. This 'temperament' would at the most provide a paper guarantee: Cromwell's search for security was satisfied by a separate agreement with the province of Holland which strained, but perhaps technically did not break, the constitutional prohibition on single provinces concluding treaties with foreign powers. The States of Holland was to pass an Act of Seclusion excluding William from holding any office in the province. Until this was done Cromwell, now lord protector, would not ratify the peace treaty. However, Holland had been given an inducement to do so; the treaty did not contain the kind of provisions that the mercantilist Rump MPs had advocated to discriminate against Dutch trade. Indeed the commissioners had been sent instructions from the Hague to seek the repeal of the Navigation Act, revealing not only extraordinary naivety (since they were not authorized to offer anything in return) but also the extent of their concern for their trade. But the suggestion was to be repeated in 1660 when the 1651 Act lapsed with the restoration of the monarchy: this was to provoke a different English reaction, a belief that Dutch anxiety about their trade could be exploited.[30]

De Witt and Holland could not maintain the Act of Seclusion after Charles II was restored. There was a general expectation, not

29 Ibid., vol. i, pp. 182–4, 188; R. Geikie and I.A. Montgomery, *The Dutch Barrier* (Cambridge, 1930), pp. 377–86.

30 Rowen, *De Witt*, pp. 206–7, 215–17; Thurloe, vol. i, pp. 290, 296, 302–3, 306; Wicquefort, *Histoire*, vol. ii, 296, 301–3, 306; Israel, *Dutch Republic*, pp. 722–6.

confined to Orangists, that Charles would exert pressure on William's behalf, but he did not. He gave Downing, who returned to the Hague as envoy in 1661 having served Cromwell there earlier, carefully limited instructions. Charles needed to consolidate his authority before engaging in foreign policy initiatives, and he had inherited a run-down navy. So instead of collaborating with Zeeland, which in August 1660 asked the States General to name the boy William as captain general, and suggested to Holland that he should be appointed Stadtholder of the two provinces, Downing was merely to encourage the other provinces to persuade the States of Holland to promise that, when he reached the age of discretion (presumably in 1668, when he became 18), William would be 'provided' with the same offices as his ancestors. The word 'provided' avoided any implication of election or creation that would recognize the States General or provincial States as his sovereign.[31]

Charles's initial caution was realistic. The Orangist party had declined in strength and militancy since 1650–53, but it was bound to revive as William approached manhood. In the longer term both Charles and Clarendon wanted to secure De Witt's elimination from politics, but only after a treaty had been concluded to settle outstanding trade disputes. Characteristically it was Clarendon, rather than Charles, who detested De Witt, not only as the personification of Dutch republicanism but also because he had established an identity of interest with Cromwell. Clarendon believed that the secret negotiations which had preceded the Act of Seclusion could be used to convict De Witt of breaking the Dutch constitution, and so clear a way for William.[32]

By contrast Downing, although certainly ready to use William's position in order to bring pressure on De Witt, aimed at extorting trading concessions from the Dutch. His main political strategy was to exploit what he described as 'the infinite advantages upon the account of the form of the government of this country, which is such a shattered and divided thing'.[33] He found many ways in which dissensions could be exacerbated. Downing sponsored propaganda to 'disabuse' the people, that is to inflame them against their Regent oligarchs, particularly in 1665 when he stayed on at the Hague for several months after hostilities began. Downing loaded blame for the

31 Japikse, *Verwikkelingen*, pp. xix, xxiii–xxiv; Israel, *Dutch Republic*, p. 751.
32 Japikse, *Verwikkelingen*, pp. xxxiii–xxxiv; T.H. Lister, *The Life and Administration of Edward, first Earl of Clarendon*, vol. iii (1838), pp. 167, 172.
33 Japikse, *Verwikkelingen*, p. liv.

war on the two monopoly companies, the VOC and WIC, in order to increase the reluctance of the landward provinces to support and help finance the war, and to play on the jealousy against the companies on the part of middling merchants and shipowners. But his main aim was to isolate and denigrate De Witt and his associates, whom he constantly stigmatized as his 'juncto'.[34]

The blatant aggressiveness of English policies and actions in 1664–65 reduced the effectiveness of Downing's propaganda. His greatest successes were in intelligence or espionage work. He boasted that because of the permeability of all parts of the Dutch government and administration, their inability to maintain secrecy, no decision remained safe from his network of informants. This forced De Witt to deceive members of the naval committee of the States General in order to deceive Downing, and keep secret the orders which were sent in August 1664 to De Ruyter in the Mediterranean, instructing him to carry out a reprisal raid on the English in west Africa. But Downing did learn immediately of the further orders sent early in 1665 to De Ruyter to carry out raids on English plantations in the Caribbean and North America. Downing also got hold of the instructions for the conduct of the fleet, the war plan, given to Obdam who commanded the fleet in the first campaign. His penetration of the Dutch diplomatic correspondence was such that the French ambassador at the Hague protested that full details of the crucial and sensitive negotiations for Louis to enter the war on the Dutch side, which were taking place in Paris, had been reported to London as a result of leaks at the Hague by men in the inner circles of government, who had access to despatches from the Dutch ambassador to France. Downing described such informants as 'friends', covert Orangists who hated De Witt, although some of them did receive payment for their information. Downing also deployed a network of paid agents. These men talked to officers and seamen, and monitored work in the navy yards, to ascertain when the Dutch fleet would be ready for sea, or how long it would take to repair battle damage.[35]

Downing was right to try to isolate and denigrate De Witt. His leadership more than any other factor enabled the Dutch to recover from the initial, disastrous defeat off Lowestoft. No important deci-

34 Ibid., pp. xxxiii–xxxiv, li; *Cal.Cl.SP*, pp. 412–13, 417, 449; Lister, *Life of Clarendon*, p. 203.

35 Lister, *Life of Clarendon*, pp. 361n, 363, 371–3, 388; *CSPVenetian 1664–65*, p. 52; see also Thurloe, vol. i, pp. 260, 301–2, 316–17, 359, 549.

sion was made without reference to him. Downing had reluctantly to admit that De Witt worked almost continuously with little sleep, taking on an immense burden of responsibility. Like William later he never appeared to be discouraged, but unlike William he had the ability to persuade doubters and to sway the States of Holland and the States General, but then they were the source of his power. His indispensability meant that there was no alternative: Orangist sentiment was less of a danger than in 1653. The proposition to send William to England to negotiate for peace, based on the obviously fallacious assumption that Charles would give him far more generous terms than could be obtained in ordinary diplomatic negotiations, was risibly unrealistic.[36]

De Witt's leadership during the war of 1665–67, the way in which he made government according to the principles of the True Freedom work, even in crisis conditions, represented the summit of his achievement. However, he could not overcome the accumulating difficulties of the years afterwards. His own misjudgements also contributed directly to the catastrophe of 1672, but so did the divisions that undermined the effectiveness of the Regent party.[37]

William's claims to some form of office were bound to increase as he approached maturity. De Witt's attempts to block him were doomed to failure. In August 1667 the States of Holland passed the ludicrously (and indeed provocatively) mistitled Perpetual Edict. This erected a paper barrier to William's career advancement. The States abolished the office of Stadtholder 'for ever' in the province of Holland. It imposed an oath on all existing and future members of town governments to respect this abolition, and also to permit no authority to intervene by determining the composition of these bodies. This looked back to William II's attempted interference with the town governments and was intended to block any person purporting to act as Stadtholder from setting out to pack the States. The danger was real. First, the Edict was aimed at preventing the kind of purges which the Orangists forced through in 1672 and which William III immediately ratified. Second, the States of Holland announced its intention to veto anyone holding the offices of captain and admiral general from becoming Stadtholder of any province as well. It set out to obtain a similar pledge from the other provinces and succeeded

---

36 *CSP Venetian 1664–65*, p. 221; Wicquefort, *Histoire*, vol. iii, p. 210; Lister, *Life of Clarendon*, p. 388.

37 Israel, *Dutch Republic*, pp. 784–5, 792–4, 799–803; H.H. Rowen, *The Ambassador Prepares for War* (The Hague, 1957), pp. 53, 134, 161–2, 164.

with Utrecht, Gelderland and Overijssel. An oath to observe this provision was imposed on all appointed to offices. This extended to William himself when in 1670 he accepted the invitation to become a member of the Council of State – an advisory, not an executive, body. But in the crisis of 1672 he was understandably to ignore this oath: to have let the fatherland perish for the sake of an imposed oath was not something that would have been in character for a great-grandson of Henri IV.[38]

The Perpetual Edict embodied the principle that liberty requires the subordination of the military forces of the state to its representative institutions – ironically something that William was going to have to accept in England in 1689. De Witt, although he was faced with a new military threat from France from 1667 onwards, still gave the highest priority to preventing the army from becoming an Orangist instrument – as it had been in 1650 at the time of William II's attempted coup. He secured politically complaisant higher officers, Maurice and Wirtz, disbanded new forces that had been raised in a hurry in 1668 without careful political vetting, and reduced the proportion of foreign troops because they could not be relied on to have durable loyalty towards the True Freedom regime. He fought a rearguard action when it became clear that it would be difficult to deny William the captain generalship indefinitely; De Witt wanted an appointment for a single campaign only. This would put William in an impossible position – a command carrying full responsibility but only probationary powers.[39]

The outcome of treating the army as a political danger, relegating all questions of its efficiency and state of preparedness to second place, was disastrous. Patronage disputes created divisions within the officer corps. In an attempt to exert pressure Orangist obstruction delayed the payment of contributions by several provinces, which were earmarked for new troops, until the end of 1671, so that when the French invaded many of the defence forces were raw recruits. De Witt delayed enlisting mercenary contingents from neighbouring German princes. A significant number of the politically safe officers proved to be incompetent or even traitorous, which was to lead to wild Orangist charges that De Witt was engaged in a conspiracy to betray the Republic to France.[40]

38 Rowen, *De Witt*, 788–90; DLC, p. 371; Baxter, *William III*, p. 54; Israel, *Dutch Republic*, pp. 791–3; Geyl, *Orange and Stuart*, pp. 270–1.

39 Wicquefort, *Histoire*, vol. iv, pp. 61, 74, 349, 391, 394–6, 401.

40 Ibid., vol. iv, pp. 352–3; Geyl, *Orange and Stuart*, p. 357; Israel, *Dutch Republic*, p. 794.

When William was finally made captain general on 25 February 1672 – De Witt had tenaciously but almost suicidally tried to delay the appointment further, until his twenty-second birthday in November – he found the army in poor condition, whereas the fleet was superbly prepared. Traditionally the Regent party, like the Country party in England, distrusted the army and its aristocratic and foreign officers as a potential threat to the constitution. Despite the Orangist sympathies of most officers, and nearly all seamen, the navy did not constitute such a threat, and on its efficiency the trade and therefore the survival of Holland depended. The comparative neglect of the army was also due to De Witt's reluctance to recognize that France, the ally of 1666–67, was now pursuing policies that were as antagonistic to the vital interests of the Dutch Republic as any threat from England.[41]

In the last two years before the war of 1672 De Witt's leadership, which had saved the Republic in the two English wars, lost much of its effectiveness. Admittedly he faced problems to which he had no solution; the new threat from France added to the revived threat from England, Colbert's *petite guerre* of discrimination against Dutch trade and shipping, a split in the Regent governing elite which must benefit William and the Orangists. It is not surprising that after two decades of unremitting pressures the conviction that everything which he had achieved was now at increasing risk should have affected De Witt, making him less decisive and more obstinate.

The consequences of De Witt's declining effectiveness were extremely damaging. Divisions which were the result of different trading interests delayed and weakened the institution of reprisals for Colbert's tariffs and prohibitions. De Witt persisted in playing down the mounting evidence of Louis XIV's hostility and failed to take sufficient notice of the astonishingly accurate information which he received in February 1671 from De Groot, his ambassador in Paris, about Anglo-French intentions.[42] Historians have been influenced in their judgement of De Witt by their knowledge of his appalling end, and have tended to discount the Orangist charges of treason that helped to inflame the Hagenaar mob against him and his brother. But such had been the prestige and pre-eminence of Johan De Witt that it was credible for pamphleteers to depict him as having wilfully left the Republic defenceless rather than admit William to a share of power.

---

41 Baxter, *William III*, pp. 58, 61, 62–4; Israel, *Dutch Republic*, p. 794.

42 Wicquefort, *Histoire*, vol. iv, pp. 346, 349, 352–3, 354, 357; F.J.L. Krämer, *Lettres de Pierre de Groot à Abraham de Wicquefort* (The Hague, 1894), pp. 15–37.

The hysteria against the De Witt brothers was a natural reaction in the middle of a catastrophe, and the True Freedom could not have survived the French invasion of 1672, just as the Second Empire was bound to collapse in 1870 and the Third Republic in 1940.[43]

Furthermore in terms of harsh political realism there was no reason for William to regret the permanent elimination of De Witt, as distinct from the way in which this was done. As late as the spring of 1671 De Witt had tried to re-establish a political understanding with Louis on what would have been French terms, and this despite De Groot's warnings. With De Witt at their head the Regent partisans would have been a more formidable threat when, after 1674 and the French retreat from Dutch territory, Louis renewed his approaches to them.[44]

William was greatly helped in consolidating his authority by the collaboration of the 'middle' party, Regents who had become increasingly dissatisfied with De Witt's leadership and policies. William had no wish to be dependent on the popular forces who coerced the Regents of the Holland towns into repealing the Perpetual Edict and granting William the Stadtholderate and the offices of captain and admiral general. Serious disturbances had erupted as the French approached, with crowds preventing rich citizens leaving with their portable assets for the perhaps illusory safety of Zeeland or, more damagingly, for Hamburg or even England. The Orangist clergy whipped up popular anger against the Regents. Under threats of violence from crowds who assembled outside each Stadthuis, first in Dordrecht – De Witt's hometown – the demoralized magistrates were forced to denounce the Perpetual Edict and agree to William's appointment. In the States of Holland some deputies insisted that if their promises were not honoured their own lives would be in danger. One deputation argued that necessity required action, whether inside or outside the strict limits of the law – a contention that could be used to justify and order changes of the most drastic kind.[45]

Clearly the situation in June and July 1672 was one of such dire crisis that William could have gone far beyond an 'alteration', that is a sweeping change of personnel, and broken the hold of the wealthy urban oligarchs, opening offices to the middling sort who constituted the Orangist party's main support in the towns. Many

43 Colenbrander, vol. ii, pp. 130, 187.

44 Rowen, *Ambassador Prepares for War*, pp. 163–4; Israel, *Dutch Republic*, pp. 793–4.

45 Israel, *Dutch Republic*, pp. 799–806; Colenbrander, vol. ii, p. 129.

Orangists would have welcomed his assuming the position and powers of a hereditary, sovereign prince.[46] But such moves would have created confusion and in-fighting. Most Orangist partisans lacked administrative experience to replace De Witt's associates in urban offices. Alienation of the entire urban elite would have made the raising of loans difficult if not impossible. The willingness of the 'middle' party to serve William, to fill the vacancies created by the purges of the urban ruling bodies, ensured the survival of the existing governmental structures at all levels. These were to continue to function for more than another century, both for good (stability) and ill (stagnation, ossification). And during this third war it was the constitutional uncertainties of the English, not the Dutch, state that were to have more effect on the outcome.

<hr>

[46] Colenbrander, vol. ii, p. 155; DLC, pp. 339–41, 371.

5   WAR AND THE ENGLISH STATE

Any impression of a continuity of policies through the three wars on the part of successive English governments, and particularly that they were each inspired by mercantilist principles or interests, is misleading. The character of the governments that fought them could hardly have been more dissimilar. The first began under the Rump, was prosecuted by the Nominated or Barebones Parliament, but was ended by the Protectorate. The second war, under the restored monarchy, was launched with parliamentary cooperation, the third without it. There were considerable variations in the influence that mercantile, or any popular, interests could exert on policy decisions. City of London interest groups did not bring about the first war, but they tried vainly to make it a commercial war, and in 1664–65 renewed calls for pressure to be threatened, or used, to extort major concessions from the Dutch. But in contrast the war of 1672–74 was entirely a royal or Court war, with only a fraudulent pretence that commercial advantage remained a major objective.

In 1649–51 the Rump followed an outdated tradition in regarding the Dutch Republic as England's natural friend. The Long Parliament had sent an envoy, Walter Strickland, to the Hague in 1642 and proposed a strict alliance to the States General. The Dutch did not respond. Concerned to protect their interests they astutely established relations on two levels of diplomacy while declaring themselves neutral. They continued to recognize Charles's ambassador. The States General refused to receive Strickland, but the States of Holland did, in order to negotiate over matters of trade, such as the seizure of Dutch vessels with contraband, but this did not imply any degree of recognition: it sent an envoy to negotiate with the Irish Catholic Confederates over similar disputes. In March 1649 the Rump, speaking for the newly established Commonwealth, made a new approach for good relations, floating the idea of a 'nearer Union', that is a permanent and close alliance. Only Holland, fearful for its trading interests, advocated recognition but William II's support for the Stuarts and the Scots made this impossible, and only after his death in November 1650 was recognition at last given to the regicide Commonwealth.[1]

In London William's death seemed to transform the entire situation. Almost immediately, in February 1651, the Rump sent the St John-Strickland mission to offer the States General a union or coalition between the two republics for the purpose of conserving religion and liberty in both. In making this offer the Rump was naively ignoring current realities. First, the protestant religion no longer constituted a common bond between the two nations. One Rump MP hopefully referred to the 'godly party' in the Dutch Republic, but no influential body of protestants existed there which remotely resembled the Independents and the sects. The influential and militant clergy of the Dutch Reformed Church were passionate Orangists who denounced the execution of Charles I. They and the plebeian members of their congregations, unlike the Regents, abominated religious toleration, what they saw as the irreligious licence produced by the sects in England and sympathized with the English and Scottish presbyterians. Some of them organized threatening demonstrations against the St John mission.[2]

Second, the death of William II and the conclusion of peace with Spain meant that Dutch liberty no longer needed English guarantees. On the contrary alignment with the regicide Commonwealth could lead to involvement in hostilities against its many enemies. More fundamentally English and Dutch concepts of liberty, and the constitutions of the two republics reflecting them, were incompatible. The Union of Utrecht provided a loose federal framework of government. Each of the eight provinces retained sovereignty: the seven which sent delegates (not representatives) to the States General had equal voting power and unanimity was required for decisions.[3] By contrast the Commonwealth's Rump and Council of State possessed and constantly exercised more highly centralized powers than had ever been known under the monarchy, and which no contemporary European sovereign actually exercised in practice. The Long Parliament had

---

1 Thurloe, vol. i, pp. 116, 123, 133.

2 Ibid., vol. i, p. 387; J.I. Israel, *The Dutch Republic: Its Rise, Greatness and Fall 1477–1806* (Oxford, 1995), pp. 637–40, 662–5, 673; it is not clear who the 'godly' party could be; the clergy of the Reformed Church opposed the Regents because of their tolerant attitude towards the sects.

3 Israel, *Dutch Republic*, pp. 700–13; the eighth province, Drenthe, did not send deputies to the States General.

abolished the regional councils of Wales and the North. During the civil war it established tightly controlled committees to administer the counties. Municipal corporations, whose autonomous rights were fundamental to the Dutch republican concept of liberty – the True Freedom – were in England defenceless against arbitrary invasion and manipulation by the Rump. An innovatory High Court of Justice, which had the power to act in provincial centres of disaffection, administered exemplary political justice to protect the security of the regime. Ireland and Scotland, after being conquered, were forcibly incorporated in a unitary state totally dominated by England – a fate that the Dutch feared would be theirs when they faced defeat in 1653. It is impossible to see how such a centralized state could have been united in any meaningful or acceptable form with a republic which existed primarily to conserve the liberties, and promote the interests, of its constituent provinces and towns. In addition the disparity in size, population, natural resources and potential was such that English domination would be difficult to avoid.[4]

The objections of the States of Holland to any union centred on their fears that their trading interests would be adversely affected. The other provinces had ideological objections. The Orangist States of Gelderland argued that the essential maxims or principles of the Commonwealth were as pernicious and dangerous as those of Philip II. The pensionary of Zeeland objected to the notion that there was any similarity between the origins of the Commonwealth and those of the Dutch Republic, between the abjuration of Philip II and the execution of Charles I. The Dutch constitution existed to protect traditional liberties against centralization, whereas the Rump had since December 1648 carried out a total alteration of government. The justification given for its changes, that they represented the 'just judgement of God', could be used again and again in the future. One of the Dutch negotiators described the renewal of the Union proposals by the English in 1653 as a 'proposal made by men of war', mostly colonels, 'who after abolishing the monarchy . . . were now entered into a vision and imagined that nothing was impossible'.[5]

Repeatedly defeated at sea during 1653 the Dutch saw political instability in England as the only hopeful development, although they were as baffled by the changes as the rest of Europe. The Orangists interpreted them as evidence of an impending collapse of the Commonwealth. Consequently they advocated an intensification

4 Thurloe, vol. i, p. 438.
5 Ibid., vol. i, pp. 230–2, 325, 469, 490.

of hostilities, an alliance with France and the exiled Stuarts, and assistance for the insurgents in the Scottish Highlands. De Witt hoped that Cromwell's dissolution of the Rump (April 1653) would facilitate a negotiated settlement, but the new Nominated or Barebones Parliament contained a strong bloc of millenarians who wanted the war continued until the Dutch were crushed and forced into abject submission. However, the final political change of 1653, the voluntary abdication of Parliament by its moderates, and the new constitution (the Instrument of Government) which made Cromwell lord protector, opened a way for an agreed peace settlement.[6]

Although Cromwell's position as a ruler installed by military power was comprehensible, neither the Dutch negotiators with whom he had frequent meetings, nor De Witt, had a full understanding of his personality and intentions. Cromwell used his entire repertoire of idiosyncrasies to keep them baffled: he offered concessions but then behaved as if he had not done so; he engaged in endless heart-to-heart conversations, often accompanied by prayers and floods of tears. But at the end of 1653, as he came to personify the state, the Dutch negotiators began to see that Cromwell might be prepared to end the war on terms that were lenient in view of the desperate Dutch situation, provided that the security of the Commonwealth was strengthened. He had not been directly concerned with the declaration of war. Cromwell did not depend on the London 'New Merchants' who had tried to influence the Rump into making the war a mercantilist campaign to ruin the Dutch trading economy and appropriate at least part of its wealth.[7]

Slingsby Bethel spoke retrospectively for these mercantilists in his pamphlet, *The World's Mistake in Oliver Cromwell*, claiming that he had thrown away an optimum opportunity to enrich England by impoverishing the Dutch. In reality Cromwell did recognize the necessity of expanding English trade. Believing that the Dutch must accept England's right to make greater use of its natural advantages he dismissed the persistent Dutch calls for withdrawal of the Navigation Act. Unlike contemporary and later mercantilist enthusiasts for pressure or war against the Dutch, Cromwell accepted the reality that trade was the supreme interest, the *salus populi* and 'soul and welfare' of the Dutch nation and state, and above all of the province of Holland, and the Regent party who governed it. Realistically Cromwell saw that the Dutch would take the earliest opportunity

---

6 Ibid., vol. i, pp. 236, 255, 283, 449; *FDW*, vol. ii, pp. 265–6.
7 Thurloe, vol. i, pp. 386, 394–5, 417, 438–9, 450.

to repudiate a harsh, dictated peace and would seek allies to enable them to do so. Similarly he understood eventually that a close union was unacceptable, although he had argued that no other ally could help protect Dutch trade as England could, because of fear of domination. After abandoning the idea of a union (in November 1653) Cromwell switched to reliance on an oblique deal with the province of Holland. It lived by trade. The peace would contain no new discriminatory measures against its trade, provided that in return Holland contributed to the strengthening of Commonwealth security. This it did by passing the Seclusion Act, barring the House of Orange from holding provincial office as Stadtholder, and effectively barring its members from becoming captain general. If the war was to be intensified Cromwell and Thurloe knew that the inevitable consequence of further Dutch naval defeats would be the installation of the Orangists in offices and power, and they were the bitterest external enemies that the Commonwealth possessed.[8]

Cromwell disappointed mercantilist expectations. But although mercantilist interests could influence parliaments to get legislation passed – notably the Navigation Acts of 1651 and 1660 – their influence on the conduct of government was variable and intermittent. The desperately deep depression which affected the English economy in 1648–49 united MPs, members of the Council of State and the mercantile community in attempts to undertake remedial action. A number of cogently argued and widely circulated pamphlets – in themselves an indication of the pervasiveness and severity of the crisis – suggested a range of legislative measures.[9] In effect a partnership was established between politicians, merchants and shipowners, but very much on the Rump's terms. In August 1650 it set up the Council of Trade to 'maintain and advance the traffic-trade and several manufactures of this nation'; it consulted widely but had only advisory, not executive, powers. In 1650 foreign vessels were barred from trading with Virginia and the West Indian plantations: during the civil wars the Dutch had achieved a near monopoly with these then royalist-occupied colonies. Another Act that year imitated Dutch practice by allocating a proportion of customs revenue for the provision of regular convoys. In early 1652 the decision was made

8 Ibid., vol. i, pp. 438–9, 559.

9 Henry Robinson, *Brief Considerations concerning the Advancement of Trade and Navigation* (1649); Thomas Violet, *Mysteries and Secrets of Trade* (1653); *The Advocate* (1651, sometimes attributed to Benjamin Worsley); *The Case Stated between England and the United Provinces* (1652).

to maintain a permanent fleet in the Mediterranean, on a rota basis, to protect English shipping from French and Algerine privateers in order to enable the Levant Company to win back lost markets from the Dutch. The most important measure, the Navigation Act of 1651 barring the import into England and Ireland of all goods from Asia, Africa and America in any but English vessels, and from Europe in any except English vessels and those of the country where the goods were produced only, was intended to eliminate the Dutch entrepôt trades. The complementary policy of encouraging the operation of English entrepôts to encourage re-exports and compete with the Dutch was discussed, but war broke out before any action could be taken.[10]

Two leading groups can be identified as active in prosecuting these measures. In the Rump Thomas Chaloner, a member of the Council of State during this time, was tirelessly busy and received support from a group of merchants who worked closely with prominent MPs – Sir Henry Vane, Sir Arthur Haselrige and Thomas Scot. Both groups of MPs had connections with a distinct interest group of City merchants who held radical political opinions: their case found expression in Thomas Violet's 1651 pamphlet, *The Advocate: or a Narrative of the State and Condition of Things between the English and Dutch Nations in relation to Trade*. This gave a detailed picture of Dutch domination and led to the conclusion that actions were necessary, and the suggestion that even the Navigation Act might not be enough to alter the deeply unfavourable situation.[11]

These groups did not actually do anything to bring about hostilities, but once the war had started they were determined to use it in order to improve England's trade and shipping. Ironically they lost their ability to affect decisions only weeks before the crushing defeats suffered by Tromp made it apparently feasible to think of imposing the aggressive mercantilist policies that they had been advocating. Cromwell deprived the politicians of all influence by his dissolution of the Rump (April 1653). A month later the leading merchants associated with them – Maurice and William Thompson,

10 M. Ashley, *Financial and Commercial Policy in the Cromwellian Protectorate* (1962), p. 156; B. Worden, *The Rump Parliament* (Oxford, 1974), pp. 254–5, 299; S.R. Gardiner, *Constitutional Documents of the Puritan Revolution* (Cambridge, 1947), pp. 468–71; J. Corbett, *England in the Mediterranean* (1917), vol. i, p. 209.

11 B. Worden, *The Rump Parliament* (Oxford, 1974), pp. 30–2, 36–7, 174, 251–62, 299–303, 314; J.F. Farnell, 'The Navigation Act of 1651, the First Dutch War and the London Merchant Community', *Economic History Review* (1963), 2nd series, xvi, p. 440.

Nicholas Roberts, Thomas Andrews and William Pennoyer – subscribed a petition from the City calling on Cromwell to reinstate the Rump, an impossible demand. This defiant radical gesture annihilated the influence of the group. Only two merchants were summoned to the Barebones Parliament. The Council of Trade lost effectiveness: a Dutch merchant commented that its establishment had seemed to indicate that trade was now becoming a 'matter of state' in England, as in Holland, but that after the dissolution of the Rump it lost its sense of direction.[12]

With the elimination of those who saw the war as an opportunity to deprive the Dutch of their commercial advantages, political and ideological objectives became paramount. Harrison and the millenarians in the Barebones Parliament urged the intensification of hostilities as a holy war to purge the Dutch of their worldliness and worship of Mammon. For Cromwell and the other army generals the need for security for the Commonwealth regime continued to be the objective, and indeed after 1654 the threat from overseas intervention became negligible. There were also financial reasons for an early settlement. Expenditure on the war exhausted capital resources – the money amassed from fines and confiscations imposed on royalists – and led to a significant increase in government indebtedness. But the belief that an opportunity had existed in 1653 to enrich England at the expense of the Dutch, and had then been neglected by men intent on establishing a tyranny, was to influence opinion after 1660.[13]

The war of 1665–67 dramatically exposed the weaknesses of the restored monarchy. The earl of Clarendon as architect of the Restoration settlement aimed to restore stability, respect for authority, and a reciprocal respect by those in authority for the limitations imposed on their powers and actions by the law. He and those who thought like him, the 'friends of the constitution in church and state', limited legislation to what they thought was necessary to ensure good government and re-establish the Church. Beyond this they had nothing resembling a 'programme' of policies. Clarendon placed himself in what he regarded as the key office of lord chancellor because it enabled him to safeguard the practice of the rule of law and the integrity of the Church. He consciously rejected assuming the

---

12 C.H. Firth (ed.), *The Clarke Papers* (1899), vol. iii, p. 6; Worden, *Rump Parliament*, p. 314; Thurloe, vol. i, p. 498.

13 Worden, *Rump Parliament*, pp. 303–5; Thurloe, vol. i, pp. 316–17, 442, 519; *FDW*, vol. v, pp. 43, 63–8, 72–3.

role of chief minister; the sovereign personally should make all major decisions, and direct and supervise his ministers.[14]

However, Charles made no sustained attempt in the years 1661–67 to fulfil such time-consuming duties, and his failure to impose his authority in the way that Louis XIV (or James II later) did, produced uncertainty at Court. He frequently permitted or even encouraged junior ministers and courtiers to take initiatives that were at variance with the policies that had been formally promulgated. No one could tell whose advice would be accepted, or even was being followed. Courtiers were in two distinct age-groups: those who had served Charles I, and a younger generation hungry for office and money; all those pressing for another Dutch war fell into the latter category. The Court also contained, for the first time in nearly two centuries, a younger adult brother of the monarch. James, duke of York, discovered and developed for himself an active and important role as lord high admiral, attracting younger and ambitious courtiers and establishing a clientele of naval officers and administrators.

It was from members of James's circle, and from merchant interests associated with them, that the first calls came for pressure to be exerted on the Dutch. In his private correspondence with his sister Madame (wife to Louis XIV's brother) Charles affected to be indifferent to the anti-Dutch clamours of James's associates, but this pose concealed the fact that he was permitting the simultaneous pursuit of two entirely separate, and indeed contradictory, lines of policy in both domestic and external affairs. While Clarendon was engaged in legislating to re-establish anglican uniformity, Charles issued the 1662 Declaration of Indulgence in an attempt to introduce religious toleration. In foreign policy, after concluding a treaty in 1662 with the Dutch that provided for a negotiated resolution of all outstanding trading disputes and claims, Sir George Downing was allowed to use these disputes to put the Dutch under pressure to make concessions; Clarendon tried, with little effect, to restrain him. When engaged in his efforts to intimidate De Witt, Downing knew that James and his courtier-navalist groups of associates were intent on provoking a war if the Dutch refused to give way. Among them was a short-lived but temporarily dominant Restoration figure, whose importance has been overlooked because he was killed in the war that he helped to bring

14 P. Seaward, *The Cavalier Parliament and the Reconstruction of the Old Regime* (Cambridge, 1989), esp. pp. 15–25, 131–4, and ch. iii, 'Royalism and Conservatism'; J. Jones, 'The Friends of the Constitution in Church and State', in M. Bentley (ed.), *Public and Private Doctrine* (Cambridge, 1993), pp. 17–33.

about, and because he represented the kind of royal favourite that is associated with Tudor and early-Stuart Courts.

Charles Berkeley,[15] who became earl of Falmouth, acted as the essential link between Charles and James, who had on occasion been on extremely bad terms in the period just before 1660. Originally James's confidant, Berkeley succeeded in winning Charles's confidence also and clearly formulated the ambition of achieving supreme power: contemporaries compared him with the first duke of Buckingham, whose success had been consolidated by serving another James and another Charles, and several of the younger generation of courtiers – among them the astute William Coventry – showed themselves eager to serve him and so share in the rewards that would predictably follow. Berkeley secured the king's connivance for the aggressive colonial action against Dutch interests that James and his associates intended to take, and which initiated the escalatory process that led to war. James himself, his courtier associates, naval officers – former royalists and former Commonwealth sea-officers alike – all wanted an actual war as an end in itself. They (and the separate interest group headed by Monck, now duke of Albemarle) saw a victorious war, which they took for granted, as certain to bring them glory, career advancement and prize money. To do them justice they were all ready to risk their lives in action, but they tended to overlook the administrative and financial problems that would have to be resolved, and the diplomatic complications that war, and particularly a victorious war, would create.[16]

Those who favoured another Dutch war, which of course they assumed would end in total victory and a harsh peace, knew that they needed to enlist both parliamentary and mercantile support. Merchants engaged in the west African trade were already vocal about the need to curb Dutch malpractices, but mercantile opinion in general had been sobered by the heavy losses of vessels and the paralysis of trade caused by Cromwell's aggressive Spanish War. Coffee houses and taverns, and even the Exchange, might resonate with talk of the necessity for a war, but most merchants, shipowners and bankers knew that James's navalist group had self-interested motives. Revealingly the most influential City interest, the EIC, held back from pushing its own claims against the VOC for fear of being loaded with responsibility for a war that might prove to be expensive. By comparison with the EIC the one group that pressed for early

---

15 Pepys, vol. v, p. 345; C.H. Hartmann, *The King's Friend* (1951).
16 BL, Egerton MSS, 2538, f. 131.

action, the Company of Royal Adventurers (into Africa), was a light-weight in terms of capital and profits, but a heavyweight in political influence. It was a hybrid. Most of James's associates held nominal investments, most of the merchants involved had connections with the administration, and these made them dependent on James. Apart from Sir Nicholas Crispe, their investment in the company amounted to only a small proportion of their capital. This was understandable because the company was a highly speculative concern. West Africa represented a region in which the crudest mercantilist equation between power and profit applied: competition with the Dutch, the Danes and (later) the French involved trade wars in a literal sense – the regular use of force to intimidate the coastal tribes and destroy rival trading posts. But existing risks were outweighed by the prospect of great profits from the export of slaves to the western hemisphere, a trade which was beginning to expand phenomenally.[17]

The Court group centred on James was responsible for forcing the issues with the Dutch; far from being deterred by the possibility that their actions in Africa might lead to war in Europe they, and especially the naval officers, saw this as a desirable outcome. By comparison the mercantile interest in the City and Commons did not dispose of sufficient influence to sway governmental decisions. In the early years of the Cavalier Parliament there were fewer than thirty merchants, retired merchants and shipowners in the Commons. Not one of them can be described as commanding attention. In the Council of Trade several occupied advisory positions, but no merchant or City magnate occupied a governmental office. Indeed William Coventry, James's secretary, strongly disapproved of any such appointment, arguing that any merchant would concentrate on using office to benefit himself and his business associates.[18]

James's political associates displayed considerable tactical exper-tise in committing both the Commons and the City to aggressive policies. The chief working agent was Sir Thomas Clifford, who was taking the first steps in a meteoric rise to high office and power. He transformed a Commons committee originally instituted to investigate the causes of the decay of the cloth industry by having its terms of reference extended to cover the reasons for the general decay of all trade, and doubling its size to include MPs known to favour his line of argument putting the blame on Dutch competition.

---

17 Pepys, vol. v, pp. 107–9; K.G. Davies, *The Royal African Company* (1960), pp. 40, 63–4.
18 *CSPD 1664–66*, p. 75.

Merchant companies and interests were invited to submit evidence; Pepys found his City acquaintances busy preparing their cases. The Merchant Adventurers, the African Adventurers, the Levant and Muscovy Companies, and individual merchants trading with France and Italy presented theirs on 1 April 1664. The EIC circumspectly waited until 5 April, then with the Levant Company and the African Adventurers (who in purely mercantile terms did not belong to the same league) its representatives met the committee, which went over their cases in detail. Clifford as replacement chairman collated their grievances for his report.[19]

All this careful work paid off: the Commons accepted Clifford's report that the 'honour, safety and future wealth' of the nation demanded action against the Dutch. With some misgivings it swallowed outrageously inflated estimates of the losses attributable to Dutch actions. In the summary sent to the Lords detailed damages were put at £714,500, but an additional and completely hypothetical loss of over £4 million, allegedly due to the Dutch retention of Pulo Run in the Banda Islands was included for bargaining purposes.[20]

This brilliantly executed manoeuvre outflanked Clarendon and his 'friends to the constitution'; the emphasis on 'future wealth' could hardly be in sharper contrast to the static, legalistic and conservative principles of the Clarendonians. The invitation to Parliament to suggest action against the Dutch made it possible for Charles to claim, during the war, that he was entitled to additional votes of supply because Parliament had advised and encouraged him to go to war. But the support which the Commons was explicitly induced to give also entitled MPs to claim the right to monitor the progress of the war and to examine the use made of the money voted. Clifford as salesman for anti-Dutch policies inevitably raised excessive expectations about the war, and ensured that when it ended in failure there would be a vigorous reaction in the Commons. Coventry concluded that the acrimonious post-mortem conducted by the Commons meant that in future no war could be initiated unless Parliament approved. Clifford was to draw the opposite conclusion: the next Dutch War, which he was already beginning to plan in 1668–69, must be launched and as far as possible fought without calling Parliament at all.[21]

19 Pepys, vol. v, pp. 121, 127, 131, 137, 159; P. Seaward, 'The House of Commons Committee of Trade and the Origins of the Second Anglo-Dutch War', *Historical Journal* (1987), xxx, pp. 437–52.

20 *CSPVenetian 1664–66*, p. 18.

21 *Lords Journals*, vol. xi, p. 684; Pepys, vol. vii, p. 186.

Two central characteristics of government under the restored monarchy undermined the war effort, which collapsed during the winter of 1666–67. First, the mentality and attitude of officers and officials had changed since the first war fought by the Commonwealth. Almost all gave a higher priority to advancing their personal interests than to executing their duties, which all too many performed perfunctorily. Most office-holders were former Cavaliers who had been in the wilderness since the 1640s, and many succumbed to the temptation to compensate for lost time by maximizing their profits. They generally held a proprietorial attitude to their offices, but in reality they did not enjoy any security of tenure. The incessant in-fighting between leading figures in the Court extended to their clients in the administration and navy. The fortunate minority who had won out in the frantic scramble for offices in 1660–61 felt menaced by former and new rivals. Clarendon's failing health and his increasing inability to direct government effectively meant that at some time soon a general alteration would occur, and some of those who pressed for war consciously expected this to undermine Clarendon's position by highlighting his defects. Among these was his obstinate refusal to contemplate any change of personnel or method at the Treasury, and financial weakness was to prove the decisive factor in the war. Lord treasurer Southampton was incompetent; Sir Philip Warwick on whom he relied had acquired his financial expertise as far back as Juxon's treasurership of 1636–41 – but, if (like Clarendon) you did not believe that change necessitated adaptation, this was not relevant.[22]

In theory the Commons voted sufficient money. Clever manipulation produced large grants of supply, an initial sum of £2.5 million in the 1664–65 session, a further £1.25 million from the poorly attended Oxford session of October 1665. But the reduction in trade which was produced by the pressing of seamen, embargoes on outward sailings, the closing of the Baltic, unexpectedly high losses to Dutch privateers, war with France, and the plague which disrupted internal trade, all served to reduce receipts from customs, excises and chimney money, and slowed all payments into the Treasury. The government was unable to raise sufficient money for its immediate needs. Advances on taxes which Parliament had voted could not be obtained on the scale which prolonged operations made necessary because of political uncertainties, the plague (which drove most financiers out of London) and, fundamentally, the relatively primitive and

22 Pepys, vol. v, pp. 56, 73, 122, 345.

undeveloped state of English banking and credit operations. Whereas the States General was able to obtain loans after such major defeats as Lowestoft in 1665 because of the constant close relations between the financial interest and the government, English banking did not form a regular and accepted part of the mechanisms of Crown finances. Clarendon still affected to regard bankers as a new and undesirable phenomenon, 'never heard of before the late troubles'. English ministers and politicians generally still retained medieval prejudices. A Commons majority of landed gentry defeated a Bill to permit the charging of more than 6 per cent interest, proposed to facilitate loans to the Crown, on the grounds that higher interest rates would accentuate the existing decline in the price of land, and that it would increase the drain of money from the provinces to London. Clarendon and his supporters distrusted bankers because of their former association with Cromwell, and few of them had any understanding of the principles on which the money-market operated.[23]

Stuart apologists at the time and later blamed parliamentary niggardliness, or even blackmailing tactics, in failing to give the king the money he needed to win the war. There is no real basis for this contention. Parliament voted nearly £5 million in all, but government finances became confused when the money came in slowly. Loans were agreed – when they could be obtained – on an *ad hoc* basis, with widely varying conditions negotiated, and there appears to have been no effective control on expenditure. The Treasury lacked an overall picture of the current state of finances, and in consequence the naval administration was constantly hampered by the lack of ready money when it was most needed. Their creditors were placed in impossible difficulties. The ultimate failure came in the drafting of the 1667 Assessment Bill, which initially failed to contain unambiguous authority for the raising of loans on its security.[24] When this provided final and irrefutable proof of the utterly incompetent character of the administration and its lack of leadership, remedial action was taken by Downing, holder of a minor office, not by the lord treasurer or the Council. Downing introduced provisos to the £1.25 million Assessment Bill for which he got the king's support, but which

23 Seaward, *Cavalier Parliament and the Reconstruction of the Old Regime*, pp. 124–6; Edward Hyde, *The Life of Edward, Earl of Clarendon, being a Continuation of the History of the Great Rebellion* (Oxford, 1827) vol. iii, p. 7; Pepys, vol. viii, pp. 66–7, 73, 78.

24 C.D. Chandaman, *The English Public Revenue, 1660–1688* (Oxford, 1975), pp. 210–12; Pepys, vol. viii, pp. 66–7, 73, 78.

were strongly opposed by Clarendon. These established a system of appropriation: advances were to be registered and repaid in the order in which they had been made, and the receipts were to be negotiable. The scheme had major disadvantages. It restricted the Treasury: all the money advanced could be used only for the war. All those who had advanced money earlier would be relegated to the back of the queue for repayment. In fact suspicious City financiers hesitated until July 1666 before resuming advances.[25]

Clarendon's objections were ideological. Downing's scheme was avowedly imitative of Dutch practice; Clarendon regarded it as 'introductive to a Commonwealth and not fit for monarchy'. He and his associates had no solutions to the crisis but he criticized Downing for 'insolence' in presuming to offer one, and Charles for 'listening to fellows of his condition', and for accepting novelties and innovations. The Commons' attitude to the crisis in royal finances similarly became increasingly influenced by ideological considerations, with disastrous consequences. The Commons voted in principle for additional supply of £1.8 million in October 1666, but confused and interminable debates about the means to be used to raise this sum held up the final passage of the Bill, until even bankers' advances on the taxes eventually voted would come in too late to make possible the setting out of a full fleet in the spring of 1667.[26]

In these debates an ideological division was widened by incompatible Court and Country proposals on the ways and means of raising money. The Court proposal for a general excise, that is for a permanent tax that would continue after the end of the war, provoked the belief that its aim was to make the Crown independent from having to rely on extraordinary votes of supply. Consequently the Commons explicitly refused to vote any imposition that could involve a perpetual charge. But its own proposal to buy out the hated hearth or chimney tax was rejected by Charles as intended to make him more dependent on Commons votes of supply by reducing his permanent revenue. He also interpreted attempts by the Commons to set up a committee to inspect and report on all governmental expenditure, so as to discover whether money had been diverted from the war, as an invasion of his prerogative.[27]

In 1667–68 the Commons launched wide-ranging inquiries into the miscarriages of the war, operational and administrative as well

25 Clarendon, *Continuation*, vol. iii, pp. 7, 10, 16–19, 29–30, 241–4.
26 Clarendon, *Continuation*, vol. iii, pp. 23, 29, 30.
27 Pepys, vol. viii, p. 324; Chandaman, *English Public Revenue*, pp. 44, 86–7.

as financial. Had these been effective the power and reputation of the Commons would have been greatly enhanced, but they followed a pattern that was determined by basic seventeenth-century attitudes. As for example in Clarendon's magisterial *History of the Rebellion*, failures were seen as the result of human failings and vices. No attempt was made at an analysis of organizational, strategic or material weaknesses or mistakes – things that could be rectified. The inquiries consequently became hunts for scapegoats. Failure to exploit the victory off Lowestoft was due to cowardice. The Medway disaster was the result of Pett's putting his private property before his official duty; the division of the fleet to Coventry's indolence. Corrupt practices rather than a faulty system of government finances explained the inability to set out a fleet in 1667. However, this actually inconclusive set of inquiries had one important result. The vicious nature of the attacks by the Commons, together with the king's encouragement of the attacks on Clarendon after his dismissal, served as a warning to the group of ministers who in 1668–70 deliberately planned a third war. They saw the need for more careful planning and preparation – political, diplomatic and financial. And in all the preliminary steps Parliament was to have no part; indeed it was itself to be vanquished once the king emerged as victor over the Dutch.[28]

The covert purpose of the third Dutch War was as much to free the Crown from its existing dependence on Parliament, the Church of England and the militia in carrying out the business of government, as to reduce the Dutch Republic to dependence, or even to the status of an English protectorate. The secretary of the Venetian embassy, who had close contacts with James's entourage, described the chief objective as being to subdue Charles's own subjects.[29]

In reality the disparate group of ministers known as the Cabal did not agree on all the objectives of the war. The two who did most to bring the war about, James and Clifford, had the clearest and most far-reaching ideas of how victory was to be exploited. They wanted a permanent alliance with France, with possible financial subsidies and the assurance of aid to suppress rebellions until Charles had consolidated his authority. Both men were approaching conversion to catholicism. They welcomed the French pledge to assist Charles when – as he promised – he too declared his conversion. Historians

---

28 Pepys, vol. viii, pp. 485, 490n., 491, 493, 495, 510, 514, 524, 536; *Commons Journals*, vol. ix, pp. 13–14, 93 (Pett), 15–16 (Clarendon), 33, 36, 66 (Hearth tax commissioners), 80, 85 (Penn), 86 (Brounker).

29 *CSP Venetian 1671–7*, p. 205.

have downplayed the significance of Charles's promise in the Dover treaty, since of course he never publicly converted, but it had the advantage of committing Louis to support an English monarch who became a catholic. James certainly believed that the 'establishment' of catholicism, meaning not its imposition on the nation, as by Mary I, but the conferment of legal and indeed favoured status on the Church, was inextricably tied to the strengthening of the monarchy. For the rest of his life – as heir presumptive, sovereign and exile – James was to rely entirely on France, and in return constantly presented himself as the only person who could prevent England from being led into the pursuit of anti-French policies.[30]

Clifford's ideology was equally francophile and authoritarian, but more explicitly anti-Dutch. As in 1664–67 he pressed mercantilist policies to annihilate Dutch seapower in order to strip them of most of their wealth. His modest origins, his short tenure of office as lord treasurer and early death have resulted in Clifford being underestimated. But he was effectively in control of policy before 1672; he had blocked any settlement of outstanding disputes, and he bore the main responsibility for the Stop of the Exchequer.[31] Other ministers of the Cabal accepted, rather than willed and instigated, the war. Arlington went along with whatever Charles wanted, so as to keep his office. The three non-catholic ministers (Ashley, Buckingham and Lauderdale) were committed by a bogus (but still secret) 'simulated' treaty that omitted any reference to religion. They were motivated by career considerations: Lauderdale to retain the government of Scotland, Ashley to advance himself, Buckingham in the vain hope of becoming army general, France's trusted contact man and even Charles's chief minister. But they lacked the zeal and commitment of James and Clifford.[32]

They were both known to have an exalted view of the royal prerogative. In 1667 James asserted that in the crisis created by the Medway disaster the king could collect money 'as he pleased': the public safety dispensed with the need to seek consent from Parliament and keep within the law, and he was to argue the

---

30 Public Record Office (henceforth PRO), Baschet transcripts; Colbert de Croissy despatch, 1 April 1673.

31 A new biography of Clifford is needed: the existing study by C.H. Hartmann, *Clifford of the Cabal* (1937), although based on manuscript material that is now generally accessible, suffers from a dated and idiosyncratic approach.

32 M. Lee, *The Cabal* (Urbana, IL, 1965); K.H.D. Haley, *The First Earl of Shaftesbury* (Oxford, 1968), pp. 266–326; new studies are needed of Lauderdale and Buckingham.

same case in 1673 when Parliament tied supply to passage of the Test Bill. The preparations for the third Dutch War involved actions outside the law. In January 1672 the Stop of the Exchequer suspended the payment of orders made on the revenue, but orders secured on certain Acts were excepted, and the king gave himself the power to make other exceptions. In other words the king decided which property rights he would recognize and which he would suspend. MPs later were to denounce the Stop as an attack on property in its most vulnerable form (money). If property rights could be arbitrarily subverted in the case of a few hated bankers then all property rights were placed at risk.[33]

Second, Charles knew that by allying with the catholic Louis against the Dutch he would enable hostile critics to represent the war as one of religion, and that the Dutch would certainly incite the persecuted Dissenters to engage in subversive activity. By issuing the Declaration of Indulgence on 15 March, two days before war was declared, Charles eliminated this danger, and indeed diverted public attention from the war so far as domestic opinion was concerned. In the Declaration all the ecclesiastical penal laws were suspended; the most oppressive of these (for Dissenters) had been passed by the existing Parliament, the most severe (the second Conventicle Act) only two years earlier. Moreover enforcement of the Declaration involved ordering justices of the peace (JPs) not to enforce the laws; a few who demonstrated by prosecuting Dissenters that their first duty was to the law were summoned to appear before the Council and intimidated.[34]

The Stop and the Declaration formed as necessary a part of the preparations for the war as the fitting out of the fleet and the pressing of seamen. The anticipated victorious ending of the war in a single campaign would put the king in a strong position in relation to Parliament, when it was permitted to meet in the winter. The costs of the war would have been offset by French subsidies, prizes and a large indemnity that the Dutch would have to pay, the first instalment in October. Charles would then demand increases to his revenue, his permanent income, from a position of strength. From a royal per-

---

33 Pepys, vol. viii, pp. 292–3, 382; A. Grey, *Debates of the House of Commons* (1769) vol. viii, pp. 320–3; J.K. Horsefield, 'The "Stop of the Exchequer" Revisited', *Economic History Review* (1982), 2nd series, xxxv, pp. 511–28; PRO, Baschet transcripts, Colbert de Croissy despatch, 1 April 1673; *CSPVenetian 1673–74*, pp. 56, 69.

34 *CSPVenetian 1671–72*, p. 186.

spective the achievement of this demand was merely to restore royal authority to the state which had existed in earlier reigns. No previous sovereign had ever had to allow annual meetings of Parliament (even if it was the same Parliament since 1661). In addition Parliament had been trying to encroach on the royal prerogative – to restrain royal authority by attempting to appropriate supply to particular uses, to examine royal accounts, to question royal officers, and to attempt to cut imports from France (with whom Charles was supposed to be negotiating a commercial treaty) by the oblique method of selective increases in customs duties.[35]

These moves were usurpations from a Court perspective, unconstitutional interference in the processes of government. The king had the function of governing, Parliament must provide him with the means to do so. Arlington asserted that MPs lacked experience and knowledge, the Commons the necessary procedural techniques, to make useful contributions to the conduct of government. James's reported attitudes went further. He shared Louis XIV's view of MPs as '*canaille*', describing them as 'a mob of folk of little consequence'. The Commons should not be allowed to judge whether additional supply was necessary, or determine the amount to be voted, but only to decide what methods should be employed to raise the sum demanded of them. If the war ended in the quick victory which he expected it should be told that it would be dissolved if money was not voted. Any popular reaction could be quelled by the army. Then any gap could be covered by continuing to levy the additional taxes voted in 1669–70 beyond their expiry date, a tactic that the Commons in later sessions tried to make treasonable.[36]

Clifford, like Louvois, Louis's most influential minister at this time, vigorously opposed any reduction in the severe terms demanded of the Dutch. But the war did not end in 1672, and when Clifford got to the top of the greasy pole by becoming lord treasurer on 30 November 1672 his main task was to prepare for a parliamentary session. A challenge to the Declaration was certain. The employment of catholic army officers would be attacked. William's agents Zas and Arton were sent to attempt to compel Charles to make a separate peace by exploiting the major constitutional weakness of the English Crown, its need to call and ask Parliament for the supply which

35 *CSP Venetian 1672–73*, p. 188; Colenbrander, vol. ii, p. 142; K.H.D. Haley, *An English Diplomat in the Low Countries: Sir William Temple and John de Witt* (Oxford, 1986), p. 279.

36 *CSP Venetian 1664–66*, p. 239; *CSP Venetian 1673–75*, pp. 13–14, 195–6, 205–7; Grey, *Debates*, vol. iii, pp. 2, 320; vol. iv, p. 134.

the continuation of the war required. However, this first attempt at subversion by William in early 1673 not only failed because of the arrest of Zas and Arton but also proved to be counter-productive. The two agents were to make use of the notorious jealousies and enmities within the Cabal ministry: each of its members detested all his colleagues and differed from them in principles (if the word is applicable) and policy preferences. In the first instance they were to approach the two thought to be most likely to be receptive, lord chancellor Shaftesbury and Buckingham. Both men responded to the arrest of the agents by demonstratively identifying themselves with an intensification of the war, Shaftesbury by his ferocious and cynical anti-Dutch speech at the opening of Parliament, Buckingham sponsoring and pressing for the command of the army raised to invade Holland or Zeeland. Zas and Arton were found to have large sums of money at their disposal; it was assumed that most of this was earmarked for MPs and peers. Consequently anyone making speeches against the war itself and opposing votes of supply for it would be identifying themselves as either a collaborator or a sympathizer with the enemy.[37]

The revelation of the subversive purposes of Zas and Arton's mission inhibited Country MPs from criticizing the war, but it is doubtful whether they would have concentrated on doing so. Their first priority was to denounce as illegal the royal policies that accompanied the war; indeed they saw the war as a secondary issue. For them it was primarily a cover for the exercise of an alleged royal power of suspending statutes, as in the Declaration of Indulgence, an invasion of property rights by the Stop of the Exchequer, and a considerably expanded standing army; on the last it was said that the war was for an army, not the army for the war. Independent and Country MPs displayed great procedural skills in tying their votes of supply to royal retreats, instead of provoking confrontation by a total or large denial of money. Their strategy produced a (qualified) royal withdrawal of the Declaration and the royal assent to the Test Bill which excluded catholics – including James and Clifford – from all governmental offices, but in return Charles gained the money necessary to finance the campaign of 1673. Country MPs were unaware of their debt to an unseen ally in their partial success in countering royal ambitions, none other than Louis XIV himself. Faced with the Test Bill, James had urged Charles to dissolve Parliament, arrest leading peers and

---

37 K.H.D. Haley, *William of Orange and the English Opposition* (Oxford, 1953), pp. 76–8, 83–7; Grey, *Debates*, vol. ii, p. 11.

MPs and raise money without seeking the consent of Parliament, in effect undertake a coup against the constitution that would have required the use or threat of military force. But the turmoil which this would provoke would make it impossible to obtain in time the money or credit needed to enable the fleet to go out in April: this could come only in the form of additional French subsidies. By indicating that these would not be available, the French ambassador virtually vetoed a dissolution. Louis needed another summer's campaign at sea to absorb Dutch resources and maintain maximum pressure on William. This outweighed the alternative option of paying what were now increasingly scarce financial resources in order to enable Charles to free himself from constitutional restraints and confer toleration and equality of civil rights on catholics.[38]

Theoretically a successful campaign in 1673 could still enable Charles to achieve his domestic objectives through his own efforts, but the failure to force the Dutch into submission ruled this out. By the summer of 1673 the Dutch counter-offensive, which took the form of a well-organized campaign of propaganda and political subversion, was establishing the essential link between the war, the French alliance and the domestic policies of Charles and the Cabal administration. At the same time Spanish diplomats actively intervened in English affairs on two levels. To the public and above all mercantile interests, for whose benefit the war was supposedly launched, they emphasized the disastrous effects on trade and the economy generally if Charles followed Louis by declaring war on Spain. As a new session of Parliament approached they encouraged MPs not to respond to royal calls for them to consider further votes of supply. They also acted on behalf of the Dutch by indicating to Charles and his ministers the terms which the Dutch were ready to concede in a separate peace treaty, so bypassing the general negotiations at Cologne which the French effectively controlled and manipulated. When Charles proved to be initially unreceptive the Spanish embassy arranged for every MP to receive a printed copy of the terms being offered by the Dutch on his arrival at Westminster.[39]

---

38 L.M. Mignet, *Négociations relatives à la succession d'Espagne sous Louis XIV* (Paris, 1835–42) (henceforth Mignet), vol. iv, p. 156; PRO, Baschet transcripts, Colbert de Croissy despatch, 10 August 1673; *CSPVenetian 1673–75*, pp. 56, 174–5, 177.

39 Grey, *Debates*, vol. ii, pp. 202–3, 213, 229–32; Mignet, vol. iv, pp. 176–7, 205; Haley, *William of Orange and the English Opposition*, pp. 148–51; *CSPVenetian 1673–75*, pp. 121, 137, 143–4, 163, 191–2.

In formal terms the royal prerogative survived the peace-making process intact. But although Charles, not Parliament, concluded the peace treaty he did not do so as a free agent. The Commons declined his invitation to pass judgement on the terms which the Dutch proposed on the jesuitical grounds that this was exclusively a matter for the prerogative. But they resolved that they would not vote supply for a continuation of the war unless the obstinacy of the Dutch made it necessary – that is in their judgement, which amounted to making the crucial decision.[40] The third Dutch War, and the policies that accompanied it, raised many and vital questions about the constitution of the English state, but settled none of them. The legal validity of the Articles of War to enforce discipline in the army remained uncertain. Charles withdrew the Declaration of Indulgence but did not repudiate possession of a suspending power. Catholics were barred from office-holding, but not from the Crown. The legal position created by the Stop of the Exchequer was not determined until the 1690s. So by abandoning the war and the French alliance Charles preserved his prerogative rights (or pretensions), but all the major constitutional ambiguities persisted.

In practical terms the question of how far the sovereign could exercise his prerogative powers without Parliament's collaboration, or in the teeth of its opposition, remained open. Certainly for European rulers, ministers and diplomats, the war confirmed the impression that kings of England had less than sovereign powers in practice, that the failure of their ministers and Parliament to agree with royal policies, or to obstruct their implementation, could render them inoperative and make royal promises worthless. Or, as William was to discover in 1677–78 and 1681, policies advocated by either or both ministers and Parliament could be nullified by the king. In the words which Downing had applied to the Dutch system of government in the 1660s, government in the remainder of Charles's reign was to be a 'shattered and divided thing'. Louis drew what proved in the short term to be an appropriate conclusion – that French interests could best be served by neutralizing England, a strategy which he followed with success in 1678, 1681 and 1683 but also, with seriously adverse consequences for himself, in 1688.

The clandestine campaign of subversion waged by William in 1673–74 probably had less immediate effect than the pressure and lobbying of the Spanish diplomats in London. But it had much greater and indeed decisive long-term effects. In particular the arguments contained in the widely circulated pamphlet written by Du Moulin, *England's Appeal from the Private Cabal at Whitehall to the Great Council of the Nation, The Lords and Commons in Parliament Assembled*, planted in the minds of most people at all levels of society the belief that the war was the essential and central part of a continuing conspiracy to establish catholicism and arbitrary government with the help of France.[41] It was this thesis that the first Whigs were to use in their attempts to exclude James from the succession, and that formed the core of William's successful appeal in 1688. The failure of the third Dutch War and its effects – the disintegration of the Cabal ministry, James's enforced withdrawal from office and the termination of the official alliance with France – did seem at the time to remove the threat from the Court to liberties, religion and property. There was, it seemed, no need for an explicit conservationist move like the 1628 Petition of Right, designed to safeguard the law of the constitution against any repetition of the illegal policies and actions which, under the cover of wartime requirements, had been designed to undermine it. However, there was one exception: the Commons made repeated and serious legislative attempts to make any levying of taxes which had not received explicit parliamentary consent a treasonable offence, that is a crime comparable in enormity with murdering the king or rebelling against his authority.[42] Charles contributed to the reduction in tension by abandoning his ministers and any attempt to increase the authority of the Crown at the expense of Parliament or the Church of England. But when in 1687–88 James by his practices and policies confirmed and intensified the fears that had been generated in 1672–74 the response overwhelmed and dethroned him. William knew from his experience during the third Dutch War how an alteration of government could be conducted, and how to turn the situation to his advantage.

41 Haley, *William of Orange and the English Opposition*, pp. 88–111.
42 Grey, *Debates*, vol. ii, pp. 404–7; vol. iii, p. 320; vol. iv, p. 134.

THE COURSE OF THE ANGLO-DUTCH WARS

6   THE FIRST WAR, 1652–54

In March 1651 the Rump Parliament sent an extraordinary embassy, headed by St John and Strickland, to the Hague with the offer of a 'close union' or 'strict coalition' to the States General. The governmental forms that this would take were not spelled out in advance, but it was intended to be more comprehensive and permanent than an alliance so as to ensure that the religion and liberties of the two nations would be conserved. The offer reflected the sentiment of most English people outside the Stuart Court during the first half of the century, the belief that the Dutch were their natural and best friends in an otherwise largely hostile or indifferent Europe. A demand for a strict alliance had been included in the Nineteen Propositions of June 1642, and in November the Long Parliament sent Strickland to negotiate one. The refusal of the States General to recognize him, the supply of arms to the royalists, the pro-royalist bias of an embassy sent to mediate in 1643, the harbouring of the ships that defected to the royalists in 1648, were all blamed on the malicious hostility of the House of Orange with its Stuart connections. When William II died in November 1650, after attempting a coup against Amsterdam, the States of Holland decided explicitly against appointing a new Stadtholder, and a special Great Assembly was convened to discuss the constitutional position that this created. To English councillors and MPs these developments were seen as paralleling those in England: a ruler had tried but failed to overthrow constitutional liberties, his removal and the abolition of his office temporarily relieved the danger but his partisans still posed a threat. The time seemed opportune for the only two major republics in Europe to unite against those who threatened their constitutions. Yet within a year of the return of the St John embassy to England the two republics were at war, and the failure of this embassy, by producing a profound change of attitude towards the Dutch among England's rulers, contributed significantly to the abrupt collapse of goodwill between the two nations.[1]

1 Thurloe, vol. i, p. 123; S.R. Gardiner, *Constitutional Documents of the Puritan Revolution* (Oxford, 1947), p. 253; S. Groenveld, 'The English Civil Wars as a
Continued

The security of the Commonwealth regime was the chief objective of the English embassy – and of the war that followed its failure. In reality there was no parallel between the dangers facing the two republics. The Dutch now had no foreign enemies, the Orangists were demoralized by William's death, and the economy was booming. In contrast the Commonwealth was ringed by active enemies: Charles II held Scotland north of the Forth, parts of Ireland were still in royalist hands, royalist privateers harried trading vessels, an unofficial war closed France to trade and led to heavy mercantile losses in the Mediterranean. Only Spain recognized the Commonwealth – for purely opportunistic reasons. Everywhere else rulers and clergy denounced the regicide republic, among them the ministers of the Dutch Reformed Church who incited violent demonstrations against the embassy. Orangist in their sympathies they were incensed by the exclusion of the presbyterians from Parliament in 1648, and by Cromwell's invasion of Scotland. Besides being wary of concluding even an alliance with such an isolated and outlawed regime, the Dutch could have no confidence in its durability. These negotiations preceded Charles II's invasion of England and defeat at Worcester. The failure of the Rump to make progress on drafting a new constitution and the continued activity of political and religious radicals threatened a new period of instability. The Dutch consistently exaggerated the possibility that what they regarded as religious licence and the proliferation of the sects would lead to moral collapse and social disintegration.[2]

The States General was not prepared to go further than offering a treaty 'on the common interest', fearing that a union for a 'more intrinsical and mutual interest of each in other than hath hitherto been' would mean subordination to, or even incorporation in, a much larger state and one which was currently conquering and assimilating Scotland and Ireland. Moreover any degree of union with England would entail a fundamental change in the essential basis of the Union of Utrecht, in the location of sovereignty. This rested in the individual provinces and their States (the representative bodies), and was symbolized by their sending deputies to the States General who were delegates limited by binding instructions: on any new subjects

Continued

Cause of the First Anglo-Dutch War', *Historical Journal* (1987) xxx, pp. 544–5, 554, 555–6; V. Rowe, *Sir Henry Vane the Younger* (1970), p. 145.

2 Thurloe, vol. i, pp. 236, 449; J.J. Jusserand, *Recueil des instructions données aux ambassadeurs et ministres de France*, vol. xxiv, Angleterre i (1929), p. 86.

they had to refer back to their 'principals', the States, for new instructions. Consequently the Dutch members of the States General who negotiated with St John could not behave as plenipotentiaries, they could not give him authoritative answers and counter-proposals. This created the extremely damaging impression that although they professed friendship they would agree to nothing unless it was certain to work to their advantage.[3]

St John, the nominal head of the embassy, had little experience in foreign affairs, but Strickland had spent seven years at the Hague, and in September 1649 had warned the States of Holland of the danger of antagonizing the Commonwealth. Pointing out that Parliament had taken care to maintain 'the ancient friendship and correspondence' which had been so useful (the key word to use to persuade the Dutch) to the two countries, he warned that continued lack of reciprocal affection would make it impossible to 'maintain trade and friendship to our mutual satisfaction'. Strickland added that 'your dear and very considerable interests' would then be endangered. In 1649 this very explicit and direct warning made an impact, causing Holland to tell the States General that some Commonwealth leaders wanted a breach so that they could attack Dutch trade, which 'glitters as golden mountains' in their eyes, and that the sea would be turned into 'deadly poison'. But by 1651 this threat had seemingly receded, with the Commonwealth occupied in Scotland and Ireland.[4]

Consequently the Dutch negotiators adopted a wary and procrastinating attitude during the negotiations. They tabled thirty-six Articles whose main emphasis was on the renewal of the ancient union, or rather links, connected with the Magnus Intercursus of 1495. St John replied that this was insufficient and insisted on 'a nearer union than formerly hath been', demanding that the States General should declare itself on this main issue, 'and with all speed'. The failure of the Dutch negotiators to address the issue of a union led not just to the failure of the negotiations but to a sharp deterioration in Anglo-Dutch relations. The Dutch accused the ambassadors of intimidation, of setting arbitrary time-limits, and of breaking off the negotiations and returning to England when progress could still have been made. The English charged the Dutch with deliberately delaying their responses, falsifying the text of articles which had been accepted as part of the Magnus Intercursus, and misrepresenting the record of

---

3 Thurloe, vol. i, pp. 176, 179; J.I. Israel, *The Dutch Republic: Its Rise, Greatness and Fall 1477–1806* (Oxford, 1995), p. 719.

4 Thurloe, vol. i, pp. 114–16.

discussions. This failure left both parties with the impression that the other had been acting in bad faith. When the Dutch attempted to revive the negotiations at the end of 1651 the English attitude was determined by the experiences of their ambassadors. Thurloe, who had acted as their secretary, described Dutch negotiating tactics as making 'huge professions and in such manner that men are almost necessitated to believe them', but with the intention of performing only those parts that they knew would be to their advantage. The English counter to their tactics was to insist that specific replies must be made even on the most contentious issues within a short time-limit, and that the demands to be put to them must be carefully and fully prepared. The extraordinary ambassadors who arrived in England early in 1652 found themselves in an impossible negotiating position. They had instructions to seek the repeal of the Navigation Act, passed the previous October, and a renunciation of the right to search neutral ships, without offering anything in return. These preposterous and impossible demands contrasted with the itemized list of claims which the English presented, accompanied by the peremptory demand that early replies must be made. The brutally direct English attitude and the continued procrastination and evasiveness of the Dutch deepened mutual distrust: had the negotiations been conducted with a genuine intention of reaching agreement war might have been averted. They were still technically in progress when the first naval clashes occurred in May 1652, but the mistimed Dutch ploy of saying that they were now ready to discuss English proposals for a union merely confirmed the impression which was now fixed and to colour all transactions with Dutch governments over the next century – a distrust of 'good' or 'fair' words and 'huge professions', a belief that settlements would be obtained only by exerting pressure and eliminating time-wasting.[5]

Inevitably the Dutch came to believe in 1651–52 that the economic policies of the Rump and the Council of State were deliberately aimed against their interests, hence their ill-conceived intention to demand repeal of the Navigation Act. Certainly English opinion was becoming hostile. For example when the Merchant Adventurers proposed moving their Staple from Holland to Flanders they justified their request to the Rump by saying that this would 'totally dissolve the clothing of Holland', that is ruin the Leiden textile industry that had captured former English markets in Europe.[6] But it would be

5 Ibid., vol. i, pp. 176, 182–4, 188–95, 205, 207, 210–11; *CSPD 1651–52*, pp. 209, 214–15, 287, 290–2, 307; Wicquefort, *Histoire*, vol. ii, p. 113.

6 Thurloe, vol. i, pp. 199–200.

wrong to see the measures taken by the Rump as being primarily motivated by anti-Dutch feeling; they were absolutely essential if the English economy was to recover quickly (or at all) from the deep depression caused by the second civil war, harvest failure, plague and the disruption of foreign trade. No government in England has ever had to operate under such pressure as the Rump in 1649–51, something that has been ignored or downplayed by historians, and especially those influenced by Marxism, who have contended that it should have undertaken radical social and political reforms. The pragmatism of the Rump and its Council, which they condemn, reflected a rational and relevant order of priorities. The first concern was to encourage a revival of manufactures and exports. Demand in the home market had contracted because of high food prices, high taxes (particularly the excise), high poor rates and irregular employment. The basis of the Rump's economic policy was to ensure 'that government and order in trade may be preserved and confusion avoided', and this required the rejection for example of Leveller demands for the dissolution of the chartered companies as monopolies. It should be added that this served the interests of the group of merchants who sat in the Rump, and their associates who served in the Council of Trade, men whose mentality and outlook found expression in Thomas Violet's pamphlet, *The Advocate*, and whose cohesiveness contributed to the influence they wielded at Westminster and in the City. At the end of 1650 they helped enact an ordinance restricting trade with the colonies (many of which were still in royalist hands) to vessels specially licensed. This was used to seize and condemn Dutch vessels and it served as a model for the wider Navigation Act of October 1651 which was primarily aimed at the elimination of the Dutch entrepôt trade: all imports must be brought directly to England from their country of origin in either English vessels or those of that country.[7] This Act (technically an ordinance) has been grandly described as a major piece of 'state-building' and as the major cause of the first Anglo-Dutch War. Their earlier experiences meant that both the English and the Dutch were fully aware of the profound consequences of such legislative restrictions of trade. Spain imposed a trade embargo on Dutch vessels and freight in 1621, when war resumed after the twelve-year truce, and on England between 1625 and 1630, which the enforcement agency, the *Almirantazgo*, made increasingly effective. But after 1630 Charles

---

7 B. Worden, *The Rump Parliament* (Cambridge, 1974), pp. 254–60; M. Ashley, *Financial and Commercial Policy in the Cromwellian Protectorate* (1962), pp. 160–1.

realigned his foreign policy to favour Spain with considerable benefits for English trade, especially with the Mediterranean from which the Dutch found themselves virtually excluded. They had to rely on an entrepôt trade through Dover for commodities from Spain which they had formerly imported direct, and silver from America was routed via the London mint for Spain's armies and allies in northern Europe. But once negotiations for peace between Spain and the Dutch Republic made progress, and the embargo was lifted in 1647, this artificial English commercial ascendancy collapsed abruptly and completely. Now in 1651 the Dutch faced the prospect that the near monopoly they had established in trade with the English colonies (and with Scotland) would be eliminated, and the difficulties caused to the WIC by a Portuguese rising in Brazil made these losses more damaging. But there was nothing that the Dutch could do once the English disregarded their demands for repeal of the Navigation Act.[8]

However, the States General was determined to resist the English claims (and practice) of searching vessels, and they had the power to do so effectively. Dutch vessels already enjoyed favoured treatment from both France and Spain, whose war continued until 1659. In 1646 France agreed that Dutch vessels could carry enemy goods, except for contraband defined narrowly as arms, powder, horses and other military equipment, and renewed this concession in 1651 although the Dutch had made a separate peace with Spain in 1648. In 1650 Spain agreed that Dutch vessels should not be subject to interference by their admiralty authorities, so consequently they could carry French goods. The explanation of course was that both combatant states depended on Dutch carriers for the export of commodities on which their economies generally, and their war finances largely, depended. These agreements reflected their dependence on the Amsterdam entrepôt, and as the Dutch exploited the advantages of neutrality their relative superiority over their English rivals would increase.[9] The English searches of Dutch vessels for French commodities, often conducted in brutal fashion, their seizure and condemnation by the admiralty court, were becoming so numerous that they seemed to constitute a deliberate policy aimed at wrecking the vital trade with the Biscay coast of France. Only 12 vessels had been taken in 1648. This rose to 22 intercepted in 1649, 50 in 1650 and this

---

8 J.I. Israel, *The Dutch Republic and the Hispanic World* (Oxford, 1982), pp. 148–9, 205–8, 210, 285–6; Israel, *Dutch Republic*, pp. 713–14.

9 Thurloe, vol. i, p. 185; Wicquefort, *Histoire*, vol. ii, p. 124.

soared to 126 in 1651 (almost equalling the worst year's losses – 1628 – to the Dunkirkers), and 106 in the first half of 1652.[10] The weak embassy sent to London, headed by the geriatric Jacob Cats, the popular demotic poet who delivered part of his address to the uncomprehending English in verse, failed to make any impression on the issue, but any chance of success was fatally undermined by the decision of the States General to protect Dutch shipping by setting out a numerically impressive fleet of 150 ships, to be ready by 1 April. This was the most provocative initiative imaginable, the single most important cause of the ensuing war. The 'protection of trade' entailed preventing English ships exercising what they regarded as their legitimate right to search vessels, and the enormous size of the fleet was bound to be interpreted as intimidatory. It would have to patrol in the Dover Straits and Channel, that is in seas over which the Commonwealth, like the monarchy, claimed sovereign rights, and it would be contesting these rights by its activities. The chief commander Tromp aroused English suspicions; he was an Orangist in political sympathies and had frequently 'invaded' English waters, destroying the Spanish armada in the Downs in 1639, seizing English vessels in 1642 on suspicion of carrying contraband to the Spanish Netherlands, protecting the ships which defected to the royalists in 1648, and shaping up to seize the Scillies in 1651.[11]

The Dutch got the worst of all worlds by the resolution for 150 ships. It was resented as bullying. Negotiations were soured. The Rump interpreted it as a gratuitous challenge to its sovereignty, and the Dutch claim that it was defensive in purpose was dismissed as double-speak. The fleet also turned out to be a paper tiger. The States General prescribed a length of 120 to 125 feet and eighteen to twenty guns for the ships, but the admiralties had discarded many when peace came in 1648 so that now merchant vessels had to be hired, and this at a time when most were being prepared for outward bound voyages. Consequently the full number could not be obtained, many were not ready by 1 April, and many were in poor

10 Groenveld, 'English Civil Wars as Cause of First Anglo-Dutch War', pp. 561, 565–6; these losses were greater than any inflicted over a similar period in the 1640s by the Dunkirkers.

11 Wicquefort, *Histoire*, vol. ii, pp. 115, 130, 151–2, 154; Thurloe, vol. i, p. 158; J.R. Powell, *The Navy in the English Civil War* (Hamden, CT, 1962), pp. 23–6; M. Baumber, *General-at-Sea: Robert Blake and the Seventeenth-Century Revolution in Naval Warfare* (1989) pp. 94–6; H.H. Rowen, *John de Witt: Grand Pensionary of Holland* (Princeton, NJ, 1978), p. 67.

condition with inadequate armament. Again the quality of captains was not impressive. These weaknesses prevented the fleet acting as a deterrent, and they showed De Witt at least that it was futile to rely on improvising a fleet when a crisis developed.[12]

By giving Tromp orders not to approach the English coast too closely and to use his discretion in whether to salute the English flag, an attempt was made by the Dutch government to lessen the dangers of a clash, but when he and a force commanded by Blake came close to each other at the end of May, off Dover, one did develop – how it is now impossible to say. This was not in fact the first engagement; another had occurred on 12/22 May off Start Point, but the Dover clash caused great if belated alarm at the Hague.[13] On 3/13 June the States General sent Adriaan Pauw, a key figure as grand pensionary, to reinforce the embassy in London. His arrival did not cause the Rump to slacken its naval preparations, and when he proposed that each side should appoint commissioners to investigate jointly the causes of the clash, with a cessation of hostilities while they did this, the English side described the proposal as 'dilatory and impracticable', intended to delude the Commonwealth and deprive it of a 'just satisfaction'. The Rump had not planned war – in the spring it had ordered the despatch of a large force to the Mediterranean to protect trade which would have left a weakened fleet in home waters – but they thought that the Dutch had, seeing Tromp's 'attack' on Blake while Dutch negotiators talked about a settlement in London as treachery, very much as the Americans did in 1941 when Kurusu and Nomura negotiated in Washington while the carriers sailed towards Pearl Harbor. The Rump, the Council of State and the commanders at sea were united in their confidence in the superiority of their fleet – in sharp contrast with the general European estimate that the Dutch navy would prove the stronger. And unfortunately for themselves the leading men in the States General and the States of Holland shared this belief which events soon proved to have no basis whatever.[14]

Initially neither side had any realistic conception of the nature of the war on which they were embarked. Their formative naval

12 *FDW*, vol. iv, pp. 313–16, 377; Wicquefort, *Histoire*, vol. ii, pp. 121–2; *CSPVenetian 1652–53*, pp. 29–30, 32–3, 38–9, 54; J.K. Oudendijk, *Johan de Witt en de Zeemacht* (Amsterdam, 1944), p. 26.

13 Wicquefort, *Histoire*, vol. ii, pp. 126–9, 140–1; G. Penn, *Memorials of Sir William Penn* (1833), vol. i, pp. 419–21.

14 Wicquefort, *Histoire*, vol. ii, pp. 130–1, 136; Thurloe, vol. i, pp. 210–11; *Commons Journals*, vol. vii, p. 69; *CSPD 1651–52*, pp. 94, 121–2, 292, 307; J. Corbett, *England in the Mediterranean* (1917), vol. i, pp. 208–9.

experiences had been in wars against a long-distance enemy, Spain, whose armadas had been defeated in 1588 and destroyed in 1639. Offensives had taken the form of attacks on fleets and ports on the coasts of Spain and Portugal. The English had not fought a set-piece naval battle since 1588, the Dutch since 1639 but they, more ominously, had never succeeded in effectively containing the privateers based on Dunkirk. Now the geographical position of the British Isles, spread out like 'eagle's wings' across the main Dutch trade routes, greatly increased the size and complexity of the problems involved in protecting their merchant shipping, and so enabling their mercantile economy to function at levels not decisively lower than those of times of peace, or the last years of the war against Spain.[15]

At the outset neither side had thought out a coherent strategy; in the first summer both followed what can be described as a crude and literal version of Clausewitz's definition of war as a continuation of policy by violent means. The English fleets were used to widen and intensify the attacks on merchant shipping that were already being made; the Dutch concentrated on escorting convoys. Both sides committed major blunders, especially by dividing their forces, which would have been expensive later, but neither had a strategic plan that would have enabled them to exploit errors. Initially Blake was sent into the northern North Sea to attack Dutch vessels homeward bound by a north-about route. This left Ayscue with a weak force in the Dover Straits, where he was under observation by Dutch agents in Calais and the crews of French fishing boats whom they employed. With a greatly superior force Tromp failed to exploit the opportunity to exploit this foolish division of the English fleet by trapping Ayscue in the Downs, where he had annihilated the Spanish armada in 1639. Blake's objective was the Dutch fishing fleet, then off Shetland, whose activity in British seas constituted a long-standing cause of resentment. He used his frigates to take all twelve escorts, but he failed to achieve the success of the Dunkirkers who in 1635 and 1637 had taken or destroyed over 100 fishing busses.[16] When Tromp followed Blake into these northern seas bad weather prevented an engagement, and the Dutch fleet with valuable vessels under escort narrowly escaped being driven on the Shetland rocks north of Sumburgh Head. Meanwhile the States General committed the same blunder as the English, ordering De Ruyter with a weak

15 *FDW*, vol. i, pp. 31–2; DLC, pp. 157–74; J.R. Bruijn, *The Dutch Navy of the Seventeenth and Eighteenth Centuries* (Columbia, SC, 1993), pp. 25–8.

16 Wicquefort, *Histoire*, vol. ii, p. 150; Baumber, *General-at-Sea*, pp. 129–33.

force to escort a convoy down Channel, and then assemble a second convoy of return vessels and bring them home. This plan represented a response to pressure from shipowners whose vessels had been laid up, and merchants whose investments had been earning no profits, but the assembling of the first convoy led to delays and a higher risk of meeting Blake's fleet when it returned south. In addition the States General repeated their pre-war error in thinking that numbers meant an effective force, regardless of the strength of the constituent ships. They collected more than thirty for De Ruyter, but only two had more than thirty guns, and his flagship the *Neptunus* had only twenty-eight. Most were converted merchant vessels, under-gunned and lightly constructed, with inferior sailing qualities, and almost all were undermanned and poorly officered.[17]

Ayscue's cautious reaction when he encountered De Ruyter's force was unique for an English fleet commander in any of the Anglo-Dutch Wars. He stood on the defensive with De Ruyter persistently attempting to attack, and retreated to Plymouth when the Dutch eventually broke into his force. Both sides exaggerated the strength of the other, both overestimated the damage they had inflicted on the enemy; each had suffered relatively heavy casualties in personnel, but no ships were lost. The States General drew what were to be misleading conclusions: their underestimate of the determination and skill of the English commanders was confirmed, as was their assumption that convoys could use the Channel route safely. In reality De Ruyter was fortunate to get his return convoy home safely, evading three English forces by following the French coast. Blake made inadequate provision for scouting and kept his fleet too far north, errors he was to repeat in 1653; he was still more a military than a naval man and owed his appointment to his proven fighting spirit, and had much to learn about fleet warfare. However, a consistent determination to make aggressive use of his forces marked his style of leadership. In the initial clash off Dover he had inflicted heavy damage on Tromp's force, two of which were lost. On 4/14 September he overwhelmed a weakly escorted French convoy taking reinforcements to Dunkirk which was consequently forced to surrender to the investing Spanish army, a dramatic illustration of the effectiveness of seapower.[18]

Although Tromp had enjoyed immense prestige since 1639, his behaviour during the summer provoked bitter criticism and led

---

17 *FDW*, vol. ii, pp. 59–60, 63–4, 79–80, 87–8, 111–12, 146–7.
18 Ibid., vol. ii, pp. 10, 110, 123, 143–8, 163, 166, 195–6, 253, 344, 346.

to his supersession as fleet commander. Regents distrusted him as an Orangist. The ambassadors in London tried to use him as a scapegoat, loading the blame on him for the first clash, and accusing him of ignoring his instructions: they even offered to punish him in order to satisfy the English Council. Tromp had complained about the instructions he had received, saying he could not be expected to defend commerce, and at the same time fight the English fleet. Consequently the States General put an itemized set of questions about his conduct, and the negative or cautious wording of his replies revealed a breakdown in mutual trust. The States General was (without realizing it) blundering into a major question, the relationship between a government that could not ignore pressure from interest groups, and a dissatisfied public, and its commanders at sea. Tromp argued that an admiral must not be tied to instructions but should have discretion to depart from them when situations changed and the unexpected happened. He rejected the criticism that he had called too many councils of war, in order to consult his captains, with the implication that this had resulted in an over-cautious conduct of operations which was judged to have been unjustified by the politicians ashore. The States General, dissatisfied with Tromp, replaced him by Witte de With, despite the fact (of which they should have been aware) that he did not command respect in the fleet, largely it would seem because of an overbearing manner which reflected, but was meant to compensate for, his feelings of insecurity; he belonged to a minority sect, he differed from most naval officers in not being an Orangist and he lacked charisma in comparison with Tromp.[19]

De With's main qualification for his political masters would seem to be that he would keep to his instructions, and that he knew that he was expected to seek out and fight the main English fleet. The politicians still greatly underestimated English strength. They persisted in believing that De Ruyter had inflicted serious damage on Ayscue's force, and believed that the officers of the English navy were riven by political and personal antagonisms. But the sea-officers knew that they had to face superior strength: De Ruyter had observed that his ships did not have the same firepower as the English great ships. Witte de With deplored the poor morale of many of his ships' companies, the result of the different rates of pay (according to the time at which they were recruited), arrears, undermanning and the presence of large numbers of soldiers with no experience of life at

19 Ibid., vol. ii, p. 219; vol. iii, pp. 22–4, 30, 78–81; vol. v, p. 403.

sea.[20] Yet when he located Blake in the Downs he knew that he must attack and was expected to repeat Tromp's victory of 1639, although the enemy was far stronger than the Spaniards had been and ready to challenge a set-piece battle. On 25 September/5 October he had to force through a resolution in a council of war for an attack. Strong winds postponed an engagement for three days and also scattered Blake's fleet after he sortied from the Downs. Consequently the main division of the Dutch fleet was able to fall on Bourne's seriously outnumbered rear division, but failed to do significant damage before Blake came up and forced his opponents to withdraw. This first battle, the Kentish Knock, had several features that were to recur in later engagements. Blake, Penn and Bourne were all determined to force an action, even though it could not begin until as late as 1600 hours (and this in October); it was the onset of darkness that enabled the Dutch to withdraw without being pursued. In contrast several Dutch captains failed to support their admirals in close action, and refused on the two following days to renew battle. Second, the Dutch received a severe battering from the controlled broadsides of the more heavily armed English ships; although only three ships were lost, their casualties in personnel were considerable – over 2,000 wounded had to be landed afterwards. The Dutch escaped disaster primarily as a result of the late hour and to some extent because of their superior seamanship and pilotage skills. Two of Blake's ships ran aground in the early stages, and his later manoeuvres were restricted by the lack of searoom and the fear of stranding. Third, the Dutch politicians failed to carry out a realistic analysis of the causes of this reverse. Instead Witte de With was loaded with the responsibility and replaced by a rehabilitated Tromp, and the States General reverted to a strategy of using the fleet primarily for the protection of convoys of merchant vessels.[21]

It was not customary during the seventeenth century to keep fleets at sea during the winter; most ships were laid up in October while a winter guard of reduced strength was maintained. This practice made it possible to discharge most seamen so that they could take service in merchant vessels; this enabled them to undertake winter voyages that would normally be made during the summer. England, with a much smaller seagoing population and a high percentage impressed

20 Ibid., vol. ii, pp. 220–1, 233, 253, 300, 302.
21 Ibid., vol. ii, pp. 218–19, 283, 294, 296–7; vol. iii, pp. 2, 53–6; Baumber, *General-at-Sea*, pp. 145–50; Penn, *Memorials of Sir William Penn*, vol. i, p. 452; *CSPD 1651–52*, p. 430.

during the summer, needed this transfer of seamen from the navy if foreign trade was not to collapse in wartime. In addition ships suffered more wear and tear from winter weather – much more severe then than in the late twentieth century – and, with the Baltic closed to all English vessels, supplies of naval stores had to be carefully conserved. The admiralty was seeking alternative sources of plank, tar, pitch and hemp in Scotland and New England, but supplies would take time to arrive, and care and maintenance work had to compete with the programme of new construction of great ships and frigates. The English decision was to lay up half the fleet, and several of the larger ships were placed in dockyard hands for major refits involving new masts and structural timbers. A task force of twenty converted merchant vessels was to be sent to the Mediterranean. Blake expressed his unhappiness at this dispersal of strength; the Council of State was committing the cardinal strategic sin of deciding on the deployment of its forces without taking into consideration likely moves by the enemy.[22]

For some unknown reason neither the Council nor Blake took action when they received ample and timely warning that the Dutch fleet under Tromp was being prepared for an early sortie, and that over 400 vessels were waiting fully freighted to sail from Dutch havens; at this time of the year they must be bound for westward destinations, not the Baltic, which was icing up.[23] Tromp sailed on 21 November/1 December, but moves such as bringing the ships detailed for the Mediterranean from Portsmouth to join Blake in the Downs were not ordered, because it would mean recasting the planned deployments for the winter. The fleet was also suffering from the government's financial problems. Seamen's wages had fallen into serious arrears, causing widespread unrest. Work in the dockyards was being slowed by shortages of ready money and ships due to join the winter guard were not ready. Signs of governmental inattention became evident before the November elections to the Council of State, which weakened the mercantile interest and are regarded as the main reason for the lack of any sense of urgency. However, it is clear that members of both the outgoing and incoming Councils underestimated (or even were unaware of) the complexity and magnitude of the problems involved in a major naval war, and the need to change decisions and policies in the light of enemy moves.

---

22 *FDW*, vol. iii, pp. 124 *passim*, 267–452; vol. iii, pp. 50, 64.
23 Ibid., vol. iii, p. 33; Baumber, *General-at-Sea*, p. 154; *CSPD 1651–52*, pp. 447, 450.

Both the Council and Blake had yet to acquire the flexibility needed to cope with situations which could change much more quickly and completely than in the much slower moving military campaigns of the time, in which most Council members and the general-at-sea had personally participated. A whiff of complacency was also evident after the Kentish Knock.[24]

In this operation the Dutch showed much greater flexibility, twice altering their instructions to Tromp in the light of new information about English naval strength and dispositions. Nevertheless their plan, based on De Ruyter's fortuitously successful operation in the summer, contained some serious flaws and questionable assumptions. Tromp would escort an enormous convoy down Channel, careen and take on provisions off St Martin de Ré on the French Biscay coast, and then assemble a large homeward-bound convoy which he was to escort using the Channel route again. This was risky, the English were bound to be ready for him, and Tromp would find himself in the same difficult situation as Oquendo, his opponent in 1639. Tromp expressed misgivings about his mission, raising the poor condition of many ships and the difficulties of a long winter cruise. But the main thrust of his representations to the States General concerned a perennial issue about the confidence and support that a commanding officer ordered to carry out a risky operation can expect from his political superiors. He knew that substantial losses of merchant vessels would result in their owners bringing pressure to bear on the States General, and he had already endured an investigation into his conduct of the previous summer's campaign, and lost his command even before this was completed, and Witte de With had been superseded after doing his utmost at the Kentish Knock. To safeguard himself he asked before sailing that he should receive a pledge that his conduct of the operation should not be made the subject of an inquisitorial examination. This was not really an impertinent or excessive demand for a man whose reputation as the servant of his 'dear fatherland' stood higher than any other Dutchman of his time, and as the greatest seaman in Europe.[25]

Important intelligence indicating that Blake's fleet was far weaker than had been thought was received before Tromp sailed, but even this did not give him freedom of action. He was now authorized to attack, if he found this information to be correct, but he was expressly forbidden to pursue the English into the Thames estuary because this

24 *FDW*, vol. iii, pp. 14, 164–5.
25 Ibid., vol. iii, pp. 20–4, 68–9.

would leave the convoy with only a weak escort as it continued down Channel. In other words for the States General the protection of trade still had priority over defeating the enemy fleet; it is significant that when De Witt assumed the direction of the war in 1653, and in 1665–67, he consistently ordered offensives into the Thames in order to strike a decisive blow that would end the war. The accident of gales resulted in Tromp's force appearing in the Dover Straits well ahead of the convoy so that he was unencumbered by merchant vessels. Blake had fewer than half Tromp's ships, and several were unreliable privateers commandeered to meet the emergency. He had instructions to sail into the Channel where he could join with ships coming from Portsmouth (although these were converted merchant vessels and of dubious strength) before attempting an attack. Consequently on 30 November/10 December the two fleets sailed on parallel courses along the Kent coast west of Folkestone. As Tromp appreciated, Blake was sailing into a trap: Dungeness lay ahead and the English would have to turn to port. As they did Tromp attacked Blake and the leading ships; many English captains slackened sail, lagged behind and stayed out of the engagement. Tromp was unable to take full advantage of his superior seamanship, which gave him superiority of numbers in the actual fire-fight, because even his larger ships carried inadequate armaments that made little impression on the stoutly constructed English great ships. Blake lost only the *Garland* and the *Bonaventure*, his casualties in personnel were otherwise light and most of his ships expended only a fraction of their powder.[26]

Nevertheless Dungeness represented a major strategic victory for Tromp, who would have been justified in hoisting the legendary broom to his masthead to symbolize his sweeping of the Channel. The convoy sailed down Channel. Troops had to be sent to protect the south coast against invasion, although the Dutch did no more than rustle Romney Marsh sheep. Blake retreated, first into the Downs, then the Thames estuary, but Tromp was prevented by his instructions from pursuing beyond the North Foreland. Psychologically Dungeness could have been a major blow to the Commonwealth. The exiled royalist Edward Hyde became euphoric, expecting it to make a deep impression on the people of England as the 'first signal overthrow those devilish rebels have sustained, either at sea or on land'.[27] He even claimed that the Dutch owed their success

26 Ibid., vol. iii, pp. 70, 75–6, 89–93, 122, 143; Baumber, *General-at-Sea*, pp. 160–1.

27 Penn, *Memorials of Sir William Penn*, p. 466.

to a refusal of the English seamen to fight because they hoped and wanted the Dutch to declare for Charles II. But in the sequel the Rump and the Council of State reacted in the most constructive and impressive fashion, undertaking both immediate improvements and lasting long-term reforms, a most remarkable achievement for men who found themselves in the middle of an unexpected crisis.

The first and best known move was to strengthen the top naval command. There was no question of accepting Blake's offer to resign, since it was not his fault that he had an inadequate fleet. The appointment on 4/14 December of the two generals-at-sea, Deane and Monck, was intended to rectify the indiscipline and lack of aggression that had been evident among many captains at Dungeness – a weakness from which the Dutch suffered and which they failed to eradicate during this first war. Monck and Deane were both disciplinarians, and experienced soldiers of proven aggressiveness, and the latter was a gunnery specialist. He was close to Cromwell, and had been his original choice to replace Warwick in 1648 as commander of the restive fleet, which had subsequently mutinied under the man appointed, the Leveller Rainsborough. It took a major effort to provide the new commanders with a fleet strong enough to oppose Tromp who must be expected to appear in the Channel with a return convoy in a matter of weeks, and this had to be done in mid-winter, a time when normally the early stages of fleet preparation were under way. In performing this emergency task Commonwealth administration can be seen at its most efficient, refitting and setting out ships, completing their complements and ensuring their provisioning months before this was usually done.[28]

Much more remarkably the Council of State carried out fundamental reforms which were to serve as the basis of centrally important aspects of naval administration for over a century. It established a new scale of pay for all rates of seamen, and it instituted a new code of naval discipline, the celebrated Articles of War. Both these reforms had immediate relevance by removing sources of weakness that threatened to impede the setting out of an effective fighting force. Inadequate pay, which was seriously in arrears in some ships, provoked disaffection and desertions. In particular anomalies resulted in insufficient reward for the skills of those categories of key personnel – bosuns, quartermasters, gunners, carpenters – which were most crucial in the fitting out of ships and in achieving maximum fighting efficiency. Able seamen were given

---

28 *Commons Journals*, vol. vii, p. 222; *FDW*, vol. iii, pp. 109–12.

an increase from nineteen to twenty-four shillings a month. In order to prevent abuses captains were to assess all seamen and record their rate. Regulations were also promulgated on the sharing out of prize money, and equivalent payments were ordered for enemy ships destroyed rather than captured. As a short-term measure a bonus was paid to all seamen who continued in, or returned to, the service in the forty days after 1 January. At this stage it was particularly important to enhance the attraction of serving in the State's ships in comparison with the gains to be made from going out in privateers, which as scavengers were certainly going to profit from snapping up stragglers and disabled vessels from Tromp's return convoy, while the warships did the hard fighting against the escort.[29]

Although the Articles of War applied to all naval personnel they were aimed particularly at captains whose incompetence or cowardice could fatally weaken the fleet, as Dungeness had shown. There were as yet no professional corps of career naval officers in either the English or the Dutch service; many captains had been taken on together with their vessels which were converted into warships, and which it was often their primary concern to conserve from damage or loss. Few had combat experience. Their incompetence and reluctance to engage the enemy were difficult to detect: English fleets did not as yet always use a line formation (the Dutch did not do so at all in this first war), and even when they did the battle usually degenerated into a mêlée, in which it was easy for an irresolute captain to hold back from the thick of the battle – whereas in eighteenth-century battles fought in line, any divergence from the formation or disregard of orders would be quickly detected. Moreover the great ships and the faster frigates were usually placed in the van, and so would be the first to engage (as at Dungeness), while the less powerful, slower and less handy converted merchant vessels were invariably placed in the rear and were expected to close the enemy as quickly as they could. Witte de With at the Kentish Knock and Blake at Dungeness suffered because many held back, or began to retire when they saw things were going badly. Articles XII–XV ordained death or other punishment for captains who failed to fight, or to encourage their men to fight, who disobeyed orders or hung back from an engagement. In the Dutch case provosts were sent out to observe, from ketches in the rear, any-one who broke away from a battle, to interrogate captains and crews and bring offenders to trial; several captains were either executed or

---

29 *FDW*, vol. iii, pp. 134, 147, 149, 267 *passim*; vol. iv, pp. 1–68; Baumber, *General-at-Sea*, pp. 165–8; *CSPD 1652–53*, pp. 39, 42–4.

imprisoned as a result. These kinds of offences were commonest in the first war when both sides employed many converted merchant vessels, some on short-term arrangements for six or nine months, with their peacetime captains. After Dungeness the English admiralty ordered that all captains and officers were to be appointed by the state, with the interests of the owners being safeguarded merely by a *reformado*, or supernumerary, officer acting as 'ship's husband'.[30]

The basic English principle held that the strength of the fleet rested in its great ships, those carrying both the most and the biggest guns. The weight of the shot fired by the broadsides of the great ships proved to be the crucial difference between the English and Dutch fleets throughout 1653, with the former discharging converted vessels in order to provide crews for the new ships that became available. Converted vessels were relegated largely to convoy protection, whereas the Dutch retained theirs despite their relatively light armaments and lightly built hulls. Some had as many as thirty-two guns, but these were light pieces firing cannon balls of only eight pounds with little penetrative power. In another realistic decision the English admiralty relegated its white elephant, the *Sovereign of the Seas*, a prestige ship *par excellence*, to the end of the list of ships to be refitted: it drew twenty-two feet and needed an exceptionally large crew of over seven hundred to sail and fight, and in early 1653 manning proved to be the most difficult problem. Wisely the admiralty concentrated on the full manning of the great ships and fast frigates, many of the latter new accessions to the fleet. By mid-February it assembled a fleet ready to confront Tromp, although the generals complained that many ships did not have sufficient able seamen, but there was no question of this being an improvised or scratch force hastily assembled.[31]

Although Tromp carried out the first phase of his sortie with complete success, the disadvantages of the Dutch strategy appeared once he arrived off St Martin. The longer he stayed the greater would be the English force ready to oppose his return voyage: he therefore communicated his decision to sail at the end of January to the merchants and skippers in the Loire and Garonne regions. But it became clear that many vessels, and especially those that had come out with him, would not be ready. Many of his warships needed refit work, but little except careening could be done, and

30 *FDW*, vol. iii, pp. 174–5, 180, 293–301, 428; Baumber, *General-at-Sea*, pp. 162–3.

31 *FDW*, vol. ii, p. 360; vol. iv, pp. 66, 278–80; Baumber, *General-at-Sea*, p. 148; D. Howarth, *Sovereign of the Seas* (1974).

provisions and powder were impossible to obtain in a region where civil war was raging. However, he kept to his timetable, sailing on 30 January/9 February with a smaller than expected convoy.

Blake sailed from the Thames on 10/20 February, in good time to intercept Tromp well down the Channel because the latter was held back by north-easterlies, and by predictable difficulties in keeping his convoy together in adverse wind conditions: an English privateer sighted him west of Ushant on 13/23 February. Blake's scouting proved to be the main English failure. He missed an advance Dutch convoy from Le Havre and Morlaix, weakly escorted, which passed to the south of him on 17/27 February. On the other hand his general strategy was very relevant; the generals emphasized to their subordinates that the primary objective was not the capture of merchant vessels, tempting as that might seem, but the destruction of Tromp's undermanned warships which must now be in poor condition. If they could be crippled by damage to masts and sails Tromp would have to leave them behind; Blake gave his captains instructions to finish them off by sinking or burning, they were not to get behind themselves by boarding and taking them. Blake was expecting his officers to put the public interest before their own advantage. A decisive victory could now be within reach: if a large number of Dutch warships were destroyed so early in the year the States General would have to realize that their fleet would be forced on to the defensive for the whole summer and all trade would be paralysed.

Blake and Tromp sighted each other at daybreak on 18/28 February. Blake was at the southernmost leg of a sweep, off the Casquets, with one division. The Dutch were to windward, the other English divisions dispersed to the north-east, downwind, which meant that they would take several hours to come up to Blake. Tromp had to make a quick decision, whether to stay close to the convoy or to attack Blake while he was still isolated. Characteristically Blake did not retire but stood to receive Tromp's attack. What followed graphically illustrates the reason why the English prevailed in this first war. For two hours Blake with four or five great ships and attendant frigates, and a few converted merchant vessels, withstood Tromp with over thirty; the latter simply lacked the firepower to overwhelm the more heavily built English ships, although these suffered heavy casualties among officers and men on the exposed upper decks. Blake was wounded and his flagship, the *Triumph*, had up to a hundred killed and wounded. Blake lost only the frigate *Samson*, with four ships damaged, Tromp lost at least eight of his ships and his failure decided him not to take offensive action again during this running battle, best described by the Dutch term, the Channel Fight.[32]

Superior seamanship enabled the convoy to make good progress during each night, but in daylight the convoy tended to lose cohesion, some vessels straggling and some captains ignoring Tromp's orders to press on all sail and get ahead of their escorts. On the second day, 19 February/1 March, Tromp fought a successful holding action south of the Isle of Wight, losing only two ships. The crisis came on 20 February/2 March when the Dutch warships began to run out of powder, several vessels ran themselves ashore on the French coast to save their cargoes and others jettisoned barrels of wine, and the English took many prizes. By nightfall the remains of the convoy – about thirty-five warships and a hundred vessels – seemed to be trapped south of Gris Nez with a north-north-west wind pinning them against the coast. Blake stood off because of the shoals, intending to sail in at dawn and annihilate them. But at this last stage the disadvantages of employing generals as commanders operated to deprive the English of a decisive victory. The generals accepted the advice of their pilots that Tromp would not be able to round Gris Nez, but he achieved this by using the incoming tide and once he reached Calais roads he was safe (unlike the 1588 armada). He was also helped by good fortune: immediately after he passed the straits a gale blew up which would have prevented his dilapidated ships doing so.[33]

Despite Tromp's achievement in saving most of his warships and about half his merchant vessels the Channel Fight had ominous consequences for the Dutch. It showed them that the Channel route could not be used in wartime, and this meant that the flow of trade using the alternative north-about route with its much greater mileage could never exceed a fraction (far less than 50 per cent) of its peacetime levels.[34] Second, the more heavily built and armed English ships had again proved to be too formidable for even the largest Dutch ships, mostly 46s and 40s, which were revealed to be too puny in a close engagement. The Dutch had also suffered very severe casualties in personnel, with reports of over 2,000 dead and 1,500 prisoners, while

---

32 *FDW*, vol. iv, pp. 48, 65, 68; Baumber, *General-at-Sea*, pp. 170–1.

33 *FDW*, vol. iv, pp. 78–84, 87–90, 108–11, 118–26, 163–7; Baumber, *General-at-Sea*, pp. 170–1.

34 The distance from Finisterre to the Texel via the Channel is approximately 1010 miles/1625 kilometres; the long way round north-about is 2200 miles/3450 kilometres.

the English had only 300 killed. Moreover there was no prospect of the situation changing in favour of the Dutch: new and more heavily armed ships were under construction, but shortages of money and materials were retarding progress and few actually became available during 1653. Defeat and losses depressed morale, especially among the very numerous foreign seamen who were not eager to face such death and destruction again. Ironically when Tromp reached Calais roads he received orders from the States General to keep his ships at sea, take on provisions and powder, and then sail to establish a blockade of the Thames! These orders, which originated in the inventive mind of Johan de Witt and do credit to his spirit, were based on the assumption that Tromp had been victorious. But neither he nor any Dutch commander were to win any victories or undertake any effective offensive action during the rest of the war.[35]

In London an exultant Council of State began to plan how to improve the victory and intensify the war. It sent the admiralty commissioners in person to congratulate the generals and the fleet. However, its members and the Rump survived for only a month to enjoy their now prosperous war. On 20 April Cromwell arbitrarily dissolved the Rump at a high point of the war, and throughout the summer he and the new Council held discussions with four commissioners sent by the States General to explore the possibility of a negotiated settlement. Cromwell's alleged failure to intensify pressure on the Dutch, despite further English victories, was to form the basis of bitter criticism.

Despite his heavy losses Tromp still believed that the best strategy was to seek and fight the enemy fleet, but he had first to provide protective cover for what his political masters (rightly) regarded as essential convoys. He escorted over 200 vessels sailing north-about to westward destinations, then waited on the Dogger to bring home some 150 from France, Spain and the West Indies which had missed his Channel convoy in February. He knew that the safe arrival of these vessels was seen, particularly in Amsterdam, as absolutely crucial for the effective continuation of the mercantile economy. During this first phase of the summer's campaign it is striking how the commanders at sea had little idea of their enemies' location, strength and intentions. Tromp sailed with his convoy on 4/14 May in the afternoon; the English fleet appeared off the Texel the next morning. After interrogating fishermen it set off in pursuit but failed

---

35 *FDW*, vol. iv, pp. 111, 115, 122–4, 136–8, 188–9; Rowen, *De Witt*, pp. 73–4.

to find him; Tromp was totally unaware that he was being hunted until he returned three weeks later. When he learnt that the English fleet had gone north, Tromp thought that a detachment would have been left to guard the Thames, and would be vulnerable to attack; the opportunity he had ignored in 1652 seemed to have been re-created. But when he swept the Downs he found no English ships; as compensation he wasted a great deal of powder in a futile bombardment of Dover (25 May/4 June). The next day the English fleet, after a fruitless northern cruise, reappeared off the Texel but soon returned to the English coast for provisions.[36]

This game of blind man's bluff continued for another week before the decisive battle of the war was fought on 2/12 June near the Gabbard shoal, twenty to twenty-five miles east of Felixstowe, that is well on the English side of the North Sea. The Dutch were far from the shelter of their shoals and havens when the battle went against them, but Tromp seems to have been confident that his tactical skill would prevail against the relatively clumsy or landlubber generals. But if he relied on personal experience and seamanship the generals had taken a great leap forward in systematizing the battle tactics which the fleet was to use henceforward. Indeed the 'Instructions for ordering the fleet' that were issued after the Channel Fight constituted a most momentous development: they were the initial step in developing the classic eighteenth-century technique of the British navy, adopting as a regular practice a line ahead formation. In the next century British admirals maintained this formation rigidly in battle, relying on increasingly sophisticated signalling codes and skilled yeomen to transmit instantly intelligible orders to their junior flag-officers and captains, and assuming (not always rightly) that a high level of professionalism would mean that orders would be obeyed without question. But during the Dutch wars signalling techniques were still rudimentary, going no further than the hoisting of a single (and outsize) flag at the main or the mizzen conveying a single order – for example for all ships to close on the admiral. The standard procedure of the next century by which ships under command hoisted the same flag or flags to signify that the order was understood, and executed it when the admiral dipped his, had not yet been adopted. Consequently the adoption of the line formation in 1653 had limited, but still very important, advantages: the aim in the Instructions was to ensure that the fleet remained in an ordered formation, and could

[36] *FDW*, vol. v, pp. 39–41, 49, 56, 59–60.

respond to orders, in the manoeuvring that preceded engagement in close combat. The Instructions represented an extended application of the principle of the division of the fleet into three divisions; the van, usually commanded by the vice-admiral, the main body commanded by the admiral, and the rear under the rear-admiral. The Instructions laid down that in each division the flag-officer should be the ship most to windward, with the other ships forming a line astern. This was the formation in which each division was to approach the enemy in line ahead; then, when the admiral hoisted a red flag to his foremast peak, all were to turn 90° and attack in line abreast. But it would then be for each ship to single out and engage an enemy ship: to this there was no alternative since the Dutch, unlike Britain's opponents in the next century, did not fight in line until 1666.[37]

Once battle was joined the admirals had only limited ability to command their ships. Single flags, even of very large size and at the peak of masts (if they had not been shot away), were less visible than the hoists of multi-coloured flags at the yardarm of the ship ahead on which the eighteenth-century navies depended. And even the largest flags became obscured in a mêlée by dense smoke from the guns and burning ships. Admirals communicated by sending messages in longboats, a very hazardous practice, and frequently captains and junior flag-officers came aboard the admiral's ship to ascertain his intentions. Smoke also made it difficult for anyone to tell how a battle was going; consequently the less resolute captains, especially those commanding vulnerable converted merchant vessels, held back from a general mêlée so as to have a good start if retirement became necessary.[38]

At the Gabbard, as generally during this first war, the Dutch fleet was organized for mêlée fighting. Tromp's ships carried a far higher proportion of soldiers in their crews than did the English, whose functions were to sweep the enemy's upper decks with musketry fire, kill the exposed officers and then board, overwhelming the comparatively few seamen who were not engaged in manning the broadside guns on the lower decks. Tromp also relied far more than the English on the use of fireships to finish off damaged or immobile ships, and on his superior seamanship to out-manoeuvre the English so as to concentrate his whole strength against a single division. A slackening of the wind frustrated this plan and enabled Monck to keep his fleet in line ahead; the captains did not find the unaccustomed task of

---

37 Ibid., vol. v, p. 109; Thurloe, vol. i, p. 277.
38 Thurloe, vol. i, p. 411.

keeping station too difficult in light winds, and the Dutch could not close. Monck's ships fired steady broadsides at medium range, doing damage to the hulls, masts and sails of their enemy and massacring the soldiers massed on the upper decks. Although Deane was killed by almost the first shot fired, the engagement turned into a one-sided affair, and when towards the end of the day a mêlée developed, Tromp's force had been too battered to be able to hold its own. During the night of 2–3/12–13 June a Dutch council of war accepted Tromp's resolution to make an early attack in order to cover an orderly retirement. This attack proved disastrous. Many Dutch ships ran out of powder. Several captains failed to give full support and the fleet lost cohesion. A group of devoted captains covered the retirement of Tromp's flagship, the *Brederode*, which was taking in water, but at least ten Dutch ships were destroyed and eleven taken, and many stragglers barely eluded pursuit, seeking refuge behind the shoals, like Highlanders fleeing to the mountains 'where we cannot follow', said one of Monck's officers.[39]

Heavy casualties in personnel made the Gabbard a shattering blow to Dutch fleet morale. Tromp did not dare send his damaged ships into ports for repair for fear of mass desertions, and an embargo on all outward merchant sailings had as a main purpose the resulting pressure on seamen to enter the naval service. The States General realized that the defeat would weaken the standing of the Republic with foreign governments. It therefore sent its diplomats abroad a propaganda version. This admitted a reverse but blamed it on natural causes, shifts in the wind, and minimized losses, claiming tendentiously that only five or six ships were missing – true only in the sense of being still unaccounted for. The English were said to have lost heavily. However, the Dutch public could not be deceived as easily. The Gabbard was followed by the first systematic blockade of the war, with Monck's fleet established off the coast of Holland for over a month, paralysing all merchant shipping movements and, at first, provoking alarm that the English would attempt a landing. The pressure exerted by this blockade made it imperative for Tromp, once he concentrated his ships, to sortie in a challenge to the victorious English fleet.[40]

39 *FDW*, vol. v, pp. 21–4, 69–70, 72–5, 80, 82–5, 121, 145; P. Cowburn, *The Warship in History* (1960), pp. 110–11.
40 *FDW*, vol. v, pp. 88–9, 403–4; Thurloe, vol. i, pp. 273–4; Wicquefort, *Histoire*, vol. ii, p. 224; *CSP Venetian 1651–52*, p. 91.

Tromp knew that a renewed challenge was politically necessary, but he was also painfully aware that the strength at his disposal was inadequate. Only two new great ships (the *Swieten* and *Kruningen*) – both originally being built for Genoa, not the States General, such had been the lack of Dutch pre-vision – became available for service: some forty great ships and frigates were under construction but making slow progress because of shortages of money and materials, and none was ready in 1653. The capture of two vessels from Sweden freighted with some four hundred cannon, mostly twelve and eighteen pounders, by Monck's blockaders made it necessary to scour provincial fortresses for guns, many of them of doubtful value in ships. Tromp clutched at straws, hoping that something might come from negotiations to take Danish warships on loan. The Danish navy had recently built some monster ships with eighty-six guns, and the *Sophia Amalia* of 1650 at times carried a hundred. However, this was a prestige ship *par excellence*, a white elephant comparable to Charles I's *Sovereign of the Seas*, and it spent nearly all its life laid up in port. The whole idea of hiring between ten and sixteen Danish ships was chimerical. The Danish king demanded compensation if any were lost and an equivalent number of Dutch ships to protect Copenhagen. How were they to reach the Texel? Who was to command and man them? Moreover Tromp rightly stipulated that any ships hired must be 'good sailers', and these excessively large ships, designed for the western Baltic, were unsuitable for service with the Dutch fleet. They had too great draughts – the *Sophia Amalia* drew over twenty feet – and so would be unable either to take refuge in the coastal shoal waters or to use Dutch bases, except after lightening ship. They proved to be as illusory a source of new strength as the 'miracle' mechanical ship which an eccentric French inventor was about to be commissioned to build in Rotterdam.[41]

Monck maintained an effective blockade of the Texel and Vlie, the northern sea-gates, for a month. This was a considerable administrative and logistical accomplishment by seventeenth-century standards, with his fleet being reprovisioned at sea by victuallers sent from England, and ships being sent back in rotation for refitting. He kept his major ships out of sight of land, at anchor, minimizing wear and tear, while his frigates patrolled close inshore. This enabled him to withdraw the great ships to the Suffolk coast for reprovisioning,

41 *FDW*, vol. v, pp. 51, 203, 216, 244–6, 254, 266–7; vol. iii, p. 448; Thurloe, vol. i, pp. 248, 299–300, 321, 439; F. Fox, *Great Ships: The Battlefleet of Charles II* (Greenwich, 1980), pp. 129–30; Israel, *Dutch Republic*, pp. 716–17.

without the Dutch becoming aware of his absence.[42] By contrast Tromp found himself beset by difficulties: the admiralties took time to meet his stated needs. He had to prevent the States General dissipating his strength by sending his best frigates on a diversionary raid into the Dover Straits. Mercantile pressure groups who wanted the blockade removed at the earliest possible time underestimated his major problem; before the Dutch fleet could encounter Monck with any chance of avoiding disaster it was necessary for Tromp to unite his ships in the Wielings with those sortieing from the Texel. This union he accomplished by a final demonstration of superb seamanship, fighting a holding action on 29 July/8 August which allowed the Texel ships to join him the next day. On 31 July/10 August his seamanship was again far superior to that of the English commanders, winning the weather gauge, but it availed him not at all in the face of the greater cohesion and superior firepower of the pugnacious Monck's fleet. The weight of the evidence supports the conclusion that this time the English fleet not only approached the enemy in line ahead but also maintained this formation in breaking through the Dutch fleet repeatedly. On each of four occasions the heavier cannons of the entire English fleet were brought to bear on individual Dutch ships, which were shattered in turn, as ship after ship passed and fired on them. Panic ensued. Tromp was killed early on, no commander could take his place in the confusion, and the ships which had not been engaged and still had plenty of powder and shot began to desert, although they were relatively undamaged; their captains were demoralized by seeing the destruction wreaked by the English on those ships which they were closely engaging. A rout followed, with only the Texel ships, which were at the rear of the fleet, withdrawing in good order.[43]

Dutch propaganda accounts of the battle claimed a success because Monck was forced to leave the coast and return to England. Although his casualties were not heavy nearly all the English ships suffered damage, particularly to their masts, and most of them needed refitting work after being at sea for months. The States General, anticipating that after a battle the English would have to withdraw, had already sent orders that the fleet should not enter the Texel. It was to stay just outside, in the safety of shoal

---

[42] *FDW*, vol. v, pp. 94, 148–50, 186–7, 209, 215–17, 228–30, 237; Thurloe, vol. i, pp. 279, 282, 294, 334, 340.

[43] *FDW*, vol. v, pp. 281–9, 321–7, 334–8, 340–5, 347–50, 354–8, 367–71; Wicquefort, *Histoire*, vol. ii, p. 214.

waters, to be ready to escort outward-bound merchant vessels, which had been waiting for long periods, northwards, and to bring back the large number of vessels sheltering in Norwegian havens and the Sound. Tromp's replacement, Witte de With, disregarded these unrealistic orders, which were a response to mercantile pressures on the politicians. His own morale was not high: in the previous month he had frankly and tactlessly told the States General that the Gabbard made the English masters of the seas, and therefore of the Dutch.[44] He had under his command those ships which had escaped damage during the battle, but in many cases this was because their officers had chosen not to fight in support of Tromp, and in every ship morale had collapsed. At least fifteen Dutch ships had been destroyed in what was a third consecutive defeat in a period of six months. Tromp was irreplaceable, his death a catastrophe. Witte de With, although judged a good seaman, did not inspire confidence in the fleet, while Evertsen was a Zeelander and therefore unacceptable to Hollanders and attracted unfair blame for the defeats; De Ruyter had not yet distinguished himself sufficiently to be acclaimed as Tromp's successor.

The run-down state of both fleets during the last phase of the war, victors and defeated alike, reflects the extremely limited financial, administrative and governmental stamina possessed by seventeenth-century states. The English fleet which sailed on 21/31 August under Lawson to reimpose the blockade contained several ships whose battle damage had only been patched up. The fleet was also undermanned because the desire to revive and expand receipts from customs had led to a lifting of the embargo on outward-bound merchant sailings. The defects of the fleet could be a serious matter at a time of year when bad weather would certainly be encountered. The English navy victuallers were getting into practical difficulties, so that a prolonged blockade could not be maintained, although they undertook to supply the fleet if the war continued into 1654. On the Dutch side the problems were far greater, indeed virtually insoluble. The three sea-battles taught the lesson that with seriously outgunned ships close engagements would lead only to disaster, but the admiralties informed the States General that virtually all construction work in the yards was stopped because the laying-off of most carpenters and labourers had become necessary for lack of ready money. Consequently the arrival of naval stores in ships which came through the blockade, and ordnance did not make it possible to resume work on the large scale that was necessary if a

44 *FDW*, vol. v, p. 147; Thurloe, vol. i, pp. 314, 448–9.

really effective fleet was to be sent out in 1654. Furthermore shortage of money meant that seamen's pay had fallen into serious arrears, and it was impossible for ships to be paid off as they came in. The general state of the Dutch fleet had deteriorated to the same abysmal condition that the English fleet was to find itself in at the end of 1666, when the fateful decision was taken not to send it out the next year, even though the war continued. In the autumn of 1653 the Dutch were at the end of their tether.[45]

When Witte de With's fleet sortied at the end of September his foul and undermanned ships could be supplied with only two months' victuals for a convoying expedition to south Norway. He had no confidence in the ability of his force to fight a major action, and when he returned (14/24 October) he wrote to the States General demanding permission for his ships to enter the Texel, that was in effect to wrap up the year's campaign. The politicians rejected his request, ordering him to revictual in the shallows outside while they finalized projects for offensive action. De Witt, who had been confirmed as grand pensionary of Holland on 23 July, was now effectively the director of policy. Committed to offensive action he was reluctant to see the fleet used primarily to convoy merchant vessels, the policy that Amsterdam mercantile interests favoured. But at this time De Witt had to compromise. A plan was worked out for the fleet to convoy outward-bound vessels past the Dover Straits, then return either to trap and destroy English ships found in the Downs, or to enter the Thames estuary, attack ships found there, and sink blockships in the main channels. Success in such a complicated operation by a demoralized and run-down fleet, in the face of a thrice-victorious enemy, was highly unlikely. Full details of the plans were immediately communicated to London by an English agent.[46]

The fleet was to be commanded by a new and totally inexperienced lieutenant admiral, Wassenaar van Obdam, a soldier. His appointment can be seen as partly inspired by the successful English employment of the generals-at-sea, especially Monck, but the main reason for it was political. Obdam had the reputation of being a stern disciplinarian but his political stance constituted his main qualification. He was something of a rarity, a republican aristocrat and soldier, whose appointment blocked the demands for William

---

45 *FDW*, vol. vi, pp. 1–3, 32–7, 64–5, 68–9, 72–3, 80–2, 85–9, 100–3, 202–3.

46 *FDW*, vol. vi, pp. 39, 58, 61, 109–11, 118–22, 134–6; Thurloe, vol. i, pp. 513, 549, 557, 560.

(now celebrating his third birthday) to be made admiral general with a lieutenant admiral of Orangist politics (Nassau-Beverweert possibly) commanding the fleet. In the critical situation it was an essential move to stem the wave of Orangist sentiment which was producing furious denunciations of the States General, especially from city pulpits, and riots in the Hague and other Holland towns. Obdam spoke publicly against the appointment of a captain general, but this could now be dismissed as self-interest, and he did not command general respect. It was known that he was poor and needed the money as well as the dignity that his office could give him. Moreover his appointment differed in one crucial way from that of the English generals-at-sea. Obdam assumed the command formerly held by Tromp, the veteran servant of his fatherland and second as a national hero only to William the Silent: the comparison between the two men made Obdam appear puny or opportunistic. By contrast Blake, Deane and Monck had not replaced a national figure – Warwick had already lost most of his authority before his removal – and all three quickly earned acceptance from all ranks. Yet De Witt was to persist with Obdam, employing him in the war against Sweden. Despite a most indifferent performance in the Sound, and disregarding his poor health, he again appointed Obdam in 1665 to command the best fleet that the Republic had ever sent out, only to meet with disaster off Lowestoft.[47]

After expressing doubts about the planned offensive sortie Obdam was ordered to convoy vessels to and from Norway with a force of the thirty available ships. But before he could join them they were struck by a predictable disaster. The politicians had kept them out of port, rejecting and condemning what they called Witte de With's 'ridiculous' letter asking that they should enter the Texel. The ships were close inshore to what in any winds from the north would be a lee shore. Very severe gales lasting four days created havoc. Eleven ships were driven ashore as total wrecks; nearly all the survivors lost masts. The death toll rivalled that of the naval defeats of the summer; an eye-witness gave a still moving account of wives and children crowding on the sea-dyke at Amsterdam, 'on the bridge between hope and fear', looking for the safe return of their men's ships, and of the wailing of hundreds on realizing that they were lost. This débâcle heightened political tension. The militant Orangist preachers denounced those responsible, ranting that the gales and

[47] Thurloe, vol. i, pp. 456, 462, 485–6, 488, 496, 498.

drownings were divine punishment for the sin of negotiating with the English regicides, and that the war must be continued until Charles II was restored to his father's throne. Contrarywise the disaster made De Witt and the republicans realize that the war was irretrievably lost, and that an early peace was imperative.[48]

As in most seventeenth-century wars the negotiations for a peace began long before hostilities ended, and the negotiating positions of the two sides altered with fluctuations in the fortunes of war. But in 1653 they were even more affected by the political background of fundamental change in England and of constant uncertainty and volatility in the Dutch Republic. The way in which each side formulated its case and demands was largely determined by the domestic political pressures which shaped the character and determined the composition of what in both states were newly established regimes: in England the Rump, then the Nominated or Barebones Parliament and finally the Protectorate; in the Dutch Republic the True Freedom or Stadtholderless state.

The States of Holland took the first initiative in March 1653, that is before the summer defeats of the fleet, agreeing to send the Rump a secret letter: in this context secret meant secret from the other provinces. They said that they were writing to dispel the impression allegedly current in England that the Dutch wanted the war to continue, and to convey their view that any continuation would be fatal to both nations and to the protestant religion. They did not mention their most important reason for wanting negotiations to start, the fear that Zeeland in particular, and Orangists generally, would succeed in pressing for a revival of the alliance with France as the only way of defeating England. But bringing France into the war would entail a commitment to assist and restore Charles II, and a renewal of the war against Spain. All possibility of a negotiated settlement with England would be destroyed and war with Spain would destroy what remained of Dutch trade (except with the Baltic). Land warfare against the Spanish Netherlands would also create an irresistible demand for William's nomination as captain general, with count William Frederick as lieutenant general commanding the army. This would mean the end of the True Freedom. Unfortunately but perhaps inevitably the English response was to exploit the letter for propaganda advantages. It was published in London under the cleverly misleading title, *Les Très humbles Supplications des Etats de Hollande, qui supplient le Parlement d'Angleterre de leur donner la*

---

48 Ibid., vol. i, pp. 569–72, 574; FDW, vol. vi, pp. 154–6, 161–9, 175.

Paix. By depicting Holland as begging for peace, and so admitting that it faced defeat, the French were warned off allying with a losing state. Publication boosted English morale. It increased distrust between Holland and the other provinces.[49]

The letter was sent to the Rump which was dissolved by force on 20 April so that the reply came from the successor regime, a new Council acting as executive for the Nominated Parliament. It stipulated that negotiations must be on the basis of the English demands of 1652 which the Dutch had found totally unacceptable. Nevertheless the States General agreed to send four deputies to London while protesting (for domestic political consumption) that these terms were still unacceptable. Beverningk, de facto chief negotiator because he had the confidence of De Witt, arrived at the end of June so that negotiations began against the background of major Dutch defeats. As the fanatic party in the Nominated Parliament, of whom Harrison was the most prominent, knew very little about foreign affairs Beverningk initially and cynically hoped to propitiate them by stressing the common zeal of both nations for the protestant religion. But the fanatic party proved to be violently anti-Dutch, condemning them for worshipping Mammon by their pursuit of material wealth, and equated the Dutch Reformed Church with the defeated presbyterians in England and Scotland whose establishment they proposed to demolish by the abolition of tithes, universities and a learned ministry. They became increasingly frenzied in their hostility as the English fleet won victories. Beverningk went to listen to the authentic fanatic message at their Monday meeting at Blackfriars, where the sermons and prayers that he heard were intended to stir up the people against the Dutch: he commented, in dismay as well as disgust, 'Good God! what cruel and abominable and most horrid trumpets of fire, murder and flame'.[50]

Unfortunately most of the others associated with the regime also exulted in the victories and they could not afford politically to recede from the demands which the ousted Rump had made. They would not transfer negotiations to a neutral location; the presence of Dutch deputies in London symbolized the advantage that the English fleet had achieved. They continued to insist on some form of union between the two republics, a form of 'coalition' must be accepted.

---

[49] Wicquefort, *Histoire*, vol. ii, pp. 205–6, 208–9, 218–19; Thurloe, vol. i, p. 299; Israel, *Dutch Republic*, pp. 719–20.

[50] Wicquefort, *Histoire*, vol. ii, p. 237; A. Woolrych, *Commonwealth to Protectorate* (Oxford, 1982), pp. 284–7; Thurloe, vol. i, pp. 442, 519.

Consequently De Witt, confirmed in his position of pensionary in July, came to despair of a negotiated peace, and knew that a continuation of hostilities would inevitably provoke an alteration of government, with the restoration of the House of Orange and the destruction of the True Freedom, and that this in turn would make the English government merciless in its hostility. Paradoxically it was this prospect of an alteration that alarmed Cromwell also, operating as the main factor in deciding him to make a compromise peace in March 1654.[51]

The English negotiators had the advantage of knowing almost as soon as the Dutch deputies in London the essential details of secret discussions in the States General and of its resolutions. They became fully aware of the very serious domestic crisis in the Dutch Republic, the frenzy of rumours and recriminations, the spread of disaffection and disorders almost comparable to those of 1672, but which the government was just able to contain. The information which reached Cromwell and the council showed that the Regents were facing an acute threat at home from their domestic enemies, and that the survival of their regime depended entirely on the loyalty of the Holland militia, its readiness to obey orders to keep the people bridled, and that this could be expected to continue only so long as they were paid. Only Utrecht supported Holland in opposing Zeeland's nomination of William as captain general. De Witt discovered that the Orangists were urging Charles II to come to the Hague to offer his 'assistance'; royalists claimed that if the Dutch declared for him many English ships would defect, as they had done in 1648, and that Scotland would rise in rebellion. De Witt blocked this gambit by getting the States of Holland to pass a resolution that no foreign potentate should enter the country, meaning Charles, and immediately notified the deputies in London so as to reassure the English Council. Although the other provinces did not follow Holland's move the effectiveness of this unilateral action made an impression on Cromwell, and was to provide the basis for the peace settlement.[52]

Cromwell, who was becoming increasingly exasperated by the behaviour and demands of the fanatic party in the Nominated Parliament, had no wish for a breakdown of the negotiations with the Dutch. He used his usual techniques on them, alternating between

---

51 Woolrych, *Commonwealth to Protectorate*, p. 280; Thurloe, vol. i, pp. 255, 411, 429, 448–50.

52 Wicquefort, *Histoire*, vol. ii, pp. 204, 214, 218–19, 228; Thurloe, vol. i, pp. 369, 375, 381, 389, 456.

optimism and depression about their likely success. He raised their expectations by saying that he knew the States General had never wanted the war, which Tromp as an Orangist had allegedly precipitated, and that expedients could be worked out 'in a form of project' to bind the two republics to guarantee each other's security. It would then become possible to resume examination of the proposals which the Dutch had advanced in 1652; this seemed to indicate that insistence on a form of union was being dropped. But Cromwell then abruptly changed his tone saying that he and the council could not find security in a treaty with the States General because of the danger that the inveterate enemies of the Commonwealth would repudiate it when they gained sufficient strength.[53]

Although the English negotiators made a concession on a union, that it should not be an incorporating union but a confederation similar to that formed by the Union of Utrecht, in which the component units retained their sovereignty, all elements of Dutch opinion persisted in seeing any form of union as reducing them to slavery, a condition in which they would no longer be masters of their own lives and interests. Their fears and suspicions were increased by the way in which, after military conquest, Scotland and Ireland were subjugated by being included in a nominal union in which only tiny minorities had any political rights. De Witt could see no solution other than a change of heart by the English Council, but this seemed a remote possibility: throughout the negotiations the deputies realized that they were dealing with resolute men of action – soldiers and administrators who had grown accustomed to making difficult decisions and imposing their policies by sheer will-power, and were genuinely convinced that their unbroken run of victories showed that God was with them.[54]

The first indication that Cromwell's heart and attitudes were changing came in a two-hour meeting with Beverningk in August, in St James's Park. Although he was arguing that the English concern for security meant that the demand for some form of coalition could not be abandoned, he incidentally made the admission that freedom of trade and navigation constituted the supreme interest for the Dutch state and people, their *salus populi*, and this this could best be safeguarded by a coalition with England. Although other remarks

---

53 Woolrych, *Commonwealth to Protectorate*, pp. 283–4; Thurloe, vol. i, pp. 370, 372–3, 395, 417.

54 Thurloe, vol. i, pp. 322–3, 382, 410, 429, 448, 457–8, 517, 535, 600–1; Wicquefort, *Histoire*, vol. ii, pp. 231–5.

indicated that Cromwell believed that the imbalance of trade must be rectified, the implication of this statement must be that he did not share the aggressive mercantilist ambitions of the City interests who had possessed so much influence in the Rump.[55] Second, when Cromwell spoke of the Dutch state he meant the Republic as represented by the States General. In mercantile and industrial terms this was inaccurate: 90 per cent of Dutch trade, and most of its industry, was concentrated in the single province of Holland, and it was the States of Holland which had repeatedly attempted to make a settlement with the Long Parliament and the Rump, to prevent war and to stop the Orangists forcing an alliance with the exiled Stuarts. On this last subject a clear convergence began slowly to emerge between the interests of the Commonwealth and those of Holland. Advice to initiate separate negotiations with Holland came to Thurloe as early as 9/19 September, and the advantages of this option were strengthened by the continuing impasse over a formal coalition, and the dangerous moves being proposed by other provincial States.[56] Zeeland had much less to lose if the war continued than Holland; in wartime its merchants converted their vessels into privateers, and these were reinforced by royalist privateers with (incongruously) the exiled bishop of Londonderry being permitted to set up a Stuart admiralty court. Zeeland was pressing for arms and money to be sent to the Highlanders who had just risen in rebellion.[57] The Orangist case was most fully stated by the States of Gelderland, a poor landward province: the Holland Regents were blamed for all the disasters of the war. All negotiations should be terminated as they were bound to be a trap; all those in the English government were dissemblers and hypocrites whose promises could never be relied on. Everyone must recognize that the war was as ideological as the Eighty Years War against Spain had been; it was being waged against the pernicious maxims of government which the Commonwealth embodied. Therefore the Stuart cause must be publicly embraced – a formula for a fight to the bitter end.[58]

A section of English opinion was equally irrational and intransigent in its belligerence. For the fanatic party in the Nominated Parliament a total war against the Dutch formed part of their apocalyptic vision. It was their preoccupation with material wealth that made

55 Thurloe, vol. i, pp. 438–9.
56 Ibid., vol. i, pp. 461–2.
57 Ibid., vol. i, pp. 463–4.
58 Ibid., vol. i, pp. 469, 485, 509.

the Dutch enemies of God and His purposes, and therefore of the godly in England. Holland was Babylon: its corrupting wealth must be destroyed but it must not be appropriated, as aggressive mercantile interests in the City and the Rump had urged, for fear of the infection of worldliness becoming stronger in England. Then after reducing the Dutch to total submission the next step would be to assault the more obvious strongholds of evil, France and Spain. This was a formula for perpetual war for righteousness sake, a forerunner of Trotskyite and Maoist theories of permanent revolution. In contrast Cromwell's pragmatism led him to reject the appeals from Condé, the frondeurs and the city of Bordeaux to intervene in the French civil wars, disregarding the inducement offered of exclusive trading privileges.[59]

By early November the Dutch negotiators were encouraged by signs of pragmatism in their discussions with Cromwell, particularly that what he now called a 'near union' between the republics need mean no more than a close alliance, with no question of fusion. Even before the Nominated Parliament dissolved itself on 12/22 December, and he became Protector under the new constitution of the Instrument of Government, they realized that he was the key figure on the English side, and consequently attempted to use men who were close to him as intermediaries, particularly Hugh Peters, the noted preacher who made no secret of his disapproval of the war, and lieutenant colonel Doleman, a veteran officer in the Dutch service.[60] Negotiations, which were concentrated on the issue of the Commonwealth's security, proceeded on two levels. A 'temperament' was agreed in the official negotiations, a clause requiring all office-holders in the Dutch Republic to take an oath to accept the peace treaty, which included a clause prohibiting either government from assisting rebels against the other. Such an oblique provision, which did not mention the House of Orange, fell far short of providing the minimum security against help for a Stuart restoration that Cromwell required, but it was the most that Zeeland, Friesland, Groningen, Overijssel and Gelderland would accept so that ratification by the States General could be obtained.[61]

The terms of the formal treaty were extremely lenient, although the Dutch were disappointed that their extraordinarily presumptuous proposal that the Navigation Act should be repealed received short

59 Ibid., vol. i, p. 621; *FDW*, vol. v, pp. 51, 77.

60 Thurloe, vol. i, pp. 260, 330–1, 394, 484, 576, 600; vol. ii, pp. 5, 9; Wicquefort, *Histoire*, vol. ii, pp. 204, 238–9; *FDW*, vol. ii, pp. 265–6.

61 P. Geyl, *Orange and Stuart* (1969), pp. 115–16.

shrift. Dutch warships would have to salute the English flag, but there was no formal recognition of English sovereignty over the narrow seas. No payment was to be exacted for fishing in them. The Dutch had to pay reparations for the Amboyna 'massacre' of EIC servants, and they chose to pay the compensation which the English owners received for the king of Denmark's detention of vessels trading with the Baltic in 1652.[62]

The treaty, which was agreed in March and ratified in April, made no mention of William and the House of Orange, but De Witt and Beverningk (alone on the Dutch side) knew that it would be a dead letter unless a private understanding with Cromwell was implemented. Beverningk had agreed that the States of Holland would explicitly exclude William and his descendants by name from holding any office to which an appointment required the province's consent: not only its Stadtholderate but also the captain and admiral general's positions would therefore be barred to him. At meetings of the States, with the deputies sworn to secrecy, De Witt had to overcome strenuous opposition, but he made these representatives of towns entirely dependent on trade realize that its resumption required passage of the Act of Exclusion. When the existence of this Act became known generally De Witt had to resist furious but ultimately fruitless protests from the other provinces that the Union of Utrecht, the constitution, prohibited any single province concluding agreements with other countries. De Witt deployed a brutally frank and unanswerable argument: if Holland repealed the Act this would mean a resumption of hostilities by the Commonwealth; although they were technically separate from each other the peace treaty would be invalidated by a rescinding of the Act. The lodging of the Act with Cromwell in June 1654 removed the danger of an Orangist restoration providing the Stuarts with the only fleet in Europe that could cover a full-scale invasion of the British Isles.[63]

If Cromwell achieved his aim of greater security for the Commonwealth regime, were any other objectives achieved? From a Dutch perspective the most important outcome of the war was that the peace treaty did not impose any formal or legal restrictions on their trade and freedom of navigation. For English merchants the only real gain came indirectly with the termination during the war of the

62 Thurloe, vol. i, p. 616; vol. ii, pp. 20, 28–9, 47–8, 51–2; *CSP Venetian 1651–52*, pp. 197, 202–3, 209.

63 Thurloe, vol. ii, pp. 7, 55, 58; Wicquefort, *Histoire*, vol. ii, pp. 239, 290–6, 301–6; Israel, *Dutch Republic*, pp. 722–6; Rowen, *De Witt*, pp. 215–16.

1645 treaty between the Dutch and Denmark which gave the former effective control of the Sound tolls and preferential rates; this would have virtually excluded English competition in the Baltic. Otherwise Cromwell accepted the continuation of a *status quo* that must continue to work to the advantage of the Dutch. His leniency was bitterly criticized by mercantile interests, and particularly by Slingsby Bethel in his influential pamphlet, *The World's Mistake in Oliver Cromwell*. Bethel attacked Cromwell for failing to exploit the domination of the seas achieved by the end of 1653 to ruin Dutch trade and wreck their entrepôt economy which, he contended, would have brought England untold (but undefined) advantages. In material terms the war inflicted considerable, but only in one respect lasting, damage on the Dutch mercantile system. They had to replace the approximately 1,200 vessels of all kinds taken or sunk by English privateers and the fleet. Captured *fluyts* enabled English shipowners to carry freight at more competitive rates, but many of these prizes were lost in Cromwell's disastrous Spanish War of 1655–60. Perhaps the most important result of the war was the final collapse of the WIC's Brazilian venture. The war against England prevented the despatch of reinforcements and supplies to the last garrisons holding forts and cities on the north-eastern coast, and this loss was compounded by an unwise continuation of war against Portugal which enabled the English to gain and expand a valuable share of the trade of both Portugal and Brazil.[64]

In more general terms the war made all Dutch politicians realize that the geographic situation of the Dutch Republic would always make their mercantile economy vulnerable to English seapower. As de la Court warned, in the study *Het Interest van Holland* to which De Witt contributed and subscribed, everything possible must be done to avoid war against the ruthlessly acquisitive English, and the danger of aggression was very considerably increased by the restoration of the Stuarts and a corrupt and predatory royal Court. De Witt acted accordingly. In 1660 the States General gave a lavish entertainment and large sums of money as presents to Charles and (ironically, considering that he was to be the champion of anti-Dutch aggression over the next fourteen years) to James as they travelled back to England. The ambassadors sent later in 1660 distributed bribes to ministers who were known to be eager to recoup their fortunes after poverty-stricken years of exile. Fortunately for the Dutch, since

---

64 Thurloe, vol. i, p. 371; C.R. Boxer, *The Dutch in Brazil* (Hamden, CT, 1973), pp. 235–41.

money achieved absolutely nothing, the other line of policy was to build a new navy of great ships with armaments comparable to those of English ships and to develop a professional naval officer corps.[65]

Fortunate because the restored monarchy quickly began to renew pressure. A new and strengthened Navigation Act was followed by an Act prohibiting Dutch vessels fishing in coastal waters, which their ambassadors tried, but failed, to persuade the Lords to reject and Charles to veto. De Witt, seeing that if Cromwell had been able to disregard pressure from anti-Dutch mercantile interests Charles could not, resolved not to employ policies of appeasement. And in England mercantile and naval interests, combined under James's leadership with aggressive interests of junior ministers and courtiers, assumed that a new war would without doubt end quickly and victoriously, and be followed by a punitive peace treaty.

---

[65] Wicquefort, *Histoire*, vol. ii, pp. 630–2, 656; DLC, p. 241.

7 THE SECOND WAR, 1665–67

According to Sir William Coventry the second war was caused by 'strange accidental things concurring from several parts and parties without any interest to help each other', but his convoluted contention is at best half true. Certainly the WIC and the Royal Adventurers, the rival trading companies competing for the now immensely lucrative slave trade from west Africa, engaged in local hostilities without seeing, or caring, that these might escalate into a formal war between the two states. Sir George Downing, who is usually loaded with the main responsibility for the war, made major miscalculations about the effects of the policy which he had originally formulated on his own initiative. He applied relentless pressure on the Dutch to make concessions, assuming that they would be so afraid of a new war that they would give way to his demands in order to avoid one. In the event his bullying tactics had the contrary effect: they convinced De Witt that if he made major concessions he would be regarded as an appeaser convinced of his state's weakness, and that this would only provoke further English demands. Instead De Witt calculated that a resolute stand, backed as it was by a greatly strengthened navy, would deter the English administration from aggression. It did not have the effect that De Witt expected, because it was not the administration of Clarendon and Charles II that was intent on pressing anti-Dutch policies but an aggressive combination of courtiers, junior politicians, naval officers and City merchants which was associated with, and led by, James, duke of York. He and his followers were able to initiate and prosecute these policies because of the peculiar characteristics of the king's administration in the first years after the Restoration. Clarendon's conscious rejection of the role of acting as a prime minister weakened his ability to insist on a single and consistent line of policy, as the king's attempt to introduce a form of religious toleration in 1662–63 demonstrated. After this failed Charles did not sponsor new policics, or ones that differed fundamentally from those approved by the Council, but he either encouraged or condoned the efforts of junior ministers and courtiers to launch new and independent lines of policy without reference to the Council, but with James's approval. Charles, then, did not originate or explicitly authorize anti-Dutch policies, but he made no effort to check their development.[1]

James and his associates shared Downing's fallacious assumption that the Dutch knew that they could not resist English pressure, but they drew a more belligerent conclusion. They concluded that there was nothing to fear from a new war because a repetition of the smashing victories of 1653 would ensure a triumphant outcome after a single campaign. Imbued with crude mercantilist notions that this use of violence could be exploited through a dictated peace treaty to annex much of the trade and wealth of the Dutch, they had every confidence that victory would lead to significant increases in the power and prestige of the monarchy and the wealth of the nation. Of course they also had personal reasons for welcoming a new war. It would bring active employment at sea, promotions, prize money, glory, reputation, contracts, the ruin of commercial competitors. However, this very general and simplistic confidence took insufficient account of the practical problems that would have to be overcome, and especially the logistical dimension of which naval administrators like Coventry and Pepys were well aware.

Although crude, this working version of mercantilism which was operated by James and his associates rested on their personal experience. Many of them had remained loyal to Charles I or went over to him during the fleet counter-revolution of 1648, and subsequently served in Rupert's wide-ranging expeditions; some sailed in Spanish privateers after 1655. In doing so they acquired a privateering mentality, and not surprisingly an appetite for prizes persisted after 1660, and even had an influence on the way in which operations were planned or conducted; there was always a danger that some captains would go 'a-cruising', that is go off in search of prizes.[2] Second, many of the most intractable causes of conflict with the Dutch were concerned with trade and navigation in distant seas and regions outside Europe – west Africa, the Caribbean, the Indian Ocean and the Indonesian archipelago. These were all areas where the

---

1 Cited, R. Ollard, *Man of War: Sir Robert Holmes and the Restoration Navy* (1969), p. 85.

2 A.W. Tedder, *The Navy of the Restoration* (Cambridge, 1916), pp. 110–11; Edward Hyde, *The Life of Edward, Earl of Clarendon, being a Continuation of the History of the Great Rebellion* (Oxford, 1827), vol. iii, pp. 469–70, BL, Egerton MSS, 2538 f. 103.

establishment of trade had been effected through the use of physical force against indigenous populations, non-European traders, local rulers, and European competitors. In particular the VOC built up a predominant position in the Indian Ocean and East Asia by a combination of commercial expertise and the ruthless use of force: English propaganda made great use of the 'massacre' of Amboyna, the atrocious judicial murder of English traders who were threatening to prevent the VOC establishing a monopoly in the spice trade with the Moluccas. These violent tactics validated Downing's charge that while the Dutch needed, and claimed, freedom of trade, *mare liberum*, in Europe they brutally enforced closed seas, *mare clausum*, in Indonesia and Ceylon. As a result the economic and military-naval strength of the VOC there was too strong to be effectively challenged: French and English expeditions sent against the VOC in India in the 1670s ended in abject failure. On the other hand all Dutch colonial trade was intensely vulnerable when homeward-bound vessels entered the Channel and North Sea: as Downing saw, only threats of action in the narrow seas could compel the States General and the VOC to make concessions in Asia, Africa and the Caribbean. Distant direct action was confined to the seizure in 1664 of the weakly defended and not very highly valued WIC possession of New Amsterdam.[3]

During the 1660s, while trade in Europe was depressed, a boom in sugar exports from the West Indies and in the connected slave trade from west Africa intensified competition between the WIC and its English competitors. In these remote regions no forms of order existed and success depended largely on the use of coercion and force. To survive and trade on the west African coast, in what closely resembled a Hobbesian state of nature, required constant recourse to methods of violence, and the directors of rival trading companies employed the crudest practices against their competitors and the indigenous population. It was no accident that the process of escalation that provoked the second war started in west Africa. The Company of Adventurers and the WIC knew that their profitability, and indeed survival, depended on the force they could deploy there, backed up by the support they could mobilize at home: the company found it in James and his associates, the WIC in the States of Zeeland, and possibly in the States General. In turn these supporters drew conclusions from what was happening in west Africa. For the English a new war against the Dutch represented an extension to the

---

3 T.H. Lister, *The Life and Administration of Edward, first Earl of Clarendon* (1838), vol. iii, pp. 256–8, 263–4, 411, 518–21; Pepys, vol. iv, p. 105n.

North Sea and Channel of the methods of violence that had proved successful in African waters, although this success proved to be only temporary. By destroying Dutch power at its source, striking at their trade and shipping in home waters, and wrecking their entrepôt trade, all their colonial trade and power would rapidly wither. On the Dutch side English aggression in Africa fortified De Witt's determination to avoid giving any impression of being ready to indulge in policies of appeasement. By failing to respond to attacks in Africa, and by offering concessions in response to Downing's relentless pressure at the Hague, he would merely encourage further attacks and demands. De Witt saw the ultimate objective of English policies as the reduction of the Dutch Republic to a political and mercantile state of dependency, which in the Dutch view had been the aim of the Rump in its 1651 offer of a union. This was confirmed by English emphasis on the right of the Crown to sovereignty over the British seas. This implied the exaction from the Dutch (and all others) of a form of tribute for leave to transit these seas and to fish in them. For James the assertion of this right was also a matter of ideology. He knew from his time in exile that all major European monarchies had far greater powers of authority than the kings of England, and were not restricted by the need to seek the consent of representative assemblies for legislation and taxation. But the right of sovereignty over the seas was a unique characteristic of the English Crown, and it was inherent: it had not been conferred on the Crown as had, for example, the Spanish and Portuguese pretensions to sovereignty in the New World. Sovereignty over the seas legitimized direct action against ships which refused to salute the English flag, and justified the coercive pressure which the fleet was to take in the last months of 1664, intercepting and seizing Dutch merchant vessels well before war was declared.[4]

Two of the assumptions which underpinned De Witt's rejection of any form of appeasement proved to be damagingly wrong. First, he believed that the Commons would never have sufficient trust in the king to vote him the large amounts of money that an all-out war would require, for fear that it would be diverted to make the Crown financially independent, and able to dispense with Parliament. This calculation was upset by the extreme skill with which James's lieutenants Bennet and Clifford managed the Commons. In the spring session of 1664 Clifford, a Devonshire country gentleman of

4 K.G. Davies, *The Royal African Company* (1960), pp. 41–3, 327, 347; T.W. Fulton, *The Sovereignty of the Sea* (1911), pp. 378, 419–21, 432–3, 465–6; Wicquefort, *Histoire*, vol. iii, p. 184.

modest means but limitless ambitions, adroitly managed a Commons committee appointed to investigate the state of trade. As chairman he invited the chartered companies and groups of merchants to submit evidence and then meet the committee to answer questions and expound their cases. By doing so he committed them to the recommendations which the committee made, and the Commons and Lords accepted, emphasizing that the Dutch were the principal obstacle to the improvement of trade, with the obvious corollary that action must be taken against them. This declaration of commercial hostility stemmed entirely from a Court initiative: mercantile interests responded favourably because they knew that they were expected to do so. Clifford himself was not a major investor or a front man for City interests, and his own ultimate objectives were political rather than economic: he planned to use the expected growth of the wealth of the nation to increase the power and authority of the Crown. Clifford also displayed considerable managerial skill in November when the Commons was persuaded to back up the committee report by voting £2.5 million for a war, so shattering De Witt's illusions.[5]

Second, De Witt was also wrong in assuming that the Dutch navy was now sufficiently strong to deter an English war of aggression. He had tried to rectify the weaknesses that had led to defeat in 1653, when even the largest Dutch ships had been greatly outgunned by the English great ships and the lack of a professional corps of sea officers had resulted in indiscipline. By 1663 the Dutch had a much more formidable navy, although their biggest ships were still less heavily armed than the English. They had vastly experienced and capable flag-officers, although the lieutenant admiral, Obdam, was a political appointment. But neither the existence of an improved fleet nor the Dutch 1662 treaty with France acted as deterrents; the latter was devalued in English eyes by Louis's offer to mediate between England and the Dutch.[6]

The first moves that led to war were made by the Company of Royal Adventurers, which received charters in 1660 and 1663 to trade with Guinea: the latter specified the slave trade as an explicit

---

5 P. Seaward, *The Cavalier Parliament and the Reconstruction of the Old Regime* (Cambridge, 1989), pp. 120–4; and 'The House of Commons Committee of Trade and the Origins of the Second Anglo-Dutch War', *Historical Journal* (1987), xxx pp. 437–52; Colenbrander, vol. i, pp. 127–8; Pepys, vol. v, pp. 105, 107–9, 127, 131; BL, Additional MSS 32094, ff. 24–7.

6 Lister, *Life of Clarendon*, vol. iii, pp. 423–4, 443; Colenbrander, vol. i, pp. 129, 131, 141, 143–4; J.R. Bruijn, *The Dutch Navy of the Seventeenth and Eighteenth Centuries* (Columbia, SC, 1993), pp. 73–4, 78.

objective. It was a hybrid body in composition, although it is an exaggeration to describe it as an aristocratic treasure hunt. Like the WIC it was a highly speculative venture. A nucleus of merchants specializing in African trade was joined by merchants whose main interests were elsewhere but who, like a number of courtiers and politicians, were attracted by the prospect of quick profits especially from the export of slaves. The expansion of this trade had the effect of increasing the violence and brutality of the Company's competition with the WIC, generating more proxy wars between the tribes allied to each company. Trading forts were attacked, but neither possessed the local resources to eliminate its competitor from the coast. But these could not resist forces sent out in some strength from Europe. With its expectations heightened by its new charter the Royal Adventurers sent out a strong expedition at the end of 1663, ostensibly to assert its rights, but in reality to drive the WIC from the entire coast. Court connections ensured official support. The Council authorized the despatch of a warship as escort and James gave the commander, Sir Robert Holmes, his instructions, which the latter was characteristically to exceed. Technically James did so as an officer of the company, not as lord high admiral, but he knew that his action would commit the king. He followed this by preparing another, separate, blow against the WIC, the despatch of the small force that sailed in May 1664 to seize its colony of New Netherland, including New Amsterdam, renamed New York.[7]

Holmes swept the coast taking all the main WIC posts except Elmina. At Aga his African auxiliaries massacred the Dutch who surrendered, and then decapitated them for trophies, an atrocity improved by Dutch propaganda into tales of cannibalism. De Witt had to respond with force in order to avoid giving the impression of resorting to appeasement. James anticipated this. Expecting that a Dutch task force would be sent from its home bases he had a squadron fitted out to challenge it as the ships passed down the Channel. He intended to demand that they acknowledge Charles's sovereignty over the seas by saluting: if they refused he would open fire and so precipitate war – as had happened in 1652. De Witt avoided the trap. He sent secret instructions to De Ruyter, who was commanding a squadron in the Mediterranean to carry out a reprisal raid in west Africa, which he did with great success, taking all the English posts

7 Ollard, *Man of War*, pp. 83–119, 128–9; Lister, *Life of Clarendon*, vol. iii, p. 439; H.H. Rowen, *John de Witt: Grand Pensionary of Holland* (Princeton, NJ, 1978), p. 463; Pepys, vol. v, pp. 287, 301.

except Cape Coast castle, and many vessels. This humiliation led Charles to order another round of reprisals. The States General had ordered Dutch vessels to keep out of English ports, but now English ships began systematically to seize all Dutch vessels encountered in the Channel and its western approaches. On instructions from Whitehall, Allin attacked the returning Dutch convoy from Smyrna as it passed Cadiz, but failed to take many prizes.[8]

This process of escalation was entirely the work of James and his associates, who committed the other members of the king's administration, and the African merchants, who paid a heavy commercial price for Holmes's adventure. The Court, not the City, brought about the war. In the Commons the mercantile interest possessed little individual or collective influence. Pepys estimated that between twenty and thirty merchants were MPs, and there were a few more with a mercantile background. Furthermore none of them were men of outstanding ability and reputation, and it was noticeable that those connected with the EIC were not prominent in calling for action against the Dutch: the most vocal were not leading magnates or even very substantial traders in their own right. For example it would be accurate to describe Sir Richard Ford, who arranged the publication in 1664 of Thomas Mun's mercantilist tract (written decades earlier), as a man whose personal difficulties made him willing to act as James's and Clifford's instrument. Ford cited personal experience in describing the depression in the Levant trade, which he explained as entirely the result of Dutch competition. He also complained about Dutch lawcourts denying justice to English claimants, of whom he was one. Ford owed his seat at Southampton to a recommendatory letter in 1661 from James and was deputy governor of the Royal Adventurers in 1664.[9]

James's responsibility for the war has been masked by the often repeated view that the prime author was Sir George Downing, envoy at the Hague in 1661–62 and 1663–65. Certainly the constant pressure which Downing exerted on the Dutch had the unintended effect of stiffening De Witt's resistance to English demands and convincing him that appeasement would not leave vital Dutch interests intact,

---

8 Rowen, *De Witt*, p. 140; J.K. Oudendijk, *Johan de Witt en de Zeemacht* (Amsterdam, 1944), p. 94; Lister, *Life of Clarendon*, vol. iii, pp. 417, 420–1, 422–4, 432–3; *CSPD 1664–66*, pp. 88, 96; R.C. Anderson, *The Journals of Sir Thomas Allin* (1939), vol. i, pp. 191–3; Colenbrander, vol. i, pp. 148, 157.

9 B.D. Henning, *The House of Commons, 1660–1690* (1983), vol. ii, pp. 344–6; Lister, *Life of Clarendon*, vol. iii, p. 398; *Cal.Cl.SP* vol. v, pp. 457–8; Thomas Mun, *England's Treasure by Forraign Trade* (1664).

but Downing consistently believed that this was a bluff and that eventually the Dutch would give way and that a war would not be necessary.[10] There could not be a sharper contrast than that between Downing and the celebrated Sir William Temple, whose periods at the Hague alternated with Downing's: Temple was there in 1668–70, was succeeded briefly by Downing in 1671–72 and then returned in 1674–79. Downing was entirely concerned with matters of trade, subordinating ordinary diplomatic matters to his campaign to improve the English share of world trade at the expense of the Dutch. For example acting on his own initiative he tried in 1661–62 to sabotage the negotiations for an end to the war between Portugal and the Dutch, in order to prevent the latter being given trading privileges equal to those enjoyed by the English. He threatened that Charles would break off the negotiations for a Portuguese marriage and withdraw support, ignoring the probability that this, and continuing hostilities with the Dutch, would lead to a Spanish reconquest of Portugal. Temple, by contrast, was almost entirely indifferent to trade matters; he was absorbed by high diplomacy, negotiating the Triple Alliance to check France, which converted the Dutch from being enemies in 1667 into the allies of 1668.[11]

Of course the differences between Downing and Temple were not just of personalities and diplomatic methods: they reflect the frequent and at times very sudden changes in the relationship between England and the Dutch Republic. Dependent on one's beliefs and interests it was possible to regard the Dutch as natural allies at one time, but enemies at another. The main concerns and interests that made the relationship closer than with any other country pulled in opposite directions: ordinary people still saw the Dutch as fellow protestants who had shared in the repulse of the Counter-Reformation. But it was equally plausible to say that first under the cover of English protection, and then during the civil wars, the Dutch had taken their opportunity to advance their trade at the expense of England. In trade they were antagonists, how then could they be reliable allies? Their religious toleration and the asylum they gave to political refugees evoked different responses. Only persons whose lives and actions were entirely determined by a dominant and consistently applied

10 Lister, *Life of Clarendon*, vol. iii, pp. 147, 181–2, 217, 250, 298–9, 306–7; N. Japikse (ed.), *De Verwikkelingen tussen de Republiek en Engeland* (The Hague, 1900), p. xxii, *CSP Venetian 1664–66*, p. 88.

11 Lister, *Life of Clarendon*, vol. iii, pp. 139–42, 147, 150–1; K.H.D. Haley, *An English Diplomat in the Low Countries: Sir William Temple and John de Witt* (Oxford, 1986), pp. 171, 216–17, 226–7, 247.

set of principles could adopt an attitude towards the Dutch which was not ambiguous. For Temple a balance of power and English independence could not be preserved in the face of increasingly dominant French power unless an alliance could be secured with the Dutch Republic. For James and his associates the Dutch must be defeated so that the Crown could be freed from its unnatural dependence upon its subjects. For Downing, simply, the Dutch were the obstacle to the expansion of trade, the only way in which an early and appreciable increase in the wealth of the nation could be secured.[12]

The starting point for Downing was his basic belief, that in the existing state of competition between Dutch and English mercantile interests, the former were bound to have a decisive advantage, so that it would be difficult for the latter even to hold on to their existing share of trade. Unlike the political mercantilists whose ambition was to increase royal (and ministerial) powers, Downing identified himself entirely with policies to increase the wealth of the nation. He knew that in the longer term England must adopt certain Dutch practices: lower interest rates could come only with a new system of banking (which he hoped in 1667 would follow his Treasury reforms), profits must be reinvested, a large entrepôt trade encouraged, commercial law reformed. But such major changes would take time, and many would encounter resistance. His ideas were understood and shared by relatively few people – that strange genius Sir William Petty was one – and in terms of domestic politics Downing was an isolated figure. But the short-term strategy on which he embarked, without being ordered to do so, was understood and approved by James and his associates, courtiers and politicians who made and influenced policy decisions. Downing's basic line was that a comprehensive trade treaty must not be concluded because it would only confirm and perpetuate the existing advantages which the Dutch possessed in both Europe and Asia. The 1662 treaty was not comprehensive and left many cases in dispute to be resolved: Downing systematically used these to bring unrelenting pressure to bear on the Dutch government, backed by threats of force if satisfaction was not given.[13]

---

12 Haley, *An English Diplomat*, pp. 274–5; J.T. Rutt, *The Parliamentary Diary of Thomas Burton* (1828), vol. iii, p. 461–2; Colenbrander, vol. i, pp. 157, 229–31; Lister, *Life of Clarendon*, vol. iii, p. 147; *CSP Venetian 1671–72*, p. 145.

13 Lister, *Life of Clarendon*, vol. iii, pp. 147, 287, 399, 411; C.H. Hull, *The Economic Writings of Sir William Petty* (New York, 1963), vol. i, pp. 254–65; Marquis of Lansdowne, *The Petty Papers* (1927), vol. ii, pp. 185–6.

Downing's strategy involved him in a massive burden of work, none of which he was prepared to delegate. He personally mastered all the detail of complex commercial cases in order to present them, often to De Witt himself or to deputies of the States General or directors of the VOC. A quirk in the way that Dutch politics worked made him the central figure in every aspect of Anglo-Dutch relations. Zeeland had the conventional right to nominate the ambassador in London, but often it was difficult to find persons willing and with the abilities to serve. In 1662–63 there was no Dutch ambassador in England; Charles affected to treat this as an affront, ordering his ministers not to transact business with the chargé. Consequently all negotiations had to be handled at the Hague by Downing; this situation persisted in 1664 when the ambassador who did arrive proved to be incapable. It meant that Downing had a remarkably free hand even before Charles in October 1663 gave formal approval to his line of applying pressure on the Dutch. This followed a piece of high-handedness which completely validated Downing's arguments that without pressure no redress was to be expected. By the 1662 treaty, Pulo Run in the Moluccas, where the EIC had maintained a trading post, should have been returned, but the local VOC authorities refused to hand over possession to a costly expedition sent all the way from England.[14]

After October 1663 Downing intensified his pressure on the Dutch because he knew that he could expect full support in making all questions of trade a matter of state. He took every advantage of the weaknesses in the Dutch constitution, concentrating on widening divisions and inflaming jealousies between towns in Holland, and between Holland and the other provinces. Although he respected De Witt personally, Downing exploited resentment against the influence which he possessed, calumniating him as a would-be dictator. Similarly he tried to increase the existing hostility to the monopoly privileges of the VOC and WIC. He argued that unless the States General made a genuine attempt to compel them to abandon their aggressive methods in Indonesia and Africa, and to rectify just English complaints, these companies would drag the Republic into a disastrous war. By April 1664 Downing reported that his pressure was beginning to become effective, that it had reduced De Witt to a readiness to offer reasonable terms. However, although he personally believed that this now meant that war could be avoided, he was well

14 Rowen, *De Witt*, pp. 459–60; Wicquefort, *Histoire*, vol. iii, pp. 131–2, 134; Lister, *Life of Clarendon*, vol. iii, pp. 256–8.

aware of the belligerence of James and his interest group of courtiers and naval officers, and of their success in committing Parliament to action against the Dutch as the obstacle to the improvement of trade. He therefore left open the question whether an advantageous settlement which still fell short of giving entire satisfaction was preferable to a 'just war', and he must have suspected by then that James would regard a Dutch denial of the king's rights – meaning sovereignty of the seas – as constituting the reason for a just war. Once local hostilities in west Africa started the process of escalation, Downing aligned himself with the warmongers at Court: he advised his masters to begin stopping all Dutch vessels at sea, as Cromwell had done. His mention of Cromwell (actually it had been the Rump, as Downing knew) was deliberate, intended to provoke Charles into action; he could not afford to be less vigorous in protecting vital English interests. And when De Witt protested against these seizures Downing fobbed him off with promises, which he knew were bogus, that the vessels would soon be released.[15]

James and his admirals were confident that the war could be won by an early set-piece battle, the only question being how to force the Dutch to give battle in open sea and preferably well away from their own shoals and harbours. The assumption that the latter would remain on the defensive, aware of a presumed inferiority in armament and remembering their defeats in 1652–53, proved to be entirely incorrect. The Dutch were equally confident with a fine new and much more heavily armed fleet, and De Witt now had reasons to believe that it could carry out the offensive strategy which he had advocated even in the darkest days of 1653. In the first weeks, conscious of his own inexperience, James wisely convened a number of councils of war at which his flag-officers discussed alternative strategies, all of which were intended to bring about the decisive battle. Again wisely, James excluded volunteers from these councils; many peers and courtiers were accompanying him, among them Buckingham, who demanded entry as a privy councillor. James also disregarded a foolish suggestion from Charles that the fleet should sail north to intercept a rich convoy from the Mediterranean. Not only was it unlikely that the convoy would be sighted in the vast tracts of open sea north of Scotland, but the Thames and the English east coast would also have been left exposed to the attack which De Witt

15 Lister, *Life of Clarendon*, vol. iii, pp. 292–8, 327; *Cal.Cl.SP*, vol. v, p. 396; Pepys, vol. v, p. 121; Japikse, *Verwikkelingen*, pp. xlvi–xlvii; Tedder, *Navy of the Restoration*, pp. 110–11; Rowen, *De Witt*, p. 66; *CSP Venetian 1664–66*, p. 66.

was urging his admirals to make. In addition Charles's advocacy of commerce raiding at the first opportunity, and before a major battle had been fought and won, was highly irresponsible. Captains and ships' companies needed no encouragement to go off prize-hunting in preference to preparing for a battle, and once dispersed (as they would have become) it would have taken weeks to reassemble the entire fleet.[16]

At the first council of war three alternative strategies were proposed. Sandwich argued that by closing the Dutch coast and intercepting merchant vessels the Dutch fleet would be provoked into coming out. Lawson objected that they would simply wait until the English had to return to the English coast for provisions and water; instead the fleet should be kept fully supplied and cross the North Sea as soon as scouting ships gave notice that the Dutch were trying to unite their Maas and Zeeland divisions with the main Texel force. Rupert wanted the fleet to anchor off Goree, half-way down the coast, to prevent any junction. At another council the possibility of an attack on the Texel, and the ships anchored within it, was raised but rejected. Because of shore batteries larger ships, not frigates, would have to enter first. The narrowness of the channels, and very shallow water in some sections, meant that they would have to enter in line ahead. If any ran aground or were crippled by the shore batteries all ships ahead of them would be trapped, and only a limited number could be sent in with a single tide. These risks deterred such an attack being attempted in all three wars, although a decisive success was to be achieved in 1799 when the fleet of the Batavian Republic was captured.[17]

Intelligence provided by Downing, who remained at the Hague for months after war was declared on 4/14 March, led directly to the first major action. From a member of the naval committee of the States General who was acting as his informant, Downing obtained the operational orders issued to Obdam, and these reached James in time for him to take appropriate action. James learned that, contrary to his assumption that the Dutch would remain initially on the defensive, Obdam had explicit instructions to sortie and seek battle. James immediately moved his fleet to Sole Bay, from where

16 R.C. Anderson (ed.), *The Journal of Edward Montagu, first Earl of Sandwich* (1929), p. 181; Colenbrander, vol. i, pp. 166, 176–7; E.M. Thompson, *Correspondence of the Family of Hatton* (1878), vol. i, p. 37.

17 Anderson, *Journal of Sandwich*, pp. 181–2, 194, 199–204, 205–6, 208, 222; F.R. Harris, *The Life of Edward Mountagu, First Earl of Sandwich* (1912), vol. i, pp. 285–7, 289–90.

he could sortie in almost all states of the wind, and topped up with supplies; he also relegated his converted merchant vessels to form a reserve force.[18] Obdam's instructions reflected Dutch confidence in the strength of their new navy. He had few converted merchant vessels in his main force, which consisted largely of great ships with armaments almost comparable with James's most powerful, although most of those provided by the North Quarter and Friesland admiralties were smaller and less well-armed. But the new ships which were nearing completion were mostly equal to all but four or five of the English. However, the Dutch fleet had one fatal weakness, its commander Obdam, who had been appointed in 1653 and retained since, despite an indifferent record, entirely on account of his republican politics. In 1659 mental as well as physical exhaustion had forced a premature return from the Sound; in 1665 his health was not good. He lacked the personality and reputation to inspire his officers and men, as Tromp had, and he was bereft of ideas. Most damagingly his continuation in command delayed the adoption of new fighting methods; it was only after his death that it followed the practice – adopted by the English in 1653 – of entering battle in line formation and, if possible, of maintaining it throughout an action. Obdam was also diminished by De Witt's interventions; he dictated orders in detail, even telling him which channel to use in sortieing from the Texel, and reproaching him with delays which were due to the deficiencies of the admiralties.

Obdam's failure effectively to unite what was still essentially a composite navy in which both the admiralties and flag-officers from Zeeland and Friesland were jealous and critical of those of Holland, underlines James's wisdom in discouraging during the war any policy of favouring officers with a royalist background at the expense of ex-Commonwealth men. His readiness to take advice flattered the self-esteem of his subordinates, and the exceptional courage and personal example of attention to duty which he displayed won the loyalty and admiration of all under his command, including the seamen whom the government was to abuse and betray in the most callous fashion. It was in major sea-battles that James's most positive qualities emerged most clearly.[19]

18 Oudendijk, *Johan de Witt en de Zeemacht*, pp. 96, 100n; Lister, *Life of Clarendon*, vol. iii, pp. 363, 372, 388; Anderson, *Journal of Sandwich*, pp. 182–8, 221; *CSP Venetian 1664–66*, p. 52.

19 Wicquefort, *Histoire*, vol. ii, pp. 514–15; Rowen, *De Witt*, p. 574; Pepys, vol. iii, pp. 121–3; vol. v, pp. 160–3; Colenbrander, vol. i, p. 160; Anderson, *Journal of Sandwich*, p. 173.

The battle of Lowestoft began at first light, 3/13 June, in good weather that allowed the heaviest guns to be used, and generally under optimum conditions for James to exploit success both tactically and strategically. He had seventeen hours of daylight, and if the Dutch could be thrown into disorder they had over seventy miles to sail before they could reach the safety of their shoals and havens. There were still at least four months of campaigning weather left. But during the morning the improved armament of the Dutch great ships enabled them to hold their own in a medium-distance gunnery duel, and their tactic of concentrating fire against flagships proved effective. Lawson's division became disorganized after he was wounded. James survived unwounded when his captain and most of his staff and accompanying volunteers were killed, but his command of the fleet was unaffected. After noon the superior English gunnery began to inflict heavy damage. At 1500 hours Obdam's flagship blew up with all hands, disorganizing and demoralizing the fleet. No flag-officer was in a position to take over command, consequently many captains simply fled, although Tromp the younger was able to organize a creditable rearguard action with some ships. In the confusion ships became entangled with each other and, with other cripples, were destroyed by fireships. Lowestoft was the heaviest Dutch defeat in all three wars: at least seventeen ships were sunk, burnt or taken, over 6,000 men were killed and captured. The English lost one ship.[20]

The Dutch fleet subsequently escaped annihilation only as the result of a bizarre incident which was to be uncovered in the post-war post-mortem into the failures of the war. James ordered a general chase. The fleet took up station to follow his flagship during the brief night. But Henry Brounker, a disreputable friend (and alleged pimp) of James, had been demoralized by the death of many of his fellow volunteers and had no desire for another day's battle. He appeared on deck during the night with what he claimed was a verbal order from James to slacken sail. The captain did so, without verifying the order, and the fleet complied with the flagship's evolution. James had intended to get between the fugitive Dutch ships – many of which were slowed by battle damage to masts, sails and rigging – and their coast. Tantalizingly he just failed to overhaul Tromp's rearguard, and many Dutch ships which had despairingly run themselves aground remained out of reach at low tide. The furthest out from the shore

20 Anderson, *Journal of Sandwich*, pp. 223–4, 227–8; *Journals of Allin*, vol i, p. 234; Colenbrander, vol. i, pp. 188–9, 192–204; *CSPVenetian 1664–66*, pp. 144–7, 150, 152.

was boarded by the resolute De Witt, who had hurried from the Hague, and stayed on the ship until the tide took her into the Texel.[21]

By putting himself in danger De Witt began the process of restoring Dutch morale. He insisted on courts martial of officers who were identified as the first to desert the fleet. He made Tromp commander of the fleet until De Ruyter returned, but acting as a deputy from the States General, with colleagues selected because they were nonentities, he assumed direction of the war personally, and effectively made all the most important decisions, remaining at the Texel. Thanks to his pre-vision new great ships were becoming available to replace losses; many of these had been of converted merchant vessels. An embargo was rigidly enforced on outward merchant sailings so as to provide seamen for the fleet. Propaganda pamphlets and officially inspired material in newssheets encouraged the public to look forward to the return of De Ruyter with his ships and the prizes he had taken off west Africa and in his raids in the Caribbean and along the north American coasts. One commentator observed that the Dutch people were waiting for him with the same high expectations as the Jews waiting for the Messiah.[22]

The Dutch recovery was aided by the failure of the English commanders to follow up their victory. In 1653 Monck established a close blockade after defeating Tromp, but now James took the fleet back to the Suffolk coast, and then went off with Rupert and most of the volunteers to Court. The volunteers had suffered heavy casualties and James had had a narrow escape, consequently Charles judged that his brother's life and status as heir presumptive made him too valuable to risk in another battle; James was not to command at sea again until 1672. The change over and a lack of any sense of urgency delayed the sailing of the fleet under its new admiral, the earl of Sandwich. Nevertheless Lowestoft made a deep impression throughout Europe. For the second time in less than a decade England suddenly emerged as the power that all states with maritime interests had cause to fear: indeed courtiers and naval officers began to talk arrogantly of asserting maximum English claims; neutral ships were

21 Colenbrander, vol. i, pp. 203, 207–8, 212; A. Grey, *Debates of the House of Commons* (1769), vol. i, pp. 139–41, 144; Pepys, vol. vi, p. 159; vol. vii, pp. 286, 406, 447, 489–92; Anderson, *Journal of Sandwich*, p. 294; *Commons Journals*, vol. ix, pp. 86, 96.

22 Rowen, *De Witt*, pp. 579–80; Wicquefort, *Histoire*, vol. iii, p. 388; Oudendijk, *Johan de Witt en de Zeemacht*, pp. 98–9, 120; *CSP Venetian 1664–66*, pp. 109, 175; Colenbrander, vol. i, pp. 270–1.

seized. Later Clarendon regretted this triumphalism and specifically 'the very foolish discourses of many of getting dominion of the whole seas'. James was culpable in this respect, telling d'Humières, an old friend accompanying the French embassy, that if the French fleet came into the Atlantic (and not just the Channel) he would oblige it to salute English ships and their flag. D'Humières replied that English ships in the Mediterranean would similarly have to salute the French flag, only to get an uncompromising rejoinder, 'I mean to exact what is due to me, and I promise not to pay elsewhere what I am not bound to pay'. The Spanish government was reported to be 'chilled with fear' now that the seas were 'reduced to servitude by the overweening power' of the English navy, fearing that their American possessions would be the next target for English aggression – as in 1655.[23]

However, the only major operation attempted during the rest of 1665, the attack on a concentration of Dutch vessels sheltering in Bergen, including extremely valuable VOC return vessels, miscarried in August. Downing was reporting from the Hague that their capture would shatter Dutch morale, and damage mercantile interests so seriously, that De Witt's position would be undermined. For officers and seamen it would bring abundant prize money. In addition, since the attack was prearranged with the king of Denmark, who was to share the spoils, he would probably be committed to going to war against the Dutch: Charles promised him naval assistance and was negotiating for a Swedish undertaking not to attack Denmark. The consequences for the Dutch would be catastrophic. War against Denmark would mean that the Baltic would be closed to their vessels and trade. Convoys and vessels returning from the west by the north-about route would no longer be able to wait in Norwegian ports and fiords. The king of Denmark would take the opportunity to repudiate his massive debts, affecting Dutch and particularly Amsterdam financiers. Lastly, the Dutch fleet carried large numbers of Norwegian seamen: few of them had obeyed a 1664 decree to leave the Dutch service, but might do so if war was declared, for fear of being treated as traitors.[24]

The Bergen attack was the outcome of a grandiose diplomatic

---

23 *CSP Venetian 1664–66*, pp. 153, 159, 165; Anderson, *Journals of Allin*, vol. i, p. 236; *Clarendon, Continuation*, vol. iii, pp. 440–2; Lister, *Life of Clarendon*, vol. iii, pp. 376, 424.

24 Colenbrander, vol. i, pp. 249–50, 254–60; *Cal.Cl.SP* vol. v, p. 440; Harris, *Life of Sandwich*, vol. i, pp. 322–30.

project to enlist Denmark and Sweden in an anti-Dutch alliance. Negotiations began in 1664 as part of the preparations for a war, but the envoys despatched for the purpose – and it was a disadvantage that there had been no diplomatic representation since 1660 – were poorly briefed and inadequately informed of developments elsewhere. Concern for likely French reactions ultimately prevented Sweden accepting an alliance. The Danes negotiated with both the English and the Dutch, fending off the latter's demands that they honour their obligations to give assistance under the 1653 treaty. Their defeat at Lowestoft brought the Danes down on the English side. Frederick III yielded to the temptation to go ahead with the project for a joint seizure of Dutch vessels sheltering in Norwegian harbours: Wicquefort his regular correspondent from the Hague commented that his decision showed that 'probity is a bourgeois virtue which kings and princes do not cherish or recognise'. The potential booty was immense, and likely to increase as all homeward-bound merchant vessels received instructions not to attempt the last leg of their voyage through the southern North Sea. VOC vessels were due shortly, and De Ruyter was also expected to put into Bergen on his return from west Africa, the Caribbean and North America with his victorious but run-down force.[25]

When Sandwich sailed with the main fleet he was told that Frederick would acquiesce in his attacks, but that the details of joint action had not been finalized. His ships were not well prepared for this long-distance sortie. Provisions were short because ships had turned away victualling tenders coming from places known to be infected by plague. A serious shortage of casks for water and beer was due to coopers having died or dispersed from London. Many seamen had inadequate clothing because fear of infection had led to the stoppage of all parcels of slops from London, the trading centre for secondhand clothes which were known to be a main agent in the spread of plague. The serious limitations imposed by these shortages stemmed from the absence of any port in Scotland where supplies in quantity could be obtained, by the certainty that bad weather would be encountered, and by the poor physical condition of most seamen. They had been refused shore leave after Lowestoft, and even conjugal visits on board, for fear of plague infecting the fleet.[26]

The first phase of Sandwich's cruise illustrates the importance

---

25 Wicquefort, *Histoire*, vol. iii, p. 231; *Cal.Cl.SP* vol. v, pp. 431–2, 438–9, 440–1, 486, 488–9, 503, 535.

26 Anderson, *Journals of Allin*, vol. i, pp. 249–50; *CSPD 1665–66*, p. 41.

and the difficulties of intelligence gathering. In a preliminary sweep he found empty seas, but was spotted by Dutch scouts who escaped northwards to give the alarm. Hypothesizing from the south-westerlies that had been blowing that no significant number of Dutch ships or vessels would come south on a direct route home, and knowing that reports by the scouts of his fleet being at sea would keep the enemy in port, he decided to attack wherever he found them. As Sandwich approached Norway he sent a messenger to Copenhagen to inform Frederick of his intention, and to ask the English envoy to obtain a promise that his governors and officers would be sent orders to assist. More neutral vessels were now being met and from them an accurate picture of the location of Dutch vessels was built up. Sandwich learnt that he had missed De Ruyter, who had sailed south-east, keeping close to the Jutland coast as far as Heligoland. However, he learnt that the next most valuable target, the VOC vessels, had arrived far later than expected, and on 30 July/9 August were known to be in Bergen.[27]

In the council of war on that day the best possible plan of blockading Bergen until despatches were received from Copenhagen, with confirmation of orders to local officers to cooperate with the fleet, had to be set aside. Ships' companies were already on reduced rations. An immediate attack had to be launched; Sandwich commented, 'unless suddenly, nothing could be attempted'. A task force of thirteen medium-size ships were to enter and attack while the rest of the fleet stayed outside the skerries to cover against any approaching Dutch fleet. Teddiman in command had Clifford with him to conduct negotiations with Danish officers: it was a distinctive feature of this war that those who had responsibility for bringing it about, and might be called warmongers, took a prominent and enthusiastic part in operations, putting their lives at risk; James, Clifford and the favourite Falmouth who was killed at Lowestoft are examples. For Sandwich and Teddiman the issues were simple and straightforward, but for Frederick and his officers at Bergen they were more ambiguous and difficult. Frederick was attracted by the prospect of booty estimated by Sandwich to be equivalent to the entire existing wealth of the Danish Crown, and thanks to the Sound tolls this was not negligible. Its acquisition would materially assist him to carry out his current policy of making himself absolute. On the other hand he did not want to be dragged into war as an English protected person.

27 Anderson, *Journals of Allin*, vol. i, pp. 244, 247.

His plan was for the English to seize the VOC and other Dutch vessels, while his officers remained inactive. The half-share which he expected was for this inactivity, not for participation. Afterwards it would be for the Dutch to decide whether to go beyond protests, but they were unlikely to declare war on Denmark, and so ensure that the Baltic was closed to their trade, and invite Frederick to repudiate his debts to Dutch financiers, which would have a catastrophic effect especially in Amsterdam.[28]

Sandwich wrote to Ahlefeldt, the governor, asking for his cooperation in the imminent attack on the VOC vessels that were drawn up in a defensive line across the harbour, but he had not received any instructions from Frederick. He replied by asking for a delay, fearing that even if orders to cooperate were on their way an unsuccessful attack, or one that set fire to a largely wooden-built town, would result in his being used as a scapegoat. But Teddiman could not afford a delay, and attacked on 3/13 August. The Danish fort commanding the harbour, as well as the Dutch, opened fire. Its plunging fire caused heavy casualties on the upper decks of Teddiman's ships, forcing him to withdraw. However, negotiations were resumed with the Danes, and in the middle of these Frederick's orders belatedly arrived. These only authorized an attack by the English fleet, which Ahlefeldt was instructed to allow and observe, but after sustaining battle damage Teddiman's ships could now overcome the Dutch only with active Danish assistance. Clifford failed to persuade Ahlefeldt to provide it, and consequently the whole operation had to be called off. Sandwich's part of the fleet had already been driven off its station by gales, and depletion of its provisions forced him to return to the English coast.[29]

Many of the Dutch vessels which helped to repulse Teddiman never got home. De Witt in person sailed with the main Dutch fleet to bring back all the vessels sheltering in the Norwegian ports and fiords, but severe gales scattered the vessels and their escorts all over the North Sea. On the last leg many of them ran into Sandwich's fleet, which had been reprovisioned, although only for a short cruise, but one that proved extremely successful. On 3/13 September he captured two VOC vessels and their escorts; on 9/19th four escorts (one a 70) and eight vessels. Finally he sighted and chased a much larger section of the dispersed convoy, under Van Nes, and would have

---

28 Anderson, *Journal of Sandwich*, pp. 250–1.
29 Ibid., pp. 240–65; Colenbrander, vol. i, pp. 250–67

overwhelmed it but for very bad weather.[30] These interceptions and the very serious losses suffered by the Dutch re-emphasized the lessons of 1653, that Dutch merchant shipping had to be kept off the North Sea whenever they had reason to suspect that the English fleet was out in force. The sequel to this brief cruise also demonstrated the acquisitive, freebooting and factional character of many of the senior English sea-officers, as well as their juniors and seamen. Sandwich feared that the Bergen failure would damage his reputation in the fleet and might be used by his rivals to engineer his removal from its command. His attempts to secure his position misfired repeatedly and badly. First, he left for the Court (then at Oxford) to canvass support, but while he was away the Dutch fleet unexpectedly appeared off the Suffolk coast. It was left to Monck to try to prepare the fleet to oppose the enemy, which improved his chances of getting the command for 1666. It was claimed that he found Sandwich's ships in too poor a condition to put to sea. Second, Sandwich tried to commit his senior officers to himself, and incidentally pocket a large sum of money himself, by sharing out the cargoes of the VOC vessels before these had been judged to be lawful prize. He must have calculated that this would be a popular move since many of the commodities had already been illegally appropriated by junior officers and seamen, understandably since none of them had received the pay due to them, and few can have had any confidence that it would be forthcoming. Little would be left for the flag-officers if they did not act, especially as the prize commissioners who would have to adjudicate were corrupt and self-serving. Later Sandwich insured himself by obtaining a retrospective authorization for his action from Charles, but this did not prevent a political storm. Four of the eleven senior officers rejected the share he offered. Allin was an open enemy of Sandwich, so too was Myngs but in his case greed overcame dislike. The other three may have anticipated the furious faction-fight which followed, first at Court and then later in Parliament. Charles thought it prudent to check this by removing Sandwich from England; he went to Madrid as ambassador.[31]

The sortie of the Dutch fleet in October 1665, which damaged Sandwich's reputation, was made in strength under De Witt's personal leadership. He insisted on taking the offensive, although it was late in the year, despite the Lowestoft defeat, and although

---

30 Colenbrander, vol. i, pp. 261–5; *CSPVenetian 1664–66*, pp. 205–6.

31 Pepys, vol. vi, p. 291; Colenbrander, vol. i, pp. 266–7; Harris, *Life of Sandwich*, vol. ii, pp. 4–5, 23; *CSPD 1665–66*, p. 17.

many ships had suffered damage in the recent gales. He imposed this offensive strategy on his admirals, and he sailed with the fleet nominally as a naval deputy of the States General but effectively as fleet commander, with De Ruyter as his adviser for seamanship, like an English admiral on a ship which was navigated and helmed by a master. Many sea-officers privately derided De Witt's pretensions to command, mocked his appearance in an ornate uniform singularly inappropriate for autumn gales in the North Sea, but perhaps envied his ingenious seabed, designed by Christian Huygens to give relief from sea-sickness. De Witt earlier humiliated his officers by going out in a rowboat to demonstrate, by sounding, that the fleet could safely use an alternative channel, the Spaanjaards gat, which they declared to be impractical. De Witt acted in the belief that his senior officers needed to be inspired and energized, that risks had to be taken, and that by failing to take the offensive whenever the opportunity presented itself the navy would relapse into the passive, defensive mode of 1653, when the fleet went to sea in the autumn only to escort merchant convoys. De Witt knew that this time there was no Cromwell, with reasons of state, to allow the war to end in a lenient peace settlement. Like Gambetta in 1870–71, De Witt knew that the survival of his country (and certainly of its republican regime) depended on himself, rather than on his officers, and that only by leading from the front could it be secured. In retrospect it is difficult to see how the Dutch Republic could have survived without him. However, it is to be suspected that command in a sea-battle would have been beyond him.[32]

De Witt had clear plans how to exploit victory in the battle which it was his objective to bring about by sortieing. The fleet would enter the Thames estuary and sink blockships in its main channels – a doubtful project in hydrographic reality. This kind of attack represented an *idée fixe* of De Witt's: he had advocated such action in 1653, and it had been included in Obdam's instructions before Lowestoft; in a variant form it was to be executed with triumphant success in the Medway attack of 1667. However, De Witt was frustrated in October 1665, ironically by the run-down state of the English fleet. Few of its ships had emerged from royal dockyards with their defects rectified. Most were undermanned and short of provisions. Consequently the English remained in their ports and anchorages. De Witt most reluctantly allowed his fleet to return to

---

32 Oudendijk, *Johan de Witt en de Zeemacht*, pp. 120, 133; Colenbrander, vol. i, pp. 286–7, 297; Rowen, *De Witt*, p. 581.

its bases with nothing to show for its weeks at sea in miserably bad weather. The contrast between the empty seas which De Witt found, and the numerous captures made by Sandwich during his much briefer cruise, provides a clear impression of the relative vulnerability of the two states and their trade. On the other hand the inability of the English government and admiralty to maintain the fleet in a condition to fight, admittedly against a background of plague, appeared as the first symptom of the weaknesses which were to produce the fatal decision not to set out a fleet in 1667.[33]

The configuration of the 1666 campaign was largely determined by the movements of a phantom fleet which never went into action during the war – the French. Louis XIV reluctantly went to war with England in January, belatedly fulfilling his obligations under the Franco-Dutch treaty of 1662, after failing by protracted negotiations to persuade Charles to abate his demands. After Lowestoft the danger of a Dutch collapse, the displacement of De Witt and the installation of William and the Orangists in office and power, which could result in the Dutch Republic becoming an English protectorate, threatened to throw up an obstacle to the realization of French ambitions. So too did English attempts to find European allies to use against the Dutch. Louis dissuaded the Swedes from concluding an alliance with Charles. But in return for promised subsidies, which Charles found himself unable to pay fully or in time, von Galen the bellicose bishop of Münster agreed in June 1665 to attack the Dutch with an army of 30,000 men; his invasion of Overijssel in September met with easy initial success against the neglected Dutch army. Arlington, the English secretary of state, planned to expand the alliance to include other German princes (notably Brandenburg), Denmark, Sweden and even the Emperor and Spain. This was moonshine, but any extension would hamper French moves to take advantage of the situation created by the momentous death on 7/17 September of Philip IV, which made the question of the inheritance to the possessions of Spain the central European issue for the next fifty years. Louis could not tolerate instability in western Germany. Consequently he sent French troops to aid the Dutch. They quickly ejected the Münster army from Dutch territory and forced the bishop to sue for peace (April 1666).[34]

33 Wicquefort, *Histoire*, vol. iii, pp. 208–9; Rowen, *De Witt*, p. 581; Pepys, vol. vi, pp. 256–60.

34 Lister, *Life of Clarendon*, vol. iii, pp. 399, 401; Mignet, vol. i, pp. 415; N. Japikse, 'Louis XIV et la Guerre Anglo-Hollandaise', *Revue Historique* (1908) 98, pp. 44–5.

By declaring war on England Louis calculated that in return De Witt and his Regent supporters would acquiesce in his plan to seize and annex important portions of the Spanish Netherlands. The Regent party attitude to France had been based on the necessity of maintaining a buffer state; France should be a friend but not a neighbour if the integrity and security of the Dutch Republic was to be secured. This obviously constituted a vital interest, but so was the continuation of trade on which the prosperity and indeed survival of Holland and Zeeland depended absolutely. The English threat to trade would continue after the war ended. Philip IV's death put De Witt in an impossibly difficult situation: both the central and permanent interests of the Republic were equally and acutely endangered; trade by the enemy, England; security by his ally, France. From this dilemma followed his later and abrupt switch of policy; in 1668 an alliance with England to check and limit French encroachments into the Spanish Netherlands.[35]

Louis was reluctant to enter the war for fear of putting his new navy at serious risk. The war caught the French navy at an early and vulnerable stage of development. In terms of materiel a formidable fleet of large, heavily armed ships was being constructed, whereas in 1660 the fleet had hardly existed. But this very rapid development meant that admirals, captains, officers and seamen lacked experience of the kind of war they now faced against the dominant navy of the age. Royal prestige and therefore royal support for continuing a programme of naval expansion would be wrecked by a heavy defeat. Louis instructed Beaufort, his commanding admiral, that conservation of his fleet must invariably be the prime consideration. But the attempt to link up with the Dutch must carry very considerable risks. The French fleet was not strong enough to meet a substantial English fleet on its own, and once it sailed past the Cotentin there was no port in which it could shelter if the Dutch were late in arriving at a rendez-vous, or the English were sighted. In addition to this injunction of extreme caution Louis added a stream of instructions to Beaufort, mostly sent from various places in the Ile de France, where the king would not even know in which direction the wind was blowing in the Channel.[36]

Most unusually Louis's decision to declare war on England met with open dissent within the French Court. His sister-in-law, Mad-

---

35 Mignet, vol. i, pp. 267–75; Haley, *An English Diplomat*, pp. 49–50, 155.

36 G. Symcox, *The Crisis of French Sea Power* (The Hague, 1974), pp. 12–71; Colenbrander, vol. i, pp. 298–301, 306–8.

ame, Charles I's daughter, did nothing to conceal her disapproval. Even more unusually her husband approved of her attitude, and a number of courtiers – but of course no ministers – expressed their disapproval of a war to protect a bourgeois republic against a fellow monarch. Louis did not suppress this naive sentiment, but turned it to his advantage. By tolerating its expression, and authorizing Madame to continue her correspondence with her brother Charles, he signalled his reluctance to go to war, and set up the main channel of communication that was to be used after 1667 in reconciling the two kings, and in initiating the secret negotiations that were to end in the Dover treaty, the reversal of alliances and the third war of 1672.[37]

Louis drew an important conclusion from the failure of his attempts in 1665 to mediate between the combatants. Charles rejected the compromise he proposed, claiming that he was committed by the belligerent attitude of Parliament and the money which it had voted: he could not afford to disappoint the expectations which he had then tacitly undertaken to fulfil. Therefore his freedom of action was restricted. Part of this was pretence, but Louis genuinely pitied Charles's position as a king whose powers and authority fell far short of being sovereign. The conclusion that he drew was that English foreign policy, being dependent in practice (if not in constitutional theory and law) on Parliament, a body that for Louis represented the *canaille*, could not be relied on for any consistency or constancy. This made it necessary for Louis, when planning the war of 1672, to concede large subsidies (larger than those paid to any other of his allies) to make Charles independent of Parliament.[38]

Louis did not want, but could not avoid, war against England. In contrast English opinion, MPs and naval officers particularly, acclaimed a war against France with uncritical enthusiasm, ignoring the practical difficulties involved in extending an already expensive war, of which ministers and naval administrators were well aware. An undeclared, unofficial war, resembling that of 1649–52, was already under way. Trade between the Biscay provinces of France and the Dutch Republic could not be continued in Dutch vessels: as a substitute French vessels (or Dutch vessels temporarily transferred to nominal French ownership) were used to carry commodities to and from Dunkirk. There they were transferred to Dutch vessels for the

37 *CSPVenetian 1666–68*, pp. 27, 239.

38 *CSPVenetian 1664–66*, p. 239; J.J. Jusserand, *Recueil des instructions données aux ambassadeurs et ministres de France*, vol. xxiv, Angleterre i (1929), pp. 386–7.

short voyage behind the shoals to Vlissingen. Acting on the principles of a continuous voyage and of an ultimate enemy destination English privateers seized French ships as lawful prizes. Colbert sent a legal expert to join the French embassy in London to argue against this doctrine, but he failed to secure restitution. Louis ordered reprisals. Much more valuable English ships were seized in the Mediterranean, on the pretence that they might be aiding the Barbary corsairs. English mercantile interests had also been antagonized by Colbert's imposition of higher tariffs which were severely reducing exports to France.[39]

The French fleet left Toulon at the end of April; the prospect of its arrival in the Channel created problems for both the English and the Dutch. It could be used to land a French army in Ireland (as was to happen in 1689). A group of Irish catholic landowners and dispossessed landowners had already approached Louis for aid, and Ormonde the lord lieutenant expressed his concern to Whitehall about the weakness of his defences. This option did not receive serious consideration; Beaufort's mission was to join his fleet with the Dutch, who welcomed this prospect of reinforcement, but knew that this junction would involve a complex and risky operation. Louis was not prepared to allow his fleet to enter the danger zone in the Channel until he could make a new estimate of the relative strength of the Dutch and English fleets, that is he waited until he could see the outcome of the first battles. Consequently Beaufort received orders to wait at Lisbon.[40]

Charles, James and the Council at Whitehall did not anticipate this extremely cautious French behaviour, and had no idea of the location of Beaufort's fleet, which they believed was about to enter the Channel, when in fact it had only just arrived at Lisbon. The hopelessly inaccurate information which they sent to the fleet led the council of war to decide to divide the fleet. Rupert sailed down Channel with twenty ships to intercept Beaufort. With the rest of the fleet Monck moved to an anchorage in the Swin, where he covered the Thames estuary, and from which he could retire if the Dutch appeared in overpowering strength. Monck was not the man to think of retreat in the face of an enemy whom he tended to underestimate, but he recognized his own vulnerability to enemies at Court who wanted officers who had served the Commonwealth

39 *CSP Venetian 1664–66*, pp. 90, 131, 137, 155, 167, 187, 233, 239, 266, 285; *CSPD 1665–66*, pp. 56–7.
40 Mignet, vol. ii, p. 508n.

removed from naval commands. This led him to write to Coventry to ask whether he should accept battle with the Dutch before he received reinforcements, and Rupert returned with his detachment. Coventry referred the letter to James, he to the king, and he to the Council, who bounced the question back to Monck, instructing him to use his discretion.[41]

On 31 May/10 June Monck sighted the Dutch fleet at anchor some way off the Flanders coast. He had the wind so he could attack them, but they could not attack him. He called a council of war at which several captains advised him not to attack a greatly superior force. Monck contemptuously disregarded what he termed their cowardice and attacked on 1/11 June. This began a prolonged battle, the Four Days Fight, in which the fleets battered each other in the most horrific and bloody of all battles during the three wars. Rupert rejoined only on the last day, by which time Monck's ships were too spent to alter the outcome. Although the surviving English admirals claimed a victory, their losses were heavier than in any other action, four ships destroyed and six captured, while a further thirty needed major repairs. Two admirals were killed, one captured. Angry recriminations followed when privately it was realized that a serious reverse had been suffered. Monck castigated the conduct of a majority of his captains; only twenty had given him full support. He was criticized for underestimating the Dutch fleet. Coventry and Arlington came under metaphorical fire for allegedly delaying the despatch of orders to Rupert to sail to Monck's assistance. Rupert was accused of a failure of leadership on the last day. And in the post-war investigation the ministers had to evade unanswerable questions about their acceptance and transmission of totally inaccurate intelligence about Beaufort's movements.[42]

De Witt also made a mistaken estimate of English losses in the Four Days Fight, and their likely effects. He greatly overestimated the damage done to the surviving ships, and the time that it would take to repair them, believing that the royal dockyards were almost destitute of materials. He expected the defeat to provoke popular disaffection; it does not seem that he had any reliable and organized contacts with English republicans, so that his exaggerated expectations were

41 Colenbrander, vol. i, pp. 370, 595–7, 600–3; *Commons Journals*, vol. ix, pp. 11, 12, 49, 52; J.R. Powell and E.K. Timings (eds), *The Rupert and Monck Letter Book, 1666* (1969), pp. 185–94, 201 *passim*.

42 Colenbrander, vol. i, pp. 332–43, 344–9, 370–2; Anderson, *Journals of Allin*, vol. ii, pp. xix–xxi; Pepys, vol. vii, pp. 148–9, 158, 177–80, 194.

probably put into his mind by political exiles in Holland. Their consequence was that he rushed the Dutch fleet to sea to exploit what proved to be imaginary opportunities. It sailed on 24 June/4 July accompanied by an unusually large number of fireships, hopefully intended for use against the English cripples that he thought would be found waiting to go up to Chatham. There were also *fluyts* carrying soldiers who were to land if an English republican, Samuel Raven, detected a readiness to rebel in the areas around the Thames estuary. The sortie proved inconclusive, finding neither cripples nor potential rebels. All it achieved was another demonstration of De Witt's offensive spirit which lifted morale in the fleet. Indeed it generated overconfidence.[43]

The English dockyards had sufficient resources to undertake a quick and efficient refit of damaged ships, so that the fleet sailed on 19/29 July in full strength to seek battle, which came six days later. Monck and Rupert as joint commanders kept their ships in line formation during the first crucial phase of the engagement, whereas the Dutch divisions in a looser crescent formation became separated from each other. This enabled the English to concentrate greatly superior strength against the single division commanded by Evertsen, which suffered severely before De Ruyter came to its aid. These two divisions were driven back in what threatened to become a rout; only by taking refuge behind the shoals off the Zeeland coast was a disaster comparable to Lowestoft prevented. Only two Dutch ships were lost but personnel casualties were heavy. Meanwhile an entirely separate action was fought between Tromp's division and a squadron commanded by Smith and Spragge, in which the latter were severely handled before Tromp made an orderly retirement.[44]

This defeat dissipated false Dutch euphoria. In his report De Ruyter rather too candidly admitted that a more audacious English pursuit could have annihilated the fleet, and Monck and Rupert paraded their victory by sailing close inshore along the coast of Holland. All outward-bound sailings were halted. Political recriminations erupted. Ships from Zeeland and Friesland had suffered the heaviest casualties; the provincial deputies blamed these on faulty leadership by De Ruyter. Rotterdam championed its native

---

43 Colenbrander, vol. i, p. 368; *Cal.Cl.SP* vol. v, p. 444; Oudendijk, *Johan de Witt en de Zeemacht*, pp. 157–8; J.R. Tanner (ed.), *Samuel Pepys's Naval Minutes* (1926), pp. 46–7.

44 Colenbrander, vol. i, pp. 413–21, 428–31, 438–40, 472–3, 479–80, 482; Powell and Timings, *Rupert and Monck Letter Book*, pp. 104–5, 112–13; Pepys, vol. vii, pp. 209, 215–16; Anderson, *Journals of Allin*, vol. ii, p. xxx.

son Tromp in a bitter dispute with De Ruyter; the latter's defenders responded by smearing Tromp as an Orangist out to make trouble, and even of having connections with the traitor Buat. At another level seamen belonging to ships from different provincial admiralties fought in the streets of Vlissingen.[45]

This defeat put out of reach the good, secure peace which De Witt had promised that a victory would bring. He hurried to the fleet to restore order and raise morale. Going by sea to the Wielings in a small boat he narrowly escaped capture when it was chased by the *Little Mary*, a sixth rate. But he had to face another very serious reverse. Characteristically after the battle all ranks in the English fleet thought the time had now come to 'go a-cruising', hunting for prizes as personal rewards. Some captains 'lost' the fleet by going off on their own, and to prevent further dispersal of strength the admirals prepared a freebooting attack on the Frisian islands of Terschelling and Vlieland. Landing parties were to loot their small towns, seize sheep and cattle, and capture vessels in which to ship off the booty. On a nastier note the better sort of inhabitants were to be kidnapped for ransom. But when Holmes, commanding the light ships and fireships, approached Terschelling he sighted an enormous mass of vessels anchored close to the sea-gate. They had disregarded warnings to retire to a safer anchorage and were so closely packed together that they could not now move to avoid the fireships which were sent in. Almost all went up in flames, together with many valuable cargoes. This loss of some 170 ships at one time in 'Holmes's bonfire', with an estimated value of £1 million, produced deep depression in Amsterdam, where an angry crowd demonstrated outside the admiralty building. In addition the landing parties looted and burnt the small town of Westerschelling.[46]

The last phase of the 1666 campaign centred entirely on the unsuccessful attempt of the French and Dutch to unite their fleets, and of the English to intercept either. This general lack of success was due to defective intelligence and poor scouting work; at each stage of the complicated manoeuvres none of the French, Dutch and English admirals, and still less Louis XIV, knew where the enemy forces were

45 Colenbrander, vol. i, pp. 440–1, 446–9, 470, 472–4, 479–80; Rowen, *De Witt*, pp. 589–90; Oudendijk, *Johan de Witt en de Zeemacht*, p. 163; Pepys, vol. vii, pp. 339–40.

46 Colenbrander, vol. i, pp. 463–5, 474; Powell and Timings, *Rupert and Monck Letter Book*, pp. 118, 121, 122–7; Pepys, vol. vii, pp. 339–40; Ollard, *Man of War*, pp. 148–58.

located. Beaufort was in constant receipt of unrealistic and obsolete instructions from his king: if he had obeyed Louis, as his army generals had to, the result would have been disastrous. Unaware that the French fleet had not yet sailed from the Biscay coast, the Dutch fleet was waiting for them in the Dover Straits on 1/11 September when the English fleet came in sight. Bad weather prevented any engagement. They resumed their vigil off Boulogne, waiting there very conscious of their vulnerability until 18/28 September. They were under the handicap of having De Ruyter hurt in an accident, but prudence dictated a retirement east to the relative safety of Dunkirk roads. Rupert also waited in vain for the French. He kept his ships too far north, on the English coast, and the scouting line which he set up to the west was dispersed by storms. Beaufort got as far as Dieppe roads, where he learnt that the Dutch had retired still further east: he therefore decided to return west to Brest, abandoning the scheme of joining with the Dutch. Fortunately for him and his fleet he had not, when taking this decision, received a letter from Louis instructing him to carry on eastwards to Calais. The cruise ended ingloriously. One ship, the *Rubis*, sailed into the English fleet, mistaking it for Beaufort's, and two forlorn ships turned up in Vlissingen. There could not be a better example of 'the fog of war' than this set of operations. Beaufort's abortive attempt to unite with the Dutch disenchanted Louis. The risks of total disaster had been so narrowly avoided, and Louis had found it so difficult to direct Beaufort in the same way as he was accustomed to direct his army generals, that he had to realize that if the navy was an instrument of policy it was unlikely to be an agent of his personal glory. He learnt, as Napoleon had to learn, that it was impossible to run a naval campaign to a prearranged plan or timetable.[47]

The year's campaign ended with yet another offensive Dutch sortie that achieved nothing. Again it was only De Witt's insistence that took the fleet to sea. De Ruyter was absent, sick ashore. De Witt again accompanied the fleet as deputy and was ready to command in battle when the English fleet was sighted (25 September/5 October). Once again bad weather prevented the fleets engaging. This constant emphasis on taking the offensive, and personal appearances with the fleet as the citizen commander, led De Witt's admirers to see and

47 Powell and Timings, *Rupert and Monck Letter Book*, pp. 154–5, 158–9, 162; Anderson, *Journals of Allin*, vol. ii, pp. 289–93; Oudendijk, *Johan de Witt en de Zeemacht*, pp. 167–9, 172–5; Japikse, 'Louis XIV et la Guerre Anglo-Hollandaise', pp. 51–3; *CSP Venetian 1666–68*, pp. 75, 78–9.

laud him as an antique Roman from the days of the Republic; others derided his behaviour, not because he was not a seaman but because he had never fought or handled weapons. All his exhortations and attempts to take the offensive which came to nothing created the impression of an amateur strategist, but in 1667 De Witt and his brother Cornelis were to impel the Dutch navy into its most spectacular victory.[48]

The Dutch attack on the great ships in the Medway (June 1667) is the best known incident in the Anglo-Dutch Wars. It would never have been attempted without De Witt's dedication to offensive action, and he had considered mounting such an action even before the war began: in 1664 he sent an agent, Ghijsen, to reconnoitre English coastal waters and the approaches to Chatham.[49] He could not accompany the attacking fleet in person because the prolonged and uncertain peace negotiations at Breda, where the French were behaving strangely, and the disturbing crisis caused by the French invasion of the Spanish Netherlands, required his constant attention to business at the Hague. Instead he sent his brother Cornelis, a member of the Maas admiralty, to instil an aggressive spirit into his flag-officers and captains, and to prevent dissensions inhibiting action and risk-taking. In the event it was entirely due to Cornelis's inspiring presence in the fleet that the attacks were pressed home, although his exacting brother expressed disappointment that he did not exploit the victory sufficiently.[50]

The De Witts eagerly seized the opportunity provided by the English decision not to set out their main fleet in 1667. This decision was only partly due to the expectation of an early peace; it also represented a shortage of money and resources. With a reduced requirement for seamen it was possible to lift the previous embargo on outward sailings by merchant vessels; this would increase revenues and help lift the economy from a deep depression. A major financial miscalculation also contributed to the decision. Parliament voted new supply in February, but most of the money was earmarked for clearing debt that had accumulated during the war, in order to prevent a collapse of government credit. Victuallers and contractors were refusing to provide any services except for payment in ready

---

48 Powell and Timings, *Rupert and Monck Letter Book*, pp. 162–3; Rowen, *De Witt*, pp. 591–2; *CSPVenetian 1664–66*, p. 176; Oudendijk, *Johan de Witt en de Zeemacht*, pp. 176, 178.

49 Rowen, *De Witt*, pp. 460, 575; Wicquefort, *Histoire*, vol. iii, p. 306.

50 Colenbrander, vol. i, p. 562.

money, which was simply not available. The dockyards had now run out of many essential supplies, their workers were going absent because they had not been paid. Only ready money in impossibly large amounts would have made it possible to set out a full fleet. Consequently only minimum-cost defences were to be prepared for a war that was thought to be winding down: task forces, mainly for trade protection, and the refurbishing of coastal forts.[51]

Important questions have to be asked about De Witt's decision to launch an offensive when peace negotiations were already in progress at Breda, and about the long-term effects. Of course in the seventeenth century most peace negotiations were long drawn out, and the combatants often tried during their prolongation to launch offensive operations that could strengthen their bargaining position. By not setting out a fleet Charles was certainly running a risk, but he was trying to secure himself by secret negotiations with Louis. In February Charles secretly undertook not to take any action in the next year, that is he promised to stand aside while Louis attacked the Spanish Netherlands: in return Louis said he would try to obtain favourable terms for England from the Dutch, and his ambassador put pressure on De Witt not to take offensive action. However, the scale of Dutch naval preparations should have warned Charles that an offensive was likely.[52]

De Witt's first objective was 'to wage war to make peace', to bring about an early settlement without having to make any major concessions to England. He told his brother Cornelis 'your excellency is the best plenipotentiary in this business, and De Ruyter with his brave officers'. Second, an early peace would free De Witt to organize diplomatic moves to contain French expansion. However, his whole strategy contained a serious flaw. He rightly expected a successful offensive and heavy English losses to generate great resentment which would be directed primarily against Charles and his ministers, and only secondarily against the Dutch. But De Witt did not see that by inflicting a humiliating defeat on Charles, and forcing him to accept a peace in which he made no gains, he would be driving the king into seeking a French alliance, and this at the time when efforts at checking France in the Spanish Netherlands would certainly damage Franco-Dutch relations. The Medway victory did not cause James

51 Seaward, *Cavalier Parliament and the Reconstruction of the Old Regime*, pp. 238–41, 258–66, 276–82, 289–94, 303–4; C.D. Chandaman, *The English Public Revenue, 1660–1688* (Oxford, 1975), pp. 147, 211.

52 Mignet, vol. ii, pp. 40, 43.

and his associates to abandon their aggressive mercantilist ambitions. Rather it taught them, and Charles, that their policies and ambitions could best be served by following Cromwell's example and allying with France, because it was the strongest power in Europe. In the triangular relationship between France, England and the Dutch Republic it was bound to be a question of two against one. In 1666–67 England faced the other two; it was therefore sense to initiate a secret set of negotiations to combine with France against the Dutch, although in public a pretend policy of allying with the Dutch to check France was adopted to gull both English opinion and the Dutch.[53]

During the spring of 1667 the English administration issued orders to strengthen coastal defences, but shortages of money and materials and general official inertia prevented much being done. The danger points were obvious enough – Sheerness (where a fort was to be built), the river Medway (to be blocked at need by a chain commanded by gun batteries), the Gravesend blockhouses on the Thames, and Harwich. Charles and James went down river on an inspection tour which was reported in the Dutch press: with facile optimism Charles believed that now that they knew about the fortifications the Dutch would not come. Monck reported that the chain would protect the great ships laid up in the Medway. But morale among those who knew most about the state of the defences plummeted; Coventry depressed Pepys by saying that when the question of money came up he responded by shrugging his shoulders, and that he would no longer put himself at risk by speaking the truth about the king's business.[54]

De Ruyter's fleet anchored in the Thames estuary on 7/17 June. The Dutch admirals urged caution, fearing that an English squadron might appear in their rear from Portsmouth, but Cornelis De Witt disregarded their opinion, ordering an attack up the Thames in the hope of burning merchant vessels sheltering there. Although panic broke out at Gravesend, the vessels withdrew further up the Thames and the attack achieved nothing but some looting and rustling on Canvey island. De Witt switched the attack with immediate success; on 10/20 June the capture of Sheerness and its fort revealed the low morale of the defenders when reinforcements refused to move

53 Oudendijk, *Johan de Witt en de Zeemacht*, p. 183; Rowen, *De Witt*, pp. 593–4; Grey, *Debates*, vol. ii, p. 10.
54 Pepys, vol. viii, pp. 84, 127n, 490–2, 505, 570–1; C. Robbins (ed.), *The Diary of John Milward* (Cambridge, 1938), p. 90.

forward. Yet Monck on the next day complacently reported that the chain, batteries and blockships would keep the Dutch out of the Medway. However, neither seamen nor dockyard workers stood by when the Dutch came up the river; on 12/22 June the crew of the *Unity* frigate which was guarding the chain jumped ship, allowing a Dutch fireship to break through. Surrenders followed by the crews of two other guardships and a skeleton crew on the *Royal Charles*. Fearing that the Dutch would take and tow away other great ships, orders were given to disable them by knocking holes in their hulls. These three ships were burnt by the Dutch on 13/23 June, but the *Royal Charles* was towed out of the river and sailed to Holland; part of it is still there today.[55]

The loss of four great ships, and eight others, was serious but not crippling. As at Pearl Harbor in 1941 a fatal blow could have been inflicted only by destroying the shore installations; the dockyard at Chatham, with its storehouses full of combustible material, would have blazed even more intensely than the City of London had done in September 1666. But the moral effects were grave. Nearly all the seamen had not even tried to resist, and why should they have risked anything? They had been betrayed by Charles and the admiralty in as shameful a fashion as anything in English history, discharged (not paid off) with tickets in lieu of money, promissory notes in which they could have no confidence, but which persons with influence could buy from them for next to nothing and get full payment. Dockyard workers made off with their tools and anything portable they could lay their hands on; they had not been paid for months. Panic gripped London, although the Thames defences were now strong. A run on the bankers occurred. Wild rumours spread; all faith in the nation's governors was shaken. If a credible alternative had existed the monarchy would have been in danger.[56]

Charles defused the crisis by two major decisions. Although Monck had failed lamentably to check the Dutch he was given plenary powers. Although privately officials and politicians despised him as a blockhead his reputation reassured a jittery public; as in 1659–60 Monck would again save England.[57] Moreover the Dutch

---

55 See P.G. Rogers, *The Dutch in the Medway* (1970); Colenbrander, vol. i, pp. 543–9, 565; Oudendijk, *Johan de Witt en de Zeemacht*, pp. 182–5; *Commons Journals*, vol. ix, pp. 12–13, 50.

56 Pepys, vol. viii, p. 501; Tanner, *Samuel Pepys's Naval Minutes*, p. 20; *CSPD 1665–66*, p. 96.

57 Pepys, vol. viii, p. 499.

fleet attack had not been accompanied by any preparations for a campaign of political subversion. De Witt sent Colonel Doleman, an officer in the Dutch service since the 1650s, to accompany the fleet commanding a force of 3,000 soldiers. Doleman, an Englishman who had helped as an intermediary in the peace of 1654, was an old friend of Monck's (and of Cromwell), and had made a political reconnaissance of England for De Witt in March 1660, but he was now employed in a purely military role. He commanded the unsuccessful landing force which attacked Landguard fort, the main defence of Harwich. The absence of a network of subversion, such as William was to organize and use in 1673–74 and 1687–88, was a delayed result of the failure to maintain an ambassador in London in 1661–64, and of the appointment of the inept and honest Van Goch.[58]

Second, Charles reversed the stance of his negotiators at Breda. Before the Medway attack they had been instructed to press for Dutch concessions, and afterwards he momentarily reacted by considering breaking off negotiations. But this assumed that England could continue the war, and without calling Parliament and its voting money this was impossible. De Ruyter controlled the Channel. Trade, including the vital supply of coal for London from the Tyne, was paralysed. Consequently peace had to be concluded as quickly as possible; the treaty, signed on 21/31 July, confirmed the status quo: the English retained New York and New Netherland; the recent Dutch occupation of Surinam was confirmed.[59] The wisdom of an early peace was shown when Parliament showed signs of falling out of royal control. It had been prorogued until October, but was recalled to meet on 25 July in case the peace was delayed. Tomkins, an MP who was the leading spokesman in the Commons for a faction led by Bristol, which worked closely with the Spanish ambassador, initiated what promised to be a ferocious and general attack on the ministers. Fortunately news arrived of the conclusion of a peace before this attack could be developed, and Parliament could be sent away, but the basis of Tomkins' speech, that the war had been used to cover an expansion of the army with the objective of setting up arbitrary government, was to be revived when the third Anglo-Dutch War also ended in failure.[60]

58 Colenbrander, vol. i, pp. 553–4, 565.
59 Wicquefort, *Histoire*, vol. iii, pp. 307, 315, 316n.
60 Henning, *House of Commons, 1660–1690*, vol. iii, pp. 577–9; *Cal.Cl.SP* vol. v, p. 339.

8 THE THIRD WAR, 1672–74

In analysing the causes of the third war of 1672–74 it is clear that disputes over trade served only as pretexts. The primary objective of Charles, James and the ministers which they tried – ultimately in vain – to conceal was to gain increased power for themselves, and to strengthen royal authority at the expense of the English nation by eliminating the existing dependence of the Crown on the cooperation of subjects, as represented by Parliament and the militia. In order to achieve this objective Charles was ready to acquiesce in the hegemony over western Europe which he knew was the primary objective of his ally Louis XIV. The alliance with France differentiated this war from the first and second. In the first, England had needed no allies; in the second, Münster on the English side, and France and Denmark on the Dutch, had not played a very important part. But in February 1673 Charles implied how important the French alliance was for him, telling Parliament that if he had not taken advantage of the conjuncture of 1672, 'perhaps I had not again ever met with the like advantage'. By conjuncture he pretended to mean the coincidence between the honour of the Crown and the interest of the kingdom, but in reality (and secret) it was the conjuncture between the interests and aims of the English and French Crowns that alone made the war of 1672 possible. Whereas important interest groups in England had pressed for anti-Dutch policies in 1650–52 and 1664–65 only individuals allowed their grievances against the Dutch to be exploited in 1670–72. The third war was solely the result of initiatives taken by the Court; parliamentary assistance (and thereby implicitly its approval) was not sought until the war had been in progress for ten months.[1]

While the French army achieved astonishing successes in its initial blitzkrieg invasion of the Dutch Republic, the English fleet, although reinforced by a strong French force, failed to win a single victory

1 *Lords Journals*, vol. xii, p. 524.

during the whole war. De Ruyter evolved and operated what was perhaps the most effective defensive strategy ever undertaken by a fleet of inferior strength. In contrast the Dutch offensive which helped to drive Charles out of the war was not unique: William was to repeat the campaign of propaganda, pressure and subversion, which he organized with great effect in 1673–74, with even greater skill and effect in 1687–88. And one of his main charges against James in 1688, that he had concluded a new secret treaty with Louis XIV aimed against the protestant religion and the liberties of the English nation, had great effect because of what had happened in 1670–72 when Charles and Louis concluded secret treaties to arrange in advance a war of aggression against the Dutch Republic.[2]

The war of 1672 was a deliberate and contrived war agreed in the secret treaty of Dover (22 May/1 June 1670). In the fifth clause Charles and Louis agreed 'to declare and wage war jointly with all their forces by land and sea' in order to humble the pride of the States General and 'reduce the power of a nation which . . . even has the insolence to aim now at setting itself up as sovereign arbiter and judge of all other potentates'. The date of the war, originally 1671, had to be postponed for a year, but this was as clear a premeditated act of aggression as any in history.[3]

The Dover treaty did not detail the grievances which justified a war against the Dutch; it merely said that each sovereign had many reasons. Charles had difficulty in 1672 in compiling a catalogue of reasons that could be published. The rights of English planters in Surinam, the loss of toll exemptions by the Merchant Adventurers, the dishonouring of Charles by an offensive medal, and a tapestry in the Dordrecht Stadthuis celebrating the Medway, and guided tours over the *Royal Charles*, which had been captured there, amounted to a thin list of pretexts.[4] The absence of any major grievances related to mercantile interests meant that the main publicly stated reason for the war was the royal claim to sovereignty over the seas. An extraordinary test case was arranged as part of the preparations for

---

2 J.R. Bruijn, *The Dutch Navy of the Seventeenth and Eighteenth Centuries* (Columbia, SC, 1993), pp. 89–90; K.H.D. Haley, *William of Orange and the English Opposition* (Oxford, 1953), especially pp. 133–84; J.R. Jones, *The Revolution of 1688 in England* (1972), pp. 198, 259–62; J.I. Israel, 'The Dutch Role in the Glorious Revolution', in Israel (ed.), *The Anglo-Dutch Moment* (Cambridge, 1991), pp. 119–20, 122.

3 A. Browning (ed.), *English Historical Documents*, vol. xii (1966), pp. 863–7; Mignet, vol. iii, pp. 222, 232, 239; *CSPVenetian 1671–72*, p. 167.

4 Wicquefort, *Histoire*, vol. iv, pp. 51, 230, 238.

the war. Captain Crow of the yacht *Merlin*, which was to transport Lady Temple, the wife of the ambassador at the Hague, received instructions to seek out a Dutch squadron that was known to be at sea and demand that it salute his tiny ship. If the Dutch refused he must fire on them until he had shot away their flag – not an easy target for the yacht's puny and low-lying guns. This he did, but when the Dutch admiral came on board to ask why he was firing he neither seized him nor reopened fire, and for this Crow was sent to the Tower. One suspects that it had been hoped that fire would be returned; a dead Lady Temple would have been an ideal *casus belli* (August 1671).[5]

Certainly Downing suspected that when he was sent to the Hague in December as Temple's replacement he too could be used as a sacrifice. His mission was to make difficulties. More subtly he was known as the champion of mercantile expansion, and anything but a francophile, so that the rift he was to engineer could be dressed up as an English quarrel. On 1/11 January 1672 he was ordered to present the States General with a memorial 'peremptorily demanding' recognition of the Crown's dominion over the seas in writing, and by instructing Dutch warships to strike their flag and topsails in salute. These demands were to be repeated after two weeks and if no reply came in the next week he was to withdraw, breaking off relations. However, this timetable got ahead of the domestic preparations: the Declaration of Indulgence which had to be published at the same time as the declaration of war, to distract attention and neutralize possible trouble among the dissenters, was not yet ready. Charles therefore ordered Downing not to withdraw until everything was ready, but the latter knew how the Dutch hated him, and feared for his life if he had to remain until war became imminent. When this danger was put to Charles he cynically replied that he was ready to take the risk on Downing's behalf, but Downing was not: saying that he had been recalled he scuttled back to London, and was put in the Tower, where ironically the chests containing part of the French subsidy were also lodged.[6]

The reasons that Louis published when he declared war were as

5 Ibid., vol. iv, pp. 236–8; W. Westergaard, *The First Triple Alliance* (New Haven, CT, 1947), pp. 51, 443, 448–9; E.M. Thompson, *Correspondence of the Family of Hatton* (1878), vol. i, pp. 63, 66–7.

6 *CSPVenetian 1671–72*, pp. 113–14; *CSPD 1671–72*, pp. 42–3, 123; Wicquefort, *Histoire*, vol. iv, pp. 352, 363; J. Beresford, *The Godfather of Downing Street* (1925), pp. 247–8, 249, 255, 263, 268.

perfunctory as the English – insults to himself, Dutch arrogance in presuming to put limits on French policies.[7] He did not refer to the economic war, *la petite guerre*, that Colbert had been waging against the Dutch for a decade. Some historians have concluded that the French motives in going to war were primarily economic, but in examining the reasons why Louis decided to attack his former allies, and bring them to submission, it is artificial to make a separation between diplomatic and economic matters. All issues concerned with both areas were matters of state, all were subject to direct control by royal authority. The only important difference between diplomatic and commercial policy-making was that Louis immersed himself in all diplomatic business, even the detail, and personally made every decision. In the case of commerce and industry Colbert submitted all important policy questions for the king's approval but possessed a greater measure of devolved authority in implementing decisions than other ministers. Louis did not constantly intervene in economic administration. There were limits to even his stamina for official business, and in this area he lacked the time to acquire the detailed knowledge that gave him equal expertise to the minister for the army (Louvois) and foreign affairs (Lionne, then Pomponne).[8]

Colbert's mercantilist policies did not form an auxiliary arm of French foreign policy. He was entirely concerned with developing French industry and foreign trade, and thereby improving the yield of royal revenues. Colbert was indifferent to their effects on other countries and impervious to consequential protests, whether these were from allied states or from those that politically were potential enemies. It was inevitable that his policies should have the greatest effect on the Dutch because of their primacy in international trade and shipping: the discriminatory policies that damaged their trade and shipping were introduced and intensified during the period when France and the Dutch Republic were allies. Similarly his prohibitive tariffs virtually wiped out English textile exports to France, provoking protests which he ignored during the years 1668–71 when the alliance

7 Wicquefort, *Histoire*, vol. iv, pp. 346, 373–4.

8 H.H. Rowen, *John de Witt: Grand Pensionary of Holland* (Princeton, NJ, 1978), pp. 741–2, 751–2; P. Sonnino, *Louis XIV and the Origins of the Dutch War* (Cambridge, 1988), pp. 125–6; A. Corvisier, 'Colbert et la Guerre', in R. Mousnier (ed.), *Un Nouveau Colbert* (1985), p. 287; E. Frémy, 'Les Causes économiques de la guerre de Hollande', *Revue d'Histoire Diplomatique* (1914) 18–19, pp. 523–51; S. Elzinga, *Het voorspel van der oorlog van 1672: de economisch-politische betrekkingen tussen Franrijk en Nederland* (Haarlem, 1926).

with England was being negotiated and concluded. Protests for Colbert were indications that his policies were working, that he was fulfilling his promises to Louis to increase his resources and reduce those of all his neighbours whether allies or potential enemies.[9]

Colbert's 'fighting tariff' of 1667 provoked intense and widespread resentment within Dutch commercial circles, but it preceded any consideration by Louis of isolating, weakening and then attacking the Dutch Republic. It followed a judgement by Colbert that his fiscal and inspectoral administration was now sufficiently efficient and comprehensive to enforce a drastically protective policy, and that he could contain any retaliatory actions. The difficulties and divisions that were to impede and delay such actions illustrate the difference between an absolute monarchy, where policy could simply be imposed, and a state dependent on representative institutions in which a variety of interests influenced policy decisions. French merchants later admitted to the Dutch ambassador that Colbert's tariffs had damaged them because of retaliation by foreign states that had the effect of reducing the volume of French trade, and they implied that industries and the royal revenue were not benefiting. But they could not influence Colbert to make any modification, and Louis treated retaliation to make him change policies which he had authorized as outrageously derogatory. By contrast in the Dutch Republic, where government existed to protect and promote interests, merchant groups were not united and exerted conflicting pressures. When a first step was proposed to ban imports of French lace and impose steep duties on other commodities Amsterdam demanded exemptions for textiles from Lille and Tournai, newly annexed by France, because these were mostly re-exported. But Leiden and Haarlem objected, claiming that their depressed industries could manufacture these products, only for Amsterdam to reply that these would not be of sufficient quality. More prolonged obstruction came from Rotterdam, which in effect was waging its own economic war against Amsterdam in the States of Holland. Similarly in the States General protracted obstruction from Groningen had a self-interested basis; it wanted a ban on French paper, although it did not manufacture enough to replace imports. Consequently no decision was reached in 1670, but when retaliation was agreed in 1671 the French response was immediate. Colbert did not have to consult interest groups when he imposed heavy duties on Dutch herrings and spices, and prohibited

9 Wicquefort, *Histoire*, vol. iv, pp. 151, 251; Corvisier, 'Colbert et la Guerre', p. 297; Frémy, 'Causes économiques', p. 523.

the export of brandy in Dutch vessels, most of which was re-exported to northern Europe.[10]

Colbert approved Louis's decision to attack the Dutch Republic, because he saw the Dutch as the main obstacle to development of the French economy, but his approval was not a precondition, nor is there any evidence to suggest that Louis regarded economic rivalry as a major reason for going to war against them. Rather a convergence existed between the objectives of the king and his finance minister. Louis wanted to reduce the Dutch to political dependence, depriving them of their capability to oppose French policies, and to organize alliances against them and particularly his designs on the Spanish Netherlands: Louis had revealed his priorities, when negotiating the secret Partition treaty with the Emperor in 1668, by insisting that the French share of Carlos II's inheritance must include the Spanish Netherlands. Subsequently relations with Vienna deteriorated, making it unlikely that the treaty would become operative, and French diplomats had to work to block moves to include the Emperor and German princes in the Triple Alliance. Victory over an isolated Dutch Republic would leave the Spanish Netherlands both militarily and diplomatically defenceless, so that they could be taken without any danger of a general European war resulting. Louis switched Pomponne from Stockholm, where he was detaching Sweden from the Triple Alliance, to the Hague embassy for the purpose of allaying De Witt's fears and suspicions. Pomponne's false assurances and chicanery deceived De Witt, who awoke to the seriousness of the Dutch position at a surprisingly late stage, in the second half of 1671.

De Witt clearly did not want to have to believe that he faced the worst possible development of an unprovoked (and therefore unavoidable) joint Anglo-French war of aggression, but he should have been warned by Colbert's *petite guerre* of undisguised economic discrimination against Dutch interests, all trade questions being treated in France as matters of state. For Colbert a victorious war could be used to disarm the Dutch commercially and so facilitate his planned expansion of French trade, shipping and manufactures. This confidence was based on one surprising assumption, that Dutch losses and damaged competitiveness would necessarily and exclusively benefit France; he left England and the advantages which France's ally might gain out of his calculations. He compiled a

10 Frémy, 'Causes économiques', pp. 534–5, 541–4, 547–8; Wicquefort, *Histoire*, vol. iv, pp. 151–5, 158n, 311.

list of alternative ways of exploiting victory on 8 July 1672, at a time when it seemed that the Dutch were at Louis's mercy. He contemplated the possibility of the annexation of the Republic in the king's dominions, in which case all economic activity would come under his ministerial control. However, if Louis allowed the Republic to survive, conditions should be inserted into a peace treaty that would bring advantages to France and its economy. The Dutch would have to withdraw all their retaliatory duties and prohibitions on French commodities, while Louis would be free to retain those he had imposed. All Dutch trade with the Levant could be prohibited which, with the enforced withdrawal of the Dutch ambassador at the Porte and all his consuls, would give the French a virtual monopoly (so much for the English Levant Company). Similarly Colbert raised the possibility of taking over all the Dutch West Indian colonies, and forts in west Africa, so as to take on the lucrative trade of providing slaves for the *asientistas*, the official syndicate with the monopoly of importing slaves into the Spanish possessions. Colbert's aim in the East Indies was more modest, the acquisition of Dutch factories and a half share of the VOC's trade with Europe (and presumably at least half the causes of conflict with the English EIC).[11]

The postponement of the war from 1671 to 1672 led to a dramatic and ambitious change in French military strategy, which had the effect of lessening the importance of the joint Anglo-French naval campaign. The plan for 1671 was for converging armies to besiege Maastricht; only after its fall would they invade the eastern Dutch provinces of Overijssel and Gelderland. The explanation is that Louis's attention was still concentrated on the Spanish Netherlands in 1670–71. Carlos II had been critically ill and was not expected to live. With Maastricht in French hands the adjacent Spanish territories would be at his mercy or, alternatively, the movement of French armies through these territories would provoke incidents that could justify a formal invasion. But the plan adopted in July 1671 involved switching the initial blow to an invasion of the Dutch Republic from the east, down the Rhine, thus outflanking the fortified river lines of defence that had held the Spaniards at bay, and were to halt the British and Americans in 1944. A military engineer sent to reconnoitre confirmed that the eastern defences were in no condition to resist a determined offensive. Moreover once the frontier defences were broken, the heart of the Dutch Republic – Utrecht and even Holland – would lie open to the invaders. As in 1667 with his invasion of Flanders, and 1670 when Lorraine was conquered, the French generals were confident that the war could be won, and the Dutch compelled to submit, in a single campaign.[12]

De Witt entirely failed to realize that the outcome of the war would be decided by military warfare, and that the war at sea would be of subordinate importance. He concentrated attention and resources on the fleet in order to deter Charles but neglected the run-down frontier fortresses. He persisted in ignoring warnings about Louis's aggressive intentions which came from a variety of sources – D'Estrades in 1670, the Elector of Brandenburg, the exiled duke of Lorraine, the Governor of the Spanish Netherlands and the burgomaster of Cologne – all admittedly interested parties.[13] Less excusably he took no action on the extraordinarily well-informed despatches sent by his ambassador in Paris, De Groot, which urged him to strengthen the eastern defences as a matter of urgency, and to agree arrangements to obtain additional troops from Brandenburg, Luneburg and Hesse. De Groot warned him that by neglecting the German princes De Witt was forfeiting their goodwill so that the Dutch would have to face the French totally on their own. He gave early warning that all attempts to dissuade Charles from joining with Louis were futile, and at a later stage provided a clear and accurate sketch of the French plans for the invasion, given him by somebody close to Louis.[14]

If De Witt clung to illusions most other Dutch politicians showed themselves even more short-sighted, putting their own particular interests before the safety of the Republic, and engaging in almost suicidal quarrels right up to the eve of the invasion. Overijssel and Gelderland – provinces that were to be overrun a few weeks later – held up the raising of new levies of soldiers. Friesland quibbled over naval expenditure. Amsterdam became embroiled in a bitter dispute with the town of Hoorn, which received interested support from other Holland towns.[15] Most damaging of all the causes of division, wrangling continued about granting William the captain generalship: the States of Holland held up the appointment for the first two months of 1672 at a critical time when it was becoming

---

12 Sonnino, *Louis XIV and the Origins of the Dutch War*, pp. 126–7, 137, 140, 158, 162, 167.

13 Wicquefort, *Histoire*, vol. iv, pp. 248, 250.

14 Ibid., vol. iv, pp. 341, 345–6, 352–7; H.H. Rowen, *The Ambassador Prepares for War* (The Hague, 1957), p. 170; Rowen, *De Witt*, pp. 810–11.

15 Wicquefort, *Histoire*, vol. iv, pp. 334–5, 361–2.

evident to all that the army was in a lamentable condition. Even then he received the appointment only for a single campaign, and was to be encumbered by deputies from the States General – the kind of men who were to be Marlborough's bugbears thirty years later: as civilians they had no more military experience than William. The army of which he took command was ill prepared for the French onslaught; last-hour attempts to strengthen the eastern defences – the so-called Ijssel line – achieved little. The States of Holland had so little confidence in the line that they ordered the construction of an inner line to defend their own province, and it was this secondary defence system together with inundations that eventually checked the French advance.[16]

The French invasion was the nearest thing to a blitzkrieg that seventeenth-century conditions allowed. Louis declared war on 6 April. Once the grass began to grow at the end of April the French armies advanced into the territories of Liège, ruled by the archbishop of Cologne, an ally: their assembly took a month. Moving through the territories of Cologne they fell on the outermost Dutch defences in the first days of June. The principal fortress – Wesel in Brandenburg territory – capitulated without a fight, the incompetent Dutch garrison officers being forced to do so by the civil population, who were terrified that they would receive the same treatment if the town put up resistance as places in Lorraine, where in 1670 the French had massacred civilians.[17] Other fortresses commanded by officers appointed by the States General on account of personal connections or political affiliations also surrendered after offering derisory resistance. By 8 June – a week after the offensive began – De Witt was publicly admitting that all resources must now be concentrated on preparing to defend Holland itself, and even hinting that it might be prudent to consider approaching the French to see if negotiations for peace could be initiated. The panic which this débâcle generated led to widely accepted accusations that it could be explained only by treachery. The abject collapse of the defences was bound to inflict fatal damage on those who had appointed the traitors who surrendered to the French, or deserted their posts.[18]

Far worse was to come. The parallel invasion by the bishop

16 Ibid., vol. iv, p. 361; S.B. Baxter, *William III* (1966), p. 71; Rowen, *De Witt*, pp. 804–8, 832, 836.

17 Wicquefort, *Histoire*, vol. iv, pp. 356–7, 383–4, 394–6.

18 Colenbrander, vol. ii, pp. 130, 132, 140–1; Rowen, *De Witt*, p. 831; *CSP Venetian 1671–72*, p. 262.

of Münster and the Elector of Cologne met no real resistance. Zwolle refused to allow its garrison to defend the town. Nobles holding provincial offices repudiated their loyalty to the Dutch Republic because Overijssel had not received assistance from the other provinces; acknowledging the bishop as their sovereign, he reciprocated by recognizing the provincial privileges and free exercise of the reformed religion. The key fortress of Coevorden surrendered, opening the way for the battling clerics to invade Groningen and Friesland.[19] A similar collapse occurred on the main front. In what French propaganda claimed as a great military feat, but which was facilitated by low water levels (the result of drought), and opposed only by weak militia forces, the French army crossed the Rhine (12 June), then took Arnhem (16th), Amersfoort (19th) and Utrecht (23rd). Utrecht had at first refused to admit William's troops, then made any defence impossible by blocking the demolition of the suburbs to create a free fire-zone.[20] Consequently William and his army retired into Holland, but neither the States of Holland nor the States General displayed any will to resist. On 22 June emissaries were sent to Louis to open negotiations, but he sent them back because they did not possess full powers to conclude as well as negotiate. On 27 June, despite strenuous opposition from Amsterdam and Zeeland, the States General agreed to send plenipotentiaries, who reached the French camp two days later.[21]

By comparison with this well-planned offensive, which achieved its objective of reducing the Dutch to submission in less than a month, the English plan of campaign contained nothing new. The fleet would bring the Dutch to battle. Reinforced by a powerful force of French ships there could be no doubt of the outcome. Then a blockade would be established, or sweeps made to capture Dutch merchantmen. In a word, opportunism. No provision was made for an invasion force to be landed; had one been prepared it could have taken advantage of the widespread panic throughout Holland and Zeeland in July. Agents had been sent to both provinces, but for espionage, not political subversion.[22]

As in 1665 the declaration of war was preceded by buccaneering attacks on Dutch merchant vessels hurrying home. Sir Robert Holmes,

---

19 Wicquefort, *Histoire*, vol. iv, pp. 412–14.
20 Ibid., vol. iv, pp. 412, 415–16; *CSPD 1672 (May–September)*, p. 213.
21 Wicquefort, vol. iv, pp. 422–34; Rowen, *De Witt*, pp. 850–1.
22 *CSPD 1671–72*, pp. 608–10; *1672 (May–September)*, pp. 257–8, 683, 685; *October 1672–February 1673*, pp. 630–1.

whose west African raid had started the process of escalation that led to the previous war, attacked the lightly escorted convoy from Smyrna in the Channel but mishandled the operation. Two of his ships received heavy damage and all the valuable Dutch vessels escaped. The real damage followed in bitter factional recriminations. Holmes accused two captains of cowardice; their friends alleged that he had deliberately failed to summon reinforcements who were in the offing, because their commander Spragge was senior to him and belonged to a hostile faction, and because he wanted to keep all the prize money for himself and his own ships. Such factionalism was to characterize the conduct of many officers throughout the war and act to the detriment of the navy and its reputation.[23]

The first phase of the campaign at sea was concerned with effecting the junction of the English fleet, which by treaty was to have a minimum strength of fifty great ships, and the French contingent with thirty. French naval administrators had made detailed provisions for the support of their contingent. Acting with impressive efficiency they sent shiploads of naval stores to be deposited in storehouses (which they had inspected) specifically designated for them so that there would not be any competition with the English when refitting became necessary. They obtained guarantees that if articles had to be obtained locally they should pay the same price as the English. Specified berths and anchorages were set aside for French ships. Finally, in October when the campaign ended the return of the French to Brest was to be covered by the English fleet.[24]

In the instructions issued to his admiral, the comte d'Estrées, Louis made a sincere effort to ensure and promote harmonious cooperation with his English allies during the campaigns at sea, but with the advantages of hindsight it is clear that nothing which he suggested in advance could have prevented the rancorous disputes that were to erupt. There were very few periods before 1941 in which the English navy had to fight in conjunction with an important allied fleet: the three examples during the seventeenth century – Buckingham's Spanish War of 1625–30, this Third Dutch War and the war of 1689–97 – all demonstrated the difficulties, especially

---

23 R. Ollard, *Man of War: Sir Robert Holmes and the Restoration Navy* (1969), pp. 173–6, 178–9; *Bulstrode Papers* (1897), p. 226; *CSPD 1671–2*, pp. 180, 189, 194; *1672 (May–September)*, p. 15; Thompson, *Hatton Correspondence*, vol. i, pp. 81–2, 84.

24 Colenbrander, vol. ii, pp. 76, 79–81, 87–8; Westergaard, *First Triple Alliance*, p. 497.

when (as in all three cases) operations went badly. Louis urged d'Estrées to ensure that all his officers worked harmoniously with their English counterparts. He put them on their mettle: the revived French naval service, with few achievements to its credit so far, must by its behaviour demonstrate the glory of the king's arms and the greatness of his reign. They would be fighting under the eyes of the navy that was regarded as the leading naval service, and enjoyed an esteem equal to that of the French army. Therefore they must seize the opportunity to equal or even surpass the English in bravery, steadiness and expertise.[25]

De Witt wanted the fleet to resume the offensive strategy that had brought victory in 1667, and sent his brother Cornelis to accompany it as States General deputy. Johan urged a repetition of an attack up the Thames and Medway estuaries to catch the English fleet before it could sail to join with the French, but delays on the part of the Zeeland admiralty prevented a sufficiently early sortie.[26] A second sortie caught the allied fleet provisioning and careening off the Suffolk coast. De Ruyter achieved a tactical surprise in what was a bold and risky offensive because if, as at Lowestoft in 1665, the Dutch got the worst of the action there would be ample opportunity for the allies to pursue them. He caught the allied fleet strung out in no kind of order along the coast of Sole Bay, with the French to the south. Although unfortunately for De Ruyter the light easterly wind faded, preventing an overwhelming victory since the allies used the tide and towing by rowboats to get into formation, a misunderstanding occurred between the English and French at the outset. The French failed to see, or understand, James's signal flag ordering them to concentrate on him. They moved south while the English with less searoom moved north. Consequently two separate actions were fought. The French engaged a weaker Zeeland division. De Ruyter with a slight superiority in strength was able to concentrate against the English, adopting a tactic of attacking their flagships, identifiable by their outsize ensigns and flags. James had his captain killed and had to move from the battered *Prince* to the *St Michael*. Sandwich's *Royal James* was set on fire, burnt down to the waterline and then sank: he was not among the few survivors. Later the failure of other captains to come to his aid was maliciously attributed to factional hostility by

25 Colenbrander, vol. ii, pp. 81–7, (1672), 208–12 (1673).

26 F.R. Harris, *The Life of Edward Mountague, First Earl of Sandwich* (1912), vol. ii, pp. 257–8; Rowen, *De Witt*, pp. 817, 820; *CSPD 1672 (May–September)*, pp. 5, 28.

men linked with James. The next day French clumsiness frustrated James's desire to renew battle; by the time they got into formation the weather deteriorated and the fleet had to return to the English coast. De Ruyter had been deprived of victory by the failure of the wind, but he won valuable time at a time of desperate crisis.[27] Refitting delayed the allied fleet for a month. Although some officers thought that the objective should be to bring De Ruyter to battle, the fleet sailed to stations where merchant vessels could be intercepted but very few were encountered: the Dutch were using a route far to the east to reach the Dollart. Consequently although the allied fleet had effective control over much of the North Sea it made extremely little use of it.

This allied control was not the result of Sole Bay, but a consequence of the collapse of resistance to the French invasion. De Ruyter had to land his marines, who formed a more important part of his ships' companies than was the case in the English navy, and many of his guns, to shore up the landward defences of Holland. Officers, seamen and small ships had to be detached to form a miniature fleet in the Zuyder Zee to guard shipping and the east coast of Holland against French attacks. One-third of the fleet had to be decommissioned by the end of June, but shortages of money and uncertainties about future payment created problems of manning. Only if an allied landing on the North Sea coast of Holland and Zeeland seemed to be imminent would the fleet sortie, and in order to be ready to do so it was stationed in the Wielings where, as was not the case with the Texel, it could not be blockaded. Fortunately from a Dutch view almost continuously bad weather, including gales of unusual severity for a summer, battered the allied fleet for the rest of the campaigning season, and these would have ruled out a landing in any case. The French contingent left early for Brest, on 18 September, and on the same day James went ashore, for the first time in three months and for the last time as lord high admiral.[28]

Before the campaign spluttered out Charles was reported as urging that 'something glorious' should be attempted: this was tantamount to admitting that the failure to formulate a coherent strategy

---

27 Colenbrander, vol. ii, p. 126; Rowen, *De Witt*, pp. 821–2; Harris, *Life of Sandwich*, vol. ii, pp. 262–3; *CSPD 1672 (May–September)*, pp. 132–3; *HMC 15th Report, app. pt 1*, vol. iii, pp. 13–23.

28 *HMC 15th Report, app. pt 1*, vol. iii, pp. 8–9; P. Blok, *The Life of Admiral De Ruyter* (1933), p. 317; *CSPD 1672 (May–September)*, pp. 267, 446–7; Colenbrander, vol. ii, p. 151.

(as well as the adverse weather) was responsible for the lack of success. Spragge did sortie in September, attacking enemy fishing busses and taking twenty. This derisory success contrasted with the onslaught on English shipping by Dutch privateers. As De Ruyter paid off ships, and merchants cancelled sailings because the seas were controlled by the allied fleet, large numbers of privateers began to operate and particularly in British coastal waters, and with considerable success. English mercantile interests became aggrieved. After all they had not been consulted about a war, as they had been in 1664, and few regarded it as likely to bring them advantages. As the war began embargoes were imposed on outward sailings so that the seamen would be available for the fleet. Subsequent petitions that these should be partially lifted – for example so that ten instead of the usual sixty vessels could sail to Newfoundland – were brusquely rejected. What incensed merchants and shipowners was the evidence that the embargoes were benefiting the French. Because they operated a rota system of maritime conscription instead of impressment, the French could maintain something approximating to peacetime levels of trade. Their vessels were assembling at Cadiz, despite strained Franco-Spanish relations, ready to take the cream of the profits (and in specie) when the flota arrived from America.[29]

Merchants also clashed with the Court and admiralty over the provision of convoys. The level of losses demanded urgent action: anticipating the tactics of the French corsairs of the 1690s and 1700s, Zeeland privateers were operating in packs. In February 1673 six of them took thirteen out of twenty-nine vessels returning from Malaga; one Vlissingen captain boasted to a master that his was the twenty-eighth prize that he had taken. These losses were serious in themselves. They also represented a sharp reversal of trends in comparison with the first two wars. In the first war very large numbers of Dutch vessels had been taken, well over 1,500 in all, although many of them were comparatively small: in the second the balance of advantage was still very much in favour of the English, but in 1672–73 English losses were not compensated by captures until the last months of the war.[30] The provision of convoys also led to mercantile disillusion. After October outward-bound sailings were again permitted, but loaded vessels had often to wait for long periods

---

29 *CSPD 1671–72*, pp. 94, 105; *1672 (May–September)*, pp. 1, 651; *1672–73*, pp. 17–18, 539; Westergaard, *First Triple Alliance*, pp. 499, 502.

30 Bruijn, *Dutch Navy*, p. 90; *Bulstrode Papers* (1897), pp. 247–8; there are innumerable references in the *CSPD* volumes to Dutch privateering activity.

before convoys sailed. Merchants blamed the admiralty for these delays. James responded by condemning merchants who clamoured for convoys but then failed to get their vessels ready and at the rendez-vous by the date fixed for departure. Criticisms of the strength of the escorts provided, and of the officers appointed to command them, infuriated him as impertinent. He wanted to send an official to the Exchange to rebuke merchants and shipowners personally, but with a parliamentary session fixed for February 1673, and an urgent need for money, more temperate counsels prevailed.[31]

Although William became admiral general in 1672 he did not exercise its powers. De Ruyter exercised command throughout the war, and the Republic owed its survival as much to him as to William. Yet in a strange postscript to the 1672 campaign the Dutch nearly lost his indispensable services. He became the target of hysterical and malicious attacks on account of his long association with the De Witt brothers. Cornelis had accompanied De Ruyter on many fleet sorties; although they had disagreements there had been effective cooperation by the two men. Johan De Witt had continuously consulted De Ruyter since Tromp's death in 1653, and this close relationship exposed the admiral to malicious misunderstanding and misinterpretation after the brothers were murdered. De Ruyter expressed his regret in his private journal, using very guarded terms, but calumnies circulated against him while he was still at sea. On 6 September a mob, encouraged by false reports that he had been dismissed, tried to wreck and loot his house, shouting that he was a traitor, would sell the fleet to the French and that he was under arrest. Militia arrived just in time to rescue his wife and property. In October an assassination attempt was foiled while he was visiting the Hague, where he had again to defend himself against criticism because in early August he had, at Johan's request, bravely and candidly defended Cornelis's conduct at Sole Bay against baseless charges of cowardice.[32]

At the beginning of the parliamentary session in February 1673 secretary of state Henry Coventry, anticipating attacks on France and the French alliance that were in the event not developed until the autumn, gave a candid explanation of Charles's foreign policy: 'we have found the danger of being against the king of France, therefore we joined with him, and he has succeeded beyond expectation'.[33] He

31 *CSPD 1672–73*, pp. 44, 108–9; *1671–72*, p. 315.
32 Blok, *De Ruyter*, pp. 316, 320; Rowen, *De Witt*, pp. 840–1, 853–5, 857–8; Colenbrander, vol. ii, pp. 184, 187.
33 A. Grey, *Debates of the House of Commons* (1769), vol. ii, p. 10.

could have added, but understandably did not, that Charles was only following the example set by Cromwell, who had consciously allied with the stronger power of France against the weaker Spain. Coventry expanded on the difficulties that would have followed had the Triple Alliance with the Dutch Republic come into effect in an attempt to check France, but again understandably he made no reference to the difficulties that Charles was experiencing in trying with very indifferent success to restrain and influence his much more powerful and successful French ally. Charles lost much of his freedom of action once he committed himself to receiving subsidies to enable him to wage war against the Dutch without calling Parliament.[34]

Charles had to reject the secret offer which William made in January 1672 to secure from the States General the rectification of all English grievances, and intern two envoys who arrived in London with instructions to offer whatever concessions were needed to avoid war.[35] And when the success of the French invasion became clear Charles began to fear that Louis would use any pretext to impose a separate settlement on the Dutch which omitted satisfaction of the English demands agreed on in the Dover treaty. He sent Halifax to assure Louis that no negotiations were being, or would be, conducted with the Dutch envoys quarantined at Hampton Court. But much more positive action was needed when Louis confirmed his fears by asking that full powers to negotiate and conclude a peace treaty should be sent to Godolphin, the future lord treasurer, who accompanied the French Court as Charles's representative when Louis joined his army in the conquered provinces. The able ambassador to France, Ralph Montagu, had been left behind in Paris. He was a match for any French minister in chicanery, but Louis would have no difficulty in out-manoeuvring and manipulating Godolphin, who was still an apprentice in diplomacy. If Charles contested the particulars of any treaty Godolphin accepted or disowned, he would put himself in the wrong, and the failure of English naval operations meant that he could not hope to achieve any objectives on his own. Therefore Charles sent a high-powered special embassy to ensure that he got what had been agreed in the Dover treaty.[36]

---

34 *HMC Le Fleming*, p. 87; C.L. Grose, 'Louis XIV's Financial Relations with Charles II and the English Parliament', *Journal of Modern History* (1929), i, pp. 177–204.

35 N. Japikse (ed.), *Correspondentie van Willem III en van Hans Willem Bentinck* (The Hague, 1932), vol. i, pp. 41, 43, 48; Mignet, vol. iv, pp. 44–5; *CSPD 1672 (May–September)*, pp. 20, 226–8, 255.

36 Wicquefort, *Histoire*, vol. iv, pp. 446–7; Colenbrander, vol. ii, pp. 142, 157.

The embassy left in early July, headed by the two leading ministers, Arlington and Buckingham. The former was secretary of state, a skilled diplomat and had recently married into an illegitimate line of the House of Orange. Buckingham had negotiated the 'simulated' treaty with France, the bogus or pretend treaty that omitted the religious clauses of the Dover treaty.[37] They conveyed to Louis Charles's insistence that 'we cannot consent to a peace, until we have some effect of the war'. What was termed 'our division' consisted of Dutch submission on the salute to the flag, symbolizing sovereignty of the seas, a rent for fishing in them, and cautionary towns (Vlissingen, Sluis and Brille) 'to be for ever in our possession'. Trade in the East Indies was to be 'adjusted' in England's favour. If they found that parts of the Dutch Republic, notably Zeeland, expressed a wish to do so they could be taken under Charles's protection – and sovereignty. They would have the same status as Wales, sending MPs to the Commons and the language being given recognition, and they would enjoy religious toleration. Finally the Dutch must pay a large indemnity to cover the expenses of the war; the first and largest instalment was to be paid in October. This demand supplies the key to Charles's domestic strategy; such an early payment would obviate the need to call Parliament in order to obtain supply.[38]

The embassy received a general welcome based on Dutch misapprehensions. The people thought they had come to rescue them from the French. Orangist politicians thought their purpose was to ensure that William received sovereignty over the Republic; in fact French advances limited what might be done for him; 'if possible' he should become prince of Holland 'and as much of the other countries [provinces] as you can', that is those areas which France and Münster did not annex. The ambassadors also encountered the first Dutch attempts to separate England from France. Van Beuningen, acting on William's behalf, emphasized that Louis was making no mention in his demands of any satisfaction of English claims, and said that Louvois had told the Dutch negotiators that Louis would make peace if his demands were met, adding that English claims were a separate matter and could be settled by conceding the salute to the flag and some money.[39]

37 Colenbrander, vol. ii, pp. 141–3; Sonnino, *Louis XIV and the Origins of the Dutch War*, pp. 114–15, 117.

38 Colenbrander, vol. ii, pp. 142, 156–7, 181; *CSPD 1672 (May–September)*, p. 289.

39 Colenbrander, vol. ii, pp. 145–6, 149, 157, 169; Wicquefort, *Histoire*, vol. iv, p. 435.

When the ambassadors met William they invited him to betray his country. Their plausible and amoral arguments, based on the assumption that self-advancement was everything, reflected the prevailing ethos of Charles's Court all too accurately, and coloured William's subsequent attitudes to English politicians. William's naive arguments that Charles should consider concluding a separate peace were rejected by the ambassadors who, after all, had been sent as emissaries to Louis to ensure that he did not conclude a separate peace from his position of strength. But they were equally naive in their misjudgement of William. They openly expressed scepticism about his belief, on which he was staking everything, that he could hold out in Holland and Zeeland. They urged him to allow himself to be established as a sovereign prince, but one who could count on continuing support from the two kings to maintain him and so would be no more than a puppet. Their advice was repeated in two letters from Charles (8/18 and 12/22 July) promising that he and Louis would establish him 'in that power which your forefathers aimed at, and I hope that your ambition is not less for being my nephew'.[40]

The embassy succeeded in its formal purpose when it went on to Louis's camp. The Heeswijk treaty stipulated that neither France nor England should conclude a separate peace treaty and that each must communicate all approaches by the Dutch to the other. Louis explicitly undertook to join in obtaining the English demands, so apparently removing the main cause of suspicion, but in private he had already decided against allowing the English to establish themselves in Walcheren, Sluis, Kadzand and Goree, the islands and places which controlled the Scheldt approaches to the port of Antwerp. The English ambassadors agreed that the demands which Louis had put to the Dutch were to stand as the basis of negotiations. These demands were extreme. Louis wanted the annexation of all Dutch territories outside the seven provinces proper, that is he would take the Generality lands and Maastricht. The intended effect was to leave the Dutch Republic and the Spanish Netherlands defenceless; the former would become a French dependency, the latter could be swallowed up at leisure. In addition the Dutch must remove all retaliatory restrictions on French commodities. Catholics were to enjoy freedom of worship, with a proportion of churches handed over to them, their clergy were to receive maintenance from the state

---

40 Colenbrander, vol. ii, pp. 154–6, 170–1; Japikse, *Correspondentie*, vol. i, pp. 71–4, 80, 86; Wicquefort, *Histoire*, vol. iv, pp. 436–7, 454.

and their laymen were to be eligible to serve as city magistrates, so creating for France a large protected constituency of support.[41]

William publicly expressed his contempt for the allied demands when addressing the States General on 20 July, when he pretended that the English demands came from the ministers, not from Charles. This statement, which he could not really have believed, was coordinated with an attempt to induce Charles to make a separate peace by offering substantial concessions – the salute, payment for the fisheries, Surinam, £400,000 – but in return Charles would have to give France no further assistance, which would entail withdrawing the English and Scottish regiments in the French service.[42] There was, however, a danger in trying to engineer a rift between Louis and Charles. If he succeeded William would be linked with the latter. Louis might respond by reviving his former connections with the Regent or Louvestein party whose chiefs had been very roughly removed from their offices by William's partisans, and using them against William (as was to happen in 1677–78). Therefore William included in his proposed deal with Charles an assumption of sovereignty for himself. This is the proposal which Geyl in his mission to rehabilitate the Regents denounced as craven and traitorous. However, the failure of this approach, coming after Charles's rejection of previous attempts to separate him from Louis, made William realize that the only way to break up the Anglo-French alliance was to stimulate and exploit the hostility which it provoked among the English people.[43]

From the beginning of the war the English government took precautions against Dutch attempts at subversion. In May 1672 searches of ships arriving from Dutch ports were ordered; the packets continued to sail between Harwich and Helvoetsluis. Following Sole Bay, rumours spread of alleged French cowardice; consequently a Proclamation was issued against the dissemination of 'false news' and 'licentious talking' on state matters. An investigation was ordered into means by which coffee houses could be regulated, and in September a campaign was started to enforce the laws against seditious literature

---

41 Mignet, vol. iv, pp. 33–5, 48–50; Colenbrander, vol. ii, p. 169; Sonnino, *Louis XIV and the Origins of the Dutch War*, p. 147; *CSPD 1672 (May–September)*, p. 289.

42 N. Japikse, *Prins Willem III*, vol. i (Amsterdam, 1930), pp. 225–7; P. Geyl, *Orange and Stuart* (1969), p. 384.

43 Geyl, *Orange and Stuart*, pp. 384–5; Japikse, *Correspondentie*, pp. 80, 86; Rowen, *Ambassador Prepares for War*, pp. 60, 67, 163–5.

and unauthorized presses.[44] Orders were issued for the arrest of two suspected Dutch agents, and in December Gerbrand Zas, who had been sent on an unofficial political reconnaissance to see what was needed to get peace negotiations started, was told to leave. Although an organized campaign of subversion had not yet begun Charles exploded with resentment, perhaps conscious of his vulnerability, saying that as William was encouraging rebellion, two could play that game, and that it would not be difficult to provoke against William the murderous anger that had recently destroyed the De Witts. Both sides realized that the opportunity for subversion would come when Parliament met on 5 February 1673.[45]

Charles ordered the intensification of precautions; all persons entering the country were to be searched and interrogated. Cargoes were to be thoroughly inspected for pamphlets, which were said improbably to be coming in contained in parcels hidden in barrels of butter addressed to the Spanish embassy. In January Zas returned and was arrested together with Willem Arton, on the basis of an intelligence report from Holland that they were to seek private discussions with those ministers thought to be less zealous for the war. It was also evident that their mission was timed to coincide with the beginning of the parliamentary session, but its effect was to prove highly counter-productive. However, the speeches made by Charles and lord chancellor Shaftesbury showed that there was a danger of opposition to the war itself being generated.[46]

The tone of Charles's speech was defensive.[47] He claimed that the war was 'necessary' and rebutted the idea that it had been provoked by 'indignities to my own person'. Shaftesbury put on a bravura performance, aggressive and confident, a brilliant rhetorical display, taking enormous risks in developing extremely sophistical arguments, many of which were to be thrown back at him during his later career. First he depicted the States General as 'the common enemies to all monarchies', dangerous neighbours to all crowned heads. As our only competitor for trade and naval power their ambition threatened the

44 *CSPD 1672 (May–September)*, pp. 30, 149, 214, 673; *Bulstrode Papers* (1897), pp. 221–2; W.D. Christie (ed.), *Letters to Sir Joseph Williamson* (1874), vol. i, p. 145; vol. ii, p. 68.

45 *CSPD 1672–73*, pp. 231, 270, 286, 293, 484.

46 *CSPD 1672–73*, pp. 427–8, 439, 480, 483–4, 505, 556–7, 595; *1673*, pp. 29, 56, 59, 127; *1673–75*, p. 11; Haley, *William of Orange and the English Opposition*, p. 99.

47 *Lords Journals*, vol. xii, p. 525.

establishment of a 'universal empire as great as Rome'; even now they were so intoxicated with ambition that they would not make peace (that is, on allied terms). Shaftesbury put the onus on the Commons to ensure that now the Dutch had been cast down the opportunity must be taken to finish them off: 'if, after this, you suffer them to get up, let this be remembered, the States of Holland are England's eternal enemy, both by interest and inclination'.[48]

The second main argument was much more daring and difficult to sustain. Shaftesbury described the war as one to which Parliament had committed itself, indeed had called on Charles to wage: ''tis your war. He [Charles] took his measures from you, and they were just and right ones, and he expects a suitable assistance'. But of course Parliament had not met since April 1671, and it had not then been told anything about a war. Shaftesbury's mental gymnastics depended on the parliamentary Address of April 1664, which had called for action (but not explicitly war) against the Dutch. To make this argument work he had to assume a binding commitment on Parliament's part to a policy of unremitting hostility to the Dutch Republic. That is why he used the infamous phrase *Delenda est Carthago* (Carthage must be destroyed). It was neither an exhortation nor a statement of royal policy, but the sentiment attributed by him to Parliament, and his quotation did not fit the situation of 1673. In the original classical model the author of the phrase, the repulsive monomaniac Cato, used it to urge the Senate to destroy Carthage, whereas Shaftesbury was putting the phrase into the mouths of the senators. His closing words plumbed the depths of cynicism and impudence: Shaftesbury called for 'a Triple Alliance of king, parliament and people, may it never be dissolved'. His listeners knew that the 1668 Triple Alliance with the Dutch Republic and Sweden for the purpose of checking French aggrandizement had been approved by Parliament, which had voted money to strengthen the navy to enforce it, not for a war against the Dutch.[49]

However, peers and MPs made no direct attack whatever on the war itself, but actually voted sufficient money for another summer's campaign. This was not because they were convinced by the two speeches at the opening of Parliament. Ironically the Dutch had only themselves to blame for this tacit parliamentary approval of the war. The arrest of Zas and Arton, the uncovering of a blatant

48 Ibid., vol. xii, p. 526.
49 Ibid., vol. xii, pp. 524–7; K.H.D. Haley, *The First Earl of Shaftesbury* (Oxford, 1968), pp. 316–18.

attempt to turn Parliament against the war, inhibited peers and MPs from outright criticism. Shaftesbury's sophistries struck a false note because everyone suspected that he was one of the ministers whom the Dutch agents had been instructed to contact, and he had therefore tried to cover himself by his total support for the war. One greatly respected independent MP (Powle) said that supply must be voted to the Crown when a foreign (and enemy) nation invaded the king's prerogative, that is by tampering with the loyalty of his people.[50] But the Commons voted money conditionally. The vote formed part of a well-planned parliamentary strategy, executed with both determination and finesse by an unofficial leadership. They were suspicious about the war's hidden objectives and loathed the French alliance, but they were even more suspicious of the Declaration of Indulgence, believing that this was intended primarily to benefit the catholics, many of whom had received civil and military offices. Even more important was their determination to take a stand on the constitutional principle that the king did not have a prerogative power to suspend valid statutes, and on this vital issue they forced a royal retreat – although not an explicit disavowal of possession of a suspending power.[51] They drew up a Test Bill to exclude all catholics from offices: its passage called for procedural finesse. The Bill went up to the Lords, who proposed amendments, some of them unacceptable. The Commons had to retain the Supply Bill in an unfinished form until the Lords passed the Test Bill. Otherwise if the Supply Bill went first to the Lords, who had no power to amend it, they would pass it and the king would give it the royal assent. Having got the money he needed Charles would then prorogue the session and the Test Bill would fall. The Commons therefore remained obdurate, deaf to the pleas of Court spokesmen, who claimed that unless money was voted immediately the Dutch would meet with no resistance at sea and could repeat their 1667 victory. The Commons justified their stand by invoking the traditional principle that redress of grievances must precede the grant of supply.[52]

In the face of this intransigence Charles considered not just proroguing but dissolving Parliament. For him, and even more for James and his associate Clifford (now lord treasurer), the Test Bill was a totally unacceptable incursion into the realm of the royal

---

50 Grey, *Debates*, vol. ii, p. 11.

51 J.P. Kenyon, *The Stuart Constitution* (Cambridge, 1966), pp. 407–10.

52 Grey, *Debates*, vol. ii, p. 137; see also pp. 48–54, 74–89, 97–100, 108–15, 137–54, 181.

prerogative, and must be defeated. But the French did not share this concern. For Louis the priority was the continuation of the war at sea by the English fleet, and this required the passing of the Supply Bill because no new French subsidies would be available as a substitute for the money that Parliament was holding in suspense. Consequently Charles found himself under pressure from Louis and the Commons to allow the Test Bill to go through, and he had to give way. A war that he and his ministers had begun with the primary objective of increasing royal powers and authority had necessitated a major surrender of power. The Test Act led both James and Clifford to resign office, paradoxically as the result of what was essentially a diktat from his French ally.[53]

In the campaign of 1673 the allies had at last an overall strategy for the war at sea. The combined fleet would seek out De Ruyter's, and by defeating it or driving it into a port that could be blockaded, the sea would be cleared for an invading army to land on the coast of Zeeland. There it could link up with French forces, particularly cavalry, thrusting west from their positions in the Generality lands. The main Dutch defences would be turned by this invasion. Charles would be able to insist on a peace that fully satisfied English as well as French demands. This general strategic concept was realistic, but of all operations an invasion of an enemy coast, especially one covered by a fleet-in-being even if in inferior strength, requires the most meticulous preparation and planning. Both were lacking in 1673 and consequently nothing was achieved, whereas in 1799 an army was got ashore in north Holland, and in 1809 on Walcheren – two expeditions that are often cited as among the most miserable failures in British military history.[54]

The first directives in April lacked any kind of realism. Rupert, commanding the fleet, was to land the soldiers who formed part of his ships' companies to attack places which could be taken easily: during the panic of 1672 some towns would have been ready to put themselves under English protection, and there were no defence forces other than militia, but this situation had changed after William became Stadtholder.[55] Then in May Charles ordered that shipping should be hired and prepared to lift a force of 10,000 infantry to the Dutch coast, where they would be joined by 5,000 soldiers from the

---

53 Mignet, vol. iv, p. 156.
54 *HMC 15th Report, app. pt 1*, vol. iii, pp. 9–11.
55 *CSPD 1673*, pp. 107–8, 175–6.

fleet. The larger force consisted of the new regiments raised during the winter, mostly raw recruits with inexperienced officers, who were concentrated for training in a camp on Blackheath, conveniently near the Thames. Their officers took their cue from their lieutenant general, Buckingham, who took no real interest in his duties and was continuously absent. Disciplinary problems resulted. On the eve of embarkation the soldiers rioted because they had been stripped of their coats (needed for other units), and the officers were inhibited from enforcing the Articles of War, the disciplinary code, because of doubts about their legality. The Articles, allegedly a translation of a French code, later provoked a furious outburst in the Commons and were cited as evidence for a Court intention to introduce arbitrary methods of government.[56]

The subsequent history of this invasion army was bedevilled by a succession of difficulties, none of which had been foreseen. Colliers were hired as transports. In the first instance they sailed to Great Yarmouth to be ready to cross the North Sea. But these small vessels were so crowded that the soldiers had to be disembarked there. The colliers could not be accommodated in the haven, weather hazards and the risk of being attacked meant that they could not anchor indefinitely in the roads outside, so they had to be sent to Harwich, and this move would prevent the mounting of an invasion at short notice.[57] The voyage to Yarmouth was not without incident. The appalling state of the army led Charles to supersede Buckingham and appoint a general from the French army, Schomberg, to improve its discipline and efficiency, and command the invasion. As captain general he possessed equal status to Rupert, commanding the fleet, and the two men would have to agree on the timing and details of the landing. Yet Schomberg made no attempt to consult Rupert, never a man noted for an equable temperament. He regarded Schomberg's neglect as an insult to his person and authority, and this was confirmed when Schomberg, while sailing with the colliers to Yarmouth, incautiously ordered the captain of his ship to hoist a flag indicating his position. Believing that only admirals could carry flags at the masthead, Rupert ordered that Schomberg's should be lowered. When this was not done immediately he fired shots at the ship carrying the general, and when its captain boarded Rupert's flagship to ask what was happening he was placed under arrest. As

---

56 Colenbrander, vol. ii, pp. 292, 297; Christie, *Letters to Williamson*, vol. i, pp. 88, 99, 107, 116–17, 123, 129, 140, 143.

57 Christie, *Letters to Williamson*, vol. i, p. 140.

a newly arrived foreigner, whose appointment had provoked alarmist complaints about the spread of French influence, Schomberg did not react but merely asked the ministers for 'protection' from the passion and violence of his co-commander as the condition of continuing in his post. It is difficult to see how a combined operation commanded by Rupert and Schomberg – both Pfalz Germans curiously – could have succeeded: at least the celebrated duel between the general and the admiral commanding the disastrous Walcheren expedition of 1809 did follow rather than precede its failure. The invasion army got no further than Yarmouth where its soldiers spent a summer 'buried in sloth and a superfluity of food' (and drink).[58]

Rupert spent the summer in a state of constant frustration and frequent ill-temper. Even before James resigned his offices on 15 June, because he would not take the oaths and the anglican sacrament as required by the Test Act, Rupert suspected that his authority was being undermined. He complained, 'if the officers of *my* fleet have any other way to apply themselves than to me, I beseech you to consider how it can be possible for me to bear any command amongst them'. His suspicions centred on the activities of Sir John Werden, a newly appointed navy commissioner, who was acting as a channel of communication between officers and James, and allegedly encouraging dissent among them. Rupert's reaction widened divisions among his officers. He went out of his way to favour those whom he believed to be loyal to himself, and disparaged those (like Spragge) who were James's protégés, and pressed for changes among his captains, asking for the promotion of men who owed everything to himself. The inevitable result was greatly to increase factionalism among the leading officers, and the tendency to recrimination when things went wrong.[59]

In addition, and even more galling, Rupert felt himself restricted throughout the campaign by a stream of instructions from Charles, who was clearly acting as mouthpiece for James. He had to ask to be allowed to depart from instructions which had been formulated in Whitehall, sometimes on points of small detail – for example to

---

58 Ibid., vol. i, p. 153; *CSPD 1673*, pp. 385, 434–5, 442–3; Colenbrander, vol. ii, pp. 283, 294, 298; *CSP Venetian 1673–75*, pp. 72, 89; J.S. Watson, *The Reign of George III* (Oxford, 1960), pp. 408, 483; see G.C. Bond, *The Grand Expedition: The British Invasion of Holland in 1809* (Athens, GA, 1979); PRO, Baschet transcripts, Colbert de Croissy–Roi, 3 August 1673.

59 *CSPD 1673*, pp. 222, 264, 373; *CSP Venetian 1673–75*, p. 5; J.D. Davies, *Gentlemen and Tarpaulins: The Officers and Men of the Restoration Navy* (Oxford, 1991), pp. 166, 169.

send two frigates, not one, as scouts.[60] The lack of success in this campaign of 1673 was partly due to the attempt made by Charles and James to dictate strategy, and the inhibiting effects this had on Rupert. When the Dutch fleet stayed in its sheltered anchorage in the Wielings he did not know whether they still wished him to mount an immediate invasion. He had to ask whether the decision of himself and his flag-officers to sail north to the Texel was approved. He was frank about his predicament: he did not know if the king had any new strategy to counter De Ruyter's fleet-in-being strategy, any plan to compel the Dutch to come out and fight in the open sea. Rupert had to ask that Charles should 'either give me his positive directions, or else leave the way of it to my management'. Underlying his complaint about his 'troubled condition' that 'either I must undertake (if his Majesty's opinion differ from mine) things against it or mine own judgement' is the apprehension that he would be loaded with the sole responsibility if reverses were suffered. When the Dutch fleet came out while Rupert's combined fleet was reprovisioning at the Nore, he asked for positive and speedy commands; should he sail to meet the enemy before his ships had received fresh seamen to replace those landed sick? When an attempt to draw De Ruyter out of his anchorage failed, Rupert asserted that if he had attacked them within their shoals, as he wanted to do, there would have been a fair chance of success, but that he had not made the attempt because of explicit restraints imposed by the king. In these frequent complaints and oblique criticism one can detect, as early as 11 July, that Rupert was beginning skilfully to disassociate himself from any responsibility for the direction of a campaign that he now expected to end in failure. When Spragge assured Rupert that he had dissuaded Charles from ordering an invasion before the Dutch fleet had been beaten, Rupert's reaction was to remind a minister that Charles, James and Spragge had all held the opposite view, and that only he himself had openly declared against a landing attempt.[61] But the exculpatory argument most frequently and vehemently advanced by Rupert concerned the allegedly cowardly or treacherous behaviour of the French admiral, d'Estrées, and most of his captains. Factionalism among officers weakened the fleet, but recriminations directed against the French had even more serious repercussions. When it became clear

---

60 Davies, *Gentlemen and Tarpaulins*, pp. 163, 166–8, 170; Colenbrander, vol. ii, pp. 297–8; *CSPD 1673*, pp. 123, 232, 537.

61 *CSPD 1673*, p. 432; Colenbrander, vol. ii, pp. 271, 310; Christie, *Letters to Williamson*, vol. i, p. 52; Davies, *Gentlemen and Tarpaulins*, pp. 170–1.

that the campaign was failing to achieve anything significant Rupert began, quite deliberately, to put the blame on the French, and in doing so inflamed the increasing hostility to France and the French alliance. As much as any other factor it was Rupert's devastating (and self-justificatory) criticisms of the conduct of the French navy that made it impossible for Charles to continue the war and fight another naval campaign in 1674.[62]

In May 1673 De Ruyter attempted to realize the offensive plan, which De Witt had often advocated, of blocking the main channels in the Thames estuary with sunken *fluyts*. The objective was to force Rupert to retire up river, and then sink the blockships to prevent him sortieing, and in this way prevent him joining with the French and Portsmouth-based ships off Dungeness, as planned. Because they were weaker than the Dutch some of Rupert's captains favoured a retreat, but he 'who never knew what it was to go back' (as an admirer commented) was ready to take great risks in going over to the offensive. Placing ketches to mark the shoals he took his fleet across the shallow waters of the Middle Grounds, on an ebbing tide and against the wind, a move that was (as he boasted) 'expressly forbidden in the rules of Trinity House'. This forced the Dutch to withdraw and as a result of the rendez-vous with the French and the Portsmouth ships the allies obtained a considerable superiority in numbers which they were to retain throughout the campaign.[63]

This allied superiority forced De Ruyter to adopt a defensive strategy, stationing his fleet in the Schooneveld, an anchorage protected by shoals to the north-west of the Wielings. Initially the allies considered sending in fireships, protected by frigates, but there was sufficient room in the Schooneveld for the Dutch ships to manoeuvre, repulsing the frigates and avoiding the fireships. On 28 May/7 June when Rupert approached, De Ruyter stood out from the shoals so as to get the advantage of the wind and be able to dictate. Rupert headed the allied fleet, and put the French as the main division; this was to prevent them becoming detached as at Sole Bay. This 'political' placing of the French had serious consequences. While Rupert and Tromp fought, the main Dutch division under De Ruyter attacked

---

62 'An Exact Relation of the Several Engagements Anno 1673', in R.C. Anderson (ed.), *Journals and Narratives of the Third Dutch War* (1946), pp. 371–86; Colenbrander, vol. ii, pp. 309–10, 335–7, 344–5, 355–8; Davies, *Gentlemen and Tarpaulins*, p. 167.

63 Christie, *Letters to Williamson*, vol. i, pp. 78, 81, 84; Thompson, *Hatton Correspondence*, p. 105; CSPD 1673, p. 222.

and broke up the French, then joined Tromp in attacking Rupert. Meanwhile poor seamanship hampered the French attempts to regain formation and aid Rupert. He commented on the French in his report with sarcasm rather than bitterness: they 'behaved as well as could be expected', they had not handled fireships with skill, but some captains had displayed great bravery. This relatively favourable judgement was made possible by the universal but erroneous belief in the fleet that the Dutch had suffered heavy losses.[64]

Neither side had lost any ships, but this first engagement of 1673 was decisive in that it validated De Ruyter's strategy. Emphasis in Rupert's report on the dangers he had run in entering shoal waters led to Charles issuing strict orders that the fleet should not try again to enter the Schooneveld, which consequently became a safe haven for De Ruyter, his 'sea-hole' in the language of English seamen. He could lie up there, sortieing only when he judged that an opportunity existed to inflict damage on the allies without himself running unduly high risks. The first opportunity came soon, on 4/14 June. From the direction of the wind he knew that the allies had not been able to do more than improvise repairs at sea. Using an easterly he took them by surprise, since they believed that they had severely weakened both the strength and the morale of the Dutch. The allies tried to get into battle formation, but never recovered from the confusion caused by each division manoeuvred independently, so that only a few ships became closely involved. Nevertheless De Ruyter achieved his objective by forcing the allies to retire from the Dutch coast for repairs and reprovisioning, Rupert taking the fleet back to the Nore. Louis expressed surprise, fearing that this would give the Dutch an opportunity to blockade the allies in the Thames. He was right. The Dutch appeared in the Gunfleet on 26 June/6 July, disproving official English claims that they were on the verge of collapse after their earlier 'defeat'. By their presence they also delayed the transit of the invasion army to Yarmouth. Moreover De Ruyter was not running any serious risks by appearing on the English coast; any wind that enabled the allies to close him would enable him to retire across the North Sea.[65]

The allied fleet was delayed in putting to sea again by the slowness of the French in refitting their ships, because they had insisted

---

64 Colenbrander, vol. ii, pp. 230, 234–5, 251–3, 261; Christie, *Letters to Williamson*, vol. i, p. 17.

65 Christie, *Letters to Williamson*, vol. i, pp. 18–19, 26; Colenbrander, vol. ii, pp. 262, 271–2; Davies, *Gentlemen and Tarpaulins*, p. 171.

206

on providing all the supplies themselves rather than obtaining them from the stocks stored in the English yards (because they thought they would be over-charged), and by a shortage of English seamen to replace the sick and casualties in Rupert's ships. De Ruyter declined to give battle because the allies had the wind, which they used to sail north close to the coast of Holland, causing great alarm, and leading the provincial militia to track along the strand the course of the enemy ships. But Rupert had then to ask Charles for instructions on what to do next. He wrote on 27 July/6 August and made suggestions of possible moves. Charles replied on 3/13 August, so over a week was wasted.[66]

Charles ruled out attempting a landing because the Dutch fleet had not been defeated, but he also advanced new reasons: the land defences had been alerted, the French army would not now be able to assist with cavalry or a diversion to tie down the enemy, and the season was too advanced. And the consequence was that it was not worth taking the risk of an all-out attack into the Schooneveld; Charles therefore repeated his order that Rupert must not attack De Ruyter 'within the banks'. By issuing this order Charles was in effect writing off any chance that the naval campaign, and indeed the war itself, could have a decisive outcome.[67]

Louis XIV had already taken a decision that would have the same effect of postponing indefinitely all possibility of imposing allied terms on the Dutch, and he had done this without consulting Charles. Louis had never wanted a successful English invasion of Zeeland because he did not wish to see them established in the towns promised to them in the Dover treaty. When drafting its terms French diplomats had been negligent: Lionne admitted that they had had no precise knowledge of the location of Vlissingen, Cadzand and Sluis. English possession of these key towns on the Scheldt would mean that when Louis took the Spanish Netherlands he would need English leave to open the port of Antwerp. This could be used as a bargaining counter, either to insist that England must be consulted on the wider issues of the future of the Spanish Empire, or at the least that Louis would have to purchase them as he had bought Dunkirk. The result was that the French demands made in July 1672 to the States General did not refer to any English acquisition of Zeeland towns, and in the early stages of the negotiations for peace which began at Cologne in the spring

---

66 Colenbrander, vol. ii, pp. 297–8.
67 Ibid., vol. ii, pp. 295, 297; CSP Venetian 1673–75, p. 72.

of 1673 the Swedish mediators (who were notoriously amenable to French direction) ruled it out as inadmissible as a claim.[68]

Louis's decision to make a major change in his war strategy was only to a minor extent influenced by his desire to exclude the English from Zeeland. The main reason was his judgement that the furtherance of French interests required a major military intervention in western Germany. As a necessary preliminary, and in order to enhance his personal glory, he switched his offensive to the south of Holland and Zeeland, undertaking a spectacularly rapid capture of the isolated fortress of Maastricht, which gave him control of the reaches of the Maas that lay between the Spanish Netherlands and any assistance that might come from the Emperor and the German princes. Louis greatly overestimated the Emperor's readiness to intervene if war broke out between France and Spain, or even in the existing war with the Dutch. He reacted to the Emperor's decision to assemble an army at Eger, in western Bohemia, and to conclude a treaty with the Dutch, by moving strong forces into the electorate of Trier. He did this against the advice of his foreign minister, Pomponne, claiming with transparent dishonesty that the occupation was the result of an unauthorized initiative by a French general. This forward move proved to be decisive and irrevocable in transforming the existing war against the Dutch into a general European war.[69]

For England the naval engagement of 11/21 August, off the Dutch coast between Camperdown and the Texel, also proved to be decisive, not because either side gained an advantage in the fight, but because the behaviour of d'Estrées and the bulk of the French contingent sparked off an explosion of anti-French hostility in England. Rupert's public and vituperative criticisms made it unthinkable that the French could serve in another campaign under his command. With hardly an exception the English officers and seamen became incensed against their French allies; their letters, and personal accounts when they returned, inflamed a public that was already turning against the war. French officers also criticized Rupert, but the effects in an absolute monarchical state were limited; the audience for such complaints

---

68 Ibid., pp. 72, 75; Sonnino, *Louis XIV and the Origins of the Dutch War*, p. 147; Rowen, *Ambassador Prepares for War*, p. 180; C.J. Ekberg, *The Failure of Louis XIV's Dutch War* (Chapel Hill, NC, 1979), p. 24.

69 Ekberg, *Failure of Louis XIV's Dutch War*, pp. 16–17, 26–7, 32–4, 39; P. Sonnino, 'Louis XIV and the Dutch', in R. Hatton (ed.), *Louis XIV and Europe* (1976), pp. 160–1; Christie, *Letters to Williamson*, p. 97; Wicquefort, *Histoire*, vol. ii, p. 570.

consisted of Louis and his ministers, they might later be included in official propaganda. But in England anti-French reports circulated verbally through the medium of coffee houses and taverns, and were published as 'relations' of the fight, and they were certain to be taken up and repeated in the Commons when it met. These reports poisoned Anglo-French relations. Charles was only exaggerating a little when he described himself and James as the only remaining friends of France. Although the Court was to pretend otherwise there was now no chance whatsoever of Parliament voting supply to finance another year's campaign.[70]

Rupert and the other reporters blamed the French for the failure to defeat the Dutch, and for the heavy casualties in personnel (but not ships). By incompetently slackening sail twice before the action began they had given the Dutch the weather gauge, but in the actual battle they had behaved in either a cowardly or a treacherous manner. By treachery was meant allegedly following secret orders not to engage the Dutch closely, so allowing the English to bear the brunt of the fighting and losses. This charge was elaborated into the claim that there was a design to let the Dutch and English weaken each other, so that the French could become the dominant naval power. The basis for these charges was that when the wind shifted, just as the action began, the main French force stood off until they were nearly six miles from Rupert, who had become heavily engaged. There they remained, failing to respond to the large flag displayed by Rupert at his mizzen-mast peak ordering them to come to his assistance. This could be regarded as the result of the distance between them, and the flag becoming obscured by smoke from the discharge of the guns, but common sense should have led the French admiral to sail to the area where a close engagement was clearly in progress. As Rupert said, he should have known what to do without being given orders. English suspicions were confirmed when a messenger arrived, as the action subsided, to ask the meaning of the signal; this indicated that it had certainly been seen. As a result, so Rupert claimed, 'the plainest and best opportunity' ever to annihilate the enemy had been thrown away, and he made it plain that he had lost confidence in d'Estrées. Most maliciously Rupert also attacked Spragge, James's protégé, and a chief member of the anti-Rupert faction, who had been killed, coupling the slowness with which his division had come to Rupert's assistance with the fact that he had visited Paris before the beginning of the campaign. Spragge's mission had been to check on the arrangements

70 Mignet, vol. iv, pp. 249, 267.

for the junction of the two fleets, but the far-fetched insinuation was that there had been collusion through his agency to let the English do the fighting.[71]

In a further piece of quite inspired mischief-making, Rupert disingenuously disclaimed any intention of trying 'to breed an animosity' between the English and French by saying that, although he blamed d'Estrées for what had happened, many of the French captains had been eager for action, but had been held back by their admiral. In insinuating that d'Estrées had been following secret orders Rupert knew that his suspicion would receive confirmation from a maverick French officer, Martel, who was engaged in a furious factional dispute with d'Estrées and had received a severe rebuke from Louis for his insubordination. Having recently arrived with a small reinforcement squadron Martel was eager to distinguish himself. In the battle on 21 August he led the initial French attack, found himself isolated in close combat with several opponents for three hours, and then rejoined d'Estrées and the main French force, expecting him to go to Rupert's assistance. In post-battle recriminations, and in his report to the Ministry of Marine, Martel said that he had seen and understood Rupert's signal, and was astonished that d'Estrées did not respond to it. This was in his view a 'craven disgrace' (*honte indigne*), and had it not been for express orders to the contrary he would have sailed to assist Rupert, even though he lacked confidence in the captains in his division, who had earlier failed to support him. This self-justificatory relation identified Martel as the kind of brave, headstrong but undisciplined and unprofessional officer that Louvois was fast eliminating from the French army, and his behaviour contravened Colbert's instruction to naval officers to discard the spirit of factionalism which the minister saw as characteristic of the 'old' navy, that is the navy before he took it in hand. Martel compounded his failings by addressing an apologetic memorandum to Rupert. In this he said that the captains who had failed to support him cited as justification 'some secret orders they will persuade us to have received' from d'Estrées. Rupert and all other critics of the French alliance did not pause to consider that this excuse could have been fabricated by the captains to cover their cowardice, which was the gloss Martel put on it in his report. They jumped to the conclusion that Martel had proved the existence of secret orders prohibiting the

---

71 Christie, *Letters to Williamson*, pp. 168–9, 170, 183, 185, 189, 191, 194; Davies, *Gentlemen and Tarpaulins*, pp. 171–3; Colenbrander, vol. ii, pp. 301–10, 327, 332, 336–7.

French from becoming involved in close engagements and risking heavy losses. This became an accepted fact in England. Consequently the failure to win a decisive victory was attributed entirely to French treachery, and treachery at the highest level. Martel's relation killed any possibility of the French and English navies fighting another campaign together. Louis described it as contrary to his glory, and prejudicial to his service, and sent Martel to the Bastille. The king published a French version of the battle, but facts had now been made irrelevant by English prejudices.[72]

The conduct of the French freed parliamentary critics of the war from the taint of behaving subversively or traitorously when they rejected the king's pleas for further financial supply. Charles tried to put them on the defensive by claiming that Dutch obstinacy in refusing to concede reasonable terms was entirely attributable to their expectation that the Commons would not vote supply.[73] By October a systematic propaganda campaign by the Dutch had established in the mind of the public the clear impression that the war and the French alliance formed part of a 'design', or conspiracy, to establish catholicism and arbitrary government in the British Isles. In addition the entire character of the war was changing. On 19 October Louis declared war on Spain, creating a very real danger that England would be dragged into this extension of the war, with totally disastrous economic effects. This danger was visible because Charles had in April formally declared that he was no longer bound by the Triple Alliance and its guarantee of the Spanish Netherlands.[74]

For critics of the war Louis was behaving as if England was 'in league with him against all the world', and as England became enmeshed in what was turning into a general European war the prospects of an early peace were receding, with Charles being reduced to the status of an ancillary unable to influence the major decisions which Louis took. Second, war against Spain would inevitably have the same damaging effects as the Cromwellian war of 1655–60. Imports of specie would stop. The Levant trade would suffer, to the advantage of French competitors. Moreover arguments about likely damage to trade made an impact because the war against the Dutch had originally been depicted as one that would produce an

---

72 Colenbrander, vol. ii, pp. 319, 322–5, 339–41, 348; Corvisier, 'Colbert et la Guerre', pp. 303–4.

73 *Lords Journals*, vol. xii, p. 593, 4 November 1673.

74 Mignet, vol. iv, pp. 176–7, 205.

expansion and greater prosperity. The ravages of Dutch privateers were disproving this possibility, and shipowners were being forced to hire foreign vessels, at a cost estimated at £300,000, because impressment was causing a shortage of seamen. Only in the Caribbean could counter-balancing gains be expected, but little of the money and loot that had been recently 'acquired' in the unofficial raids on Panama city and Cuba had reached England. Finally any decline in trade would of course reduce receipts from customs duties, and Charles could not now expect Louis to offer compensatory increases in subsidies.[75]

Charles now came under pressure from every quarter. Louis who had dissuaded him in March from dissolving Parliament (to save the Declaration of Indulgence) now exerted pressure against allowing Parliament to meet, and advised him to take all decisions himself, and compel his ministers to implement them. James forcefully supported this line of argument; he would have dissolved Parliament and arrested the politicians who were suspected of having connections with the Spanish embassy. Members of his entourage argued that a windfall gain could be used to finance at least a reduced naval armament for 1674, and that the French would be prepared to set out a rather larger contingent than the English, a development that would have made nonsense of English claims to sovereignty of the seas. The windfall followed the recapture of St Helena, when three VOC return vessels were taken, and another on the Dutch coast: they were valued at more than £300,000. But this success was counter-balanced by heavy losses to a spectacular and devastating Dutch attack on the north American plantations.[76]

James and his associates had no knowledge of the true state of royal finances. The new lord treasurer, the future earl of Danby, was telling Charles that a continuation of the war could not be financed. Consequently French arguments that a separate peace would be contrary to the Dover and Heeswijk treaties, and against Charles's reputation and honour, could have no effect because they were not backed up by promises of additional subsidies. Charles, like James, did not want to break the French alliance, but in Arlington's weasel

75 *CSP Venetian 1673–75*, pp. 143, 187–8; Christie, *Letters to Williamson*, vol. i, pp. 88, 120, 122, 143, 158; vol. ii, pp. 45, 48, 80; Grey, *Debates*, vol. ii, p. 231.

76 Mignet, vol. iv, pp. 225–6, 229–30; *CSP Venetian 1673–75*, pp. 96–7, 175, 205–7; Christie, *Letters to Williamson*, vol. i, pp. 162–3, 177–8, 181; *CSPD 1673*, pp. 506–7; D.G. Shomette and R.D. Haslach, *Raid on America: The Dutch Naval Campaign of 1672–1674* (Columbia, SC, 1988).

words to the French ambassador his adherence to it had to remain 'in his heart alone'.[77]

The Dutch propaganda campaign that turned public opinion against the war was combined with canvassing of peers, MPs and other people of influence organized by the Spanish embassy in London. At a popular level the most effective arguments exploited deep-rooted and often crude anti-papist prejudices, but French actions gave real cause for alarm. Louis restored public worship for catholics in all the conquered towns: at Utrecht the cardinal de Bouillon reconsecrated the cathedral, burnt the calvinist pews and installed a bishop (one with Jansenist sympathies!) and catholic canons and priests who would form part of the provincial States. Moreover even in 1674 Louis continued to insist that the Dutch should concede equality of religious and political rights in a peace treaty: he justified this by claiming that as the eldest son of the Church he had an obligation to do so. This suggested that he might have a similar duty in relation to the British Isles (and of course a sight of the Dover treaty would have confirmed that he had), although in reality he advanced these religious demands to embarrass the Emperor and Spain for allying with heretics.[78]

The centrepiece of the Dutch propaganda campaign, Du Moulin's pamphlet *England's Appeal*, which had been circulated just too late for the parliamentary session in the spring, reinstated anti-popery as a major influence in English politics and connected the war, the French alliance and the domestic policies of the Cabal ministers in a conspiracy against the law, the nation's liberties and the protestant religion. As the naval campaign faded, Spanish diplomats and Dutch agents found few difficulties in canvassing members of the political nation, but the real achievement of Dutch propaganda pamphlets was to create an identity in opinion between ordinary people (whether they had the right to participate in public affairs or not) and MPs who had mostly been elected in totally different circumstances back in 1661. It may be that Dutch money converted some MPs to an anti-war stance, but men of real influence, whose arguments could sway the Commons, were not likely to regurgitate secondhand arguments derived from pamphlets, nor were they merely exploiting royal

77 A. Browning, *Thomas Osborne, Earl of Danby*, vol. ii (Glasgow, 1944), pp. 63–4, 65; Mignet, vol. iv, p. 249.

78 Christie, *Letters to Williamson*, vol. ii, pp. 95, 105; Wicquefort, *Histoire*, vol. iv, pp. 416, 634, 642; Grey, *Debates*, vol. ii, pp. 189–97, 198–215; *CSP Venetian 1673–75*, pp. 175, 182–3.

difficulties. Leading MPs like Sir William Coventry, Sir Thomas Lee and Colonel Birch, who had been largely responsible for the passing of the Test Act in the previous session, now saw that liberties and religion would not be wholly secure until the war was ended and the French alliance broken off.[79]

Parliament, meeting on 27 October, was asked by Charles for 'speedy supply', 'the safety and honour of the nation requiring it'. In an attempt to put his critics on the defensive he explicitly referred to the Dutch propaganda campaign, 'the artifices of their enemies', which he hoped the loyalty of the Commons would overcome. In the back-up speech Shaftesbury tried to restore the picture of the war as one for trade against a ruthless rival, equating the Dutch trading interest with the Louvestein or Regent party (even though it was no longer in office) 'who sucked in with their milk an inveterate hatred to England'. These speeches had no effect when the Commons debated supply. MPs identified with the Country tendency cited French naval misconduct and Louis's championing of Dutch catholics as justifying a refusal of any money. But they constituted only a minority, and a blank refusal would (as the attorney general insinuated) saddle the Commons with the responsibility for any disaster that followed, and for a disadvantageous peace.[80]

In two speeches William Coventry outlined and justified a strategy that avoided any confrontation with the king, but was eventually to force him to make a separate peace. First, he exposed the artificiality of the French alliance. Citing examples of Louis breaking treaties when it suited him, he argued that Charles need not think himself under any obligation in honour or interest. He demonstrated that the French failure to support Rupert in the battle, as exposed by Martel, had been no accident but an essential part of French policy, producing a devastating peroration: 'the interest of the king of England is to keep France from being too great on the Continent, and the French interest is to keep us from being masters of the sea – the French have pursued that interest well'. In a second speech Coventry demolished the mercantilist notion that the use of naked power in the form of aggressive wars could bring increased profits or wealth in a permanent form. The Navigation Act had increased England's share of some trades at the expense of the Dutch, but 'what probability is there, if we beat the Hollander, that we shall get all trade?' This could be done

---

[79] *England's Appeal from the Private Cabal at Whitehall to the Great Council of the Nation, The Lords and Commons in Parliament Assembled* (1673).

[80] *Lords Journals*, vol. xii, pp. 588–9; Grey, *Debates*, vol. ii, p. 211.

only by 'industry and parsimony', by 'under-selling', that is reducing prices. He added that even the catastrophe of 1672 had induced few merchants to emigrate from Holland. Raw mercantilist aggression could work only in 'Guinea or other barbarous countries', but not in Europe. Coventry finally displayed his skill as a parliamentary tactician by introducing a resolution that the Commons would not consider voting any supply unless it should appear that the obstinacy of the Dutch made it necessary to continue the war, and unless the kingdom had been secured from the dangers of popery. This enabled the Commons to get round the constitutional obstacle that all questions of peace and war were exclusively a matter for the royal prerogative. It would be for the Commons to judge the acceptability of whatever concessions the Dutch offered, and they knew from their Spanish diplomatic contacts that they would not be unreasonable.[81]

The Court could not openly resist this resolution, but Charles prorogued the session on 4 November to enable those he described as 'good men' to 'recollect themselves', to free themselves from evil influences – meaning Dutch pamphlets and Spanish diplomatic contacts.[82] When Parliament reassembled on 7 January 1674 he modified his line of argument. The Dutch were relying on a breach between himself and Parliament in order to have their own way over the terms of peace: only by voting supply to finance a 'good fleet' could he obtain a 'good peace'. But the king created a bad impression by trying to defend the French alliance, which he claimed had been misrepresented 'as if there were certain secret articles of dangerous consequence', and he denied the existence of any secret treaty. MPs noted that he fumbled the delivery of this lying speech, which in some passages was said to lack coherence, but they attributed this to James's known fury at his brother for allowing Parliament to meet. In his speech the new lord keeper denounced the terms being offered by the Dutch, and their having sent printed copies of the terms to all peers and MPs.[83]

Charles tried on 24 January to put the Commons in the wrong by asking them to advise him about the latest Dutch terms; as the Dutch

81 PRO, Baschet transcripts, Colbert de Croissy to Louis XIV, 13 November 1673; Grey, *Debates*, vol. ii, pp. 203–4, 212–13; Christie, *Letters to Williamson*, vol. ii, p. 69.

82 Christie, *Letters to Williamson*, vol. ii, pp. 75, 84; *Lords Journals*, vol. xii, p. 593.

83 *Lords Journals*, vol. xii, pp. 594–5, 595–8; O. Airy (ed.), *The Essex Papers* (1890), vol. i, p. 161.

lobbyists told MPs this was a manoeuvre to pin on Parliament the responsibility for a disappointing settlement. The Commons refused to comment; as Charles had started the war he must end it. Every speech in the debate assumed that the war had been a mistake. One particularly has symbolic and ironic significance. Downing, the embodiment of aggressive mercantilism in the 1660s, and the man sent to the Hague in 1671 to precipitate this war, now favoured a peace although he criticized some of the likely terms.[84]

Considering the expenditure of lives and money on the war the peace, concluded on 9/19 February, brought derisory gains. The Dutch agreed to salute the flag, but did not recognize English sovereignty over the seas; it was no more than a courtesy. English subjects could leave Surinam. New York, retaken by the Dutch, reverted to England. The Dutch paid a modest indemnity, but most of it went back in clearing Stuart debts to the House of Orange. The Dutch took a risk in standing obstinately against paying for the right to fish in the North Sea, but rightly calculated that Charles's position was now so weak that he could not break off the negotiations on any issue.

The third war was a bogus affair from its aggressive start to its whimpering end. The fraudulent arguments used to justify it, and the French alliance which alone made it possible, had one delayed but crucial effect. When in 1688 James belatedly realized that William was about to invade he tried to rally national support against the Dutch by describing them as England's traditional enemy. His attempt failed abysmally. William trumped James by his (unfounded) assertion that in 1688, as in 1672–74, the sovereigns of England and France were bound together by a secret treaty aimed not only against the Dutch Republic but also against the liberties and religion of England and Scotland.[85]

---

84 Grey, *Debates*, vol. ii, pp. 338–41, 343–9, 350.

85 Jones, *Revolution of 1688 in England*, pp. 198–9; *A Collection of Papers Relating to the Present Juncture of Affairs* (1689), pp. 15–16.

9 CONCLUSION

One of the most perceptive reactions to the first Anglo-Dutch War came from an awestruck neutral, who exclaimed that he realized he was watching 'such war as never before was', an apparently mortal struggle of an entirely new character and on an epic scale. These were the first great oceanic wars fought by fleets composed increasingly of great ships, successors to the galleys which had dominated Mediterranean wars for two millennia but were now obsolete even within its confines. The size of the combatant fleets, the resources in men, materiel and money which they absorbed, the complexity of the logistical and administrative support which they required, the intensity of the fighting with major battles fought at short intervals despite appallingly high casualties in personnel, were all new phenomena. The course of each war saw dramatic alternations of fortunes; in 1665 after Lowestoft all other European states were faced with the prospect of total English domination of the seas, but by 1667 they had lost control of even their coastal waters. Subsequently the temporarily triumphant Dutch were reduced in 1672 to the extremity of offering capitulation before what remains as the most skilful and successful defensive naval campaign ever waged ensured their survival, and Charles II was forced by his own subjects to quit the war. This outcome emphasizes the difference between the governmental systems of the two states principally involved, England and the Dutch Republic, and all the other states of Europe, both monarchical and republican. The first war was fought by two entirely new states, the Stadtholderless Dutch Republic, which had in 1651 put the House of Orange into eclipse, and the regicide Commonwealth of England, which since 1649 was engaged in conquering Scotland and Ireland. Even after the English Restoration of 1660 few European sovereigns, or their ministers and subjects, understood the character and workings of the English system of government but were puzzled by the contrast between the naval power which Charles deployed and the political restrictions and limitations on his authority over his own subjects.

Despite being comparatively neglected by naval historians, these three wars constituted a significant stage in the development of naval warfare. They established the primacy of the great ship. Battles and wars were to be decided for the next two and a half centuries – until Midway established the primacy of the carrier – by the ships with the largest number of the heaviest guns. Such great ships, firing broadsides, and sailing in line formation for the first time, brought the Commonwealth victory in 1652–54 forcing the Dutch into belated imitation in the war of 1665–67. This practice also established the principle which the Royal Navy continued that all English flag-officers and captains should always be committed to undertaking offensive and aggressive action: in all three wars only Ayscue in the very first year showed himself an exception in this respect. The Fighting Instructions first formulated by the Commonwealth navy envisaged a disciplined compliance by the captains of individual ships to orders from their superiors, but the extremely rudimentary systems of signalling meant that flag-officers could not transmit new or changed orders during the course of action. Consequently battles tended to degenerate (that is by later standards) into mêlées in which everything depended on the initiative, courage and aggressiveness of individual captains, whereas the 'stiff formalism' of tactics in the Anglo-French Wars of the eighteenth century meant that a captain was almost invariably confined (that is, unless he was Nelson) to maintaining his station in the line. The consequences of the lack of ability by flag-officers to control their forces in action were variable but on occasion crucial. In the first war many captains of Dutch ships that had been converted from merchant vessels failed to follow orders to engage the enemy, and defected if things were seen to be going badly: the damage that their weakness and indiscipline caused precipitated the professionalization of the Dutch naval officer corps. But on occasion even junior flag-officers could, once battle was joined, make their own decisions without regard for what the other divisions of the fleet were doing. The younger Tromp fought an entirely separate action in 1666 when De Ruyter was facing disaster; the French went off on their own at Sole Bay and again in 1673 at Kijkduin/Texel.

The key to British control of the seas during the later Anglo-French Wars lay in the establishment of long-lasting blockades of the enemy's main naval bases. These were established as a matter of policy, as the initial move in a campaign, and by the 1800s were highly organized and extremely effective: by contrast blockades during the Anglo-Dutch Wars were short-lived and improvised. Unlike those in the French and Spanish wars of the next century they were established only after naval battles had been won. In these a high proportion of the ships involved had inevitably received damage and suffered casualties, which reduced the time they could continue at sea, especially if the weather deteriorated. Additionally the administrative and logistical services could not organize the despatch of sufficient supplies to keep the fleet at sea for more than a few weeks, or institute a rota for the return of a proportion of the fleet to take on supplies and water, and land the sick and wounded – commonplace tasks in the 1790s and 1800s. Moreover there existed a tempting alternative to the maintenance of blockades: the use of the fleet to search for Dutch convoys and vessels and so gain prize money for all. On the other hand the facts that the fleet kept the seas for much shorter periods, and was usually and largely paid off before winter set in, meant that the iron and severely enforced discipline of the later wars was neither necessary nor enforceable; the opportunities for desertion were far greater when the whole fleet frequently returned to the Thames estuary, and the need to recruit its manpower each spring acted as a restraint on the enforcement of discipline by officers and senior ratings who were far less professionally authoritarian than their more hierarchically minded successors of a century later.

The main theatre of operations in the wars against the Dutch – as in the German wars of the twentieth century – was clearly defined and relatively restricted in extent to the North Sea, Channel and Western Approaches.[1] It has been said that these were the first world wars, and there were major clashes (especially in 1672–73) in Asian waters and (in 1666–67) in the Caribbean.[2] But these actions in distant seas could never decide or significantly influence the outcome of the wars, or even affect the detail of the peace treaties that brought them to an end. Thanks to its dominant commercial position, and specifically the mass of merchant shipping and seamen employed in the 'country' trade between Asian countries, the VOC more than held its own against its English and French rivals, but neither these successes nor the closure of the Baltic to direct English trade in the first and second wars could counter-balance the heavy naval defeats which the Dutch suffered in the North Sea, or the lengthy dislocation of Dutch mercantile activity – both homeward and outward-bound sailings – when

1 See Map 1.

2 J.I. Israel, *The Dutch Republic: Its Rise, Greatness and Fall 1477–1806* (Oxford, 1995), pp. 721–2; C. Wilson, *Profit and Power* (The Hague, 1978), p. 128.

the focal areas off the main Dutch sea-gates became too dangerous to traverse. Indeed it can be said that the factors that contributed directly and crucially to the commercial ascendancy which the Dutch established before 1652 turned into serious disadvantages during the wars against England – as de la Court and De Witt themselves recognized. Their entrepôt trade could not be maintained beyond the capacity of their warehouses to store commodities imported from, and re-exported to, distant regions in the Baltic, the Mediterranean, Biscay, America and Asia. The disruption of Dutch trade during periods of effective English control of the seas, which proved to be relatively brief – the summers of 1653, 1665 and 1672 – severely damaged Dutch business confidence and threatened to provoke a flight of venture capital. Shipowners became alarmed that the carrying trade would be taken over by vessels based on Hamburg and other neutral ports, many of them financed by Dutch money, and they were adversely affected by higher insurance premiums and taxes. The advanced nature of the Dutch economy, with a higher degree of economic specialization and a heavier concentration of entrepreneurs, artisans and casual labour in the Holland towns than anywhere else in Europe, made it more vulnerable than the less developed economy of even south-east England. Equally Holland's society, which was predominantly urban, with a significant proportion of immigrants from abroad and from the landward provinces, in which traditional relationships and conventions had been weakened or effaced by virtually unrestricted market forces, could not have stood the strain of prolonged disruption of the economy. In periods of critical tension the role of the province's militia was to act as a bridle on the people; one unit saved De Witt in 1653 but in 1672 the Amsterdam and Rotterdam militias played a part in purging the city magistracies, and a unit at the Hague remained inactive while the De Witt brothers were torn to pieces.[3]

If the English fleet had been allowed to continue the first war into the summer of 1654, or achieved a prolonged control of the North Sea in 1665–67 and 1673, it would have been the Dutch economy and the urban society of Holland that would have been torn to pieces. In the last analysis the Dutch owed their survival to the relatively primitive state of contemporary navies and naval administration. Seventeenth-century navies were blunt instruments of power in comparison with those led by Hawke and Nelson. They had bigger, stouter ships that could keep the seas in the worst of winters,

---

3 Israel, *Dutch Republic*, pp. 801–4.

and could have coped with the gales of 1672 that nullified English superiority. Navigation improved immeasurably by their time; they had accurate charts, the means to determine longitude, and some meteorological expertise. Their ships were armed with harder-hitting and more reliable guns, they could rely on efficient service from dockyards and admiralty organizations, and their officers possessed a self-confidence and *esprit de corps* that responded to inspired leadership (when this existed) with invariably decisive effect. The difference that these developments made can be seen in the fourth Anglo-Dutch War of 1780–84, when Dutch overseas trade was paralysed and their fleet destroyed, and this at a time when Britain was also at war with France, Spain and the American colonies.

The final question to be considered is how far these three expensive and bloody wars decided anything, and specifically how far they contributed to the relative economic decline of the Dutch Republic, and its replacement by eighteenth-century Britain as the leading maritime, commercial and financial power, not just in Europe but in the world. First, it is clear that the wars disappointed the crude mercantilist expectations of the early 1650s and 1664–65 based on the belief that a significant share of world trade and actual wealth could be wrested from the Dutch by the threat, or use, of superior force against them. Experience in the first two wars showed that the total costs of aggressive wars, not only in governmental expenditure but also in the suspension of trade caused by pressing seamen and embargoes on sailings, could never be fully recovered. Mercantile losses became substantial; in the first war captures of Dutch vessels greatly exceeded losses to enemy privateers, but there was no such disparity in the second war, and in the third English losses were greater in number than prizes. Admiralty organization was not sufficiently efficient for the running of regular convoys: merchants complained of inordinate delays which kept their vessels and capital expensively idle. Moreover the Dutch recovered their dominant share of European trade immediately after the first war ended, while English trade and shipping suffered severely from the war against Spain into which Cromwell blundered in 1655, and in 1667 the Dutch were able to regain peacetime levels of commercial activity some months before the conclusion of peace.

Second, English experience during the three wars provoked critical questioning of the assumptions and formulae on which mercantilist theses depended. Mercantilist writers and politicians influenced by them believed that wealth and power were necessarily connected, and that the only way of increasing the wealth of the nation was by using the machinery of government and increasing the power of the state to win a larger share of trade. English experience during the wars exposed major fallacies in such simplistic claims. Arguing in October 1673 that Parliament should not vote money to enable Charles to continue the war into 1674, Sir William Coventry made a significant distinction between trade in Europe and that with what he termed 'barbarous countries', regions like Guinea where no settled order existed and competing European trading companies routinely used armed force.[4] In such regions the physically strongest would prosper, but in Europe an increased share of international trade could be achieved only by better organization, by ploughing back profits ('parsimony') and lowering prices by greater efficiency. Coventry also made the elementary point that Dutch losses did not automatically lead to English gains, and other Country spokesmen in the Commons implied that even if the Dutch were decisively defeated there would be little likelihood of their capital resources moving to England. The 1672 Stop of the Exchequer showed that the sovereign thought that he had the power arbitrarily to suspend the property rights of bankers. Sir William Temple, writing that year what proved to be a premature obituary of the Dutch Republic, said that trade could not grow or thrive without 'a trust in the Government from an opinion of its strength, wisdom and justice': with the last two characteristics notably absent no Dutch capitalist would invest in England.[5]

By 1673 the arguments advanced by Charles and, with blatant cynicism, lord chancellor Shaftesbury to justify the wars against the Dutch were met with almost universal disbelief. The mercantilist arguments that the power of the state must be strengthened in order to force the enemy into submission, and that substantial commercial concessions could then be extorted from them, were seen as a cover for increasing the power of the Crown and its ministers at the direct expense of Parliament and the nation. At the centre of this disquiet the army was seen not so much as a force for use abroad but as the means of suppressing liberties and religion at home. Charles, James and the Cabal ministers were suspected of intending to carry out a coup against the constitution similar to that perpetrated by Cromwell in 1653–54. At that time, so Cromwell's later critics claimed retrospectively, naval victories put the Dutch entirely at England's mercy, and they could have been deprived of much of their trade. But Cromwell

---

4 A. Grey, *Debates of the House of Commons* (1769), vol. ii, pp. 203–4.

5 Sir W. Temple, *Observations upon the United Provinces of the Netherlands* (ed. Sir G. Clark, Oxford, 1972), p. 110.

threw away this opportunity, preferring to conquer his own people with the support of his army and set himself up as lord protector and impose a constitution of his and their devising.[6] When the second war was ending in abject defeat Country MPs alleged that a hidden agenda had been pursued aimed at establishing a greatly expanded army; in their view this accounted for the fatal decision to lay up most of the fleet in 1667, so releasing resources to raise new army units. But in 1673 these kinds of suspicions became much stronger and politically more explosive. Fuelled especially by the alliance with Louis XIV, although the terms of the secret treaty of Dover were not yet known, virtually all sections of opinion came to believe that the third war was a cover not just for the establishment of arbitrary government, one freed from its dependence on Parliament and the restraints imposed by the law, but for the introduction of catholicism.

The alliance with France also had the effect of entirely under-mining the mercantilist case for the use of armed force against the Dutch, and in the longer term it altered the character of English mercantilism. Mercantilist writers and politicians in the 1650s and 1660s concentrated almost exclusively on the need for action against the Dutch because of their dominant share of trade, in the process greatly overstating the value and importance of the VOC's Asian trade. Colbert's protectionist policies altered the situation, making it impossible to sustain the argument that the Dutch alone consti-tuted the obstacle to expanding England's trade and wealth. French protectionism quickly and very substantially reduced English exports, producing a large and growing trade deficit with France which necessitated large exports of specie. This concentrated the attention of mercantilists on questions related to the damaging effects: the depletion of capital resources, the decay of the currency and the dangers to the political independence of England from the con-sequential strengthening of the already excessive military and naval power of France. The disquiet of mercantile interests was to find its expression in the Scheme of Trade, a propagandist overstatement of the imbalance of trade to justify counter-protectionist measures, but in the shorter-term Colbert's apparent success made the Dutch war irrelevant: as one MP commented, 'Fifty percent upon our goods in France, and yet the war with Holland upon account of Trade'.[7]

6 J.T. Rutt (ed.), *The Parliamentary Diary of Thomas Burton* (1828), vol. iii, pp. 111–12, 389; *CSPVenetian 1671–72*, pp. 188, 202, 205–6; *1673–75*, pp. 195–6.
7 Grey, *Debates*, vol. ii, p. 201 (Sir Thomas Lee).

As the three Anglo-Dutch Wars were being fought one of the major fallacies in current mercantilist thought was slowly becoming evident. Because of their identification of wealth with money (in the form of specie) mercantilists believed that the amount of wealth in existence was relatively static, that one country could become wealthier only by depriving others of their share. But from the late 1650s certain colonial trades began to expand, an expansion that was to continue into the eighteenth century, and of which Britain was to become the main beneficiary. Despite the fighting on the west African coast in 1664–65 and the VOC's successes in Indian and Indonesian waters, the Anglo-Dutch Wars did not affect these developments to any significant extent. Moreover the emergence of London as the leading entrepôt in commodities imported from other continents and re-exported to most parts of Europe did not in itself lead to the decline of the Amsterdam entrepôt in European commodities, which was due to quite separate causes, particularly the decline in grain shipments from the Baltic.[8] Moreover although the naval supremacy achieved and retained by the British fleet for more than a century after 1692 is the obvious reason why it became the dominant maritime power, the other principal and essential precondition is perhaps less obvious until one examines the main reason for the eventual failure of the Dutch Wars from an English perspective. They failed not because Parliament blackmailed Charles II by refusing him the money he demanded, out of factionalism or little Englander isolationism, but because the generation of men who lived through the second and third wars lost all confidence in the honesty and integrity of Charles and his ministers. Even though they did not know anything about the details of the Dover treaty Charles's subjects could see that the war had been aimed as much against their own liberties, properties and religion as against the Dutch.

During the reigns of the first four Stuart kings the lack of confidence in the integrity of the monarch and his principal advisers and servants prevented the effective mobilization of English resources in foreign wars, and of course no consensus existed in Commonwealth times. It was not until after 1688 that a consensus came into existence based on the concept of mixed government – a balance of powers within the constitution and the subordination of all branches of government to the law – which generated the confidence which was necessary for political stability. The fiscal-military state of the eighteenth century which mobilized national resources with

---

8 Israel, *Dutch Republic*, pp. 617–19, 998–1002.

far greater efficiency than the absolute monarchies of Europe, but without endangering liberties and property, was the outcome. It has been asserted that the Revolution of 1688 was only a 'petulant outburst', and that the 'Old Regime' continued in all essentials into the next century, but a comparison of Britain's conduct of the Seven Years War under the elder Pitt with the English performance in the Dutch Wars, and especially in 1665–67 and 1672–74, will show how little justification there is for such a claim.[9]

---

9 J.C.D. Clark, *Revolution and Rebellion* (Cambridge, 1986), p. 130; but see J. Brewer, *The Sinews of Power* (1989).

SELECT BIBLIOGRAPHY

The place of publication is London unless otherwise stated.

GENERAL STUDIES

Anderson, M.S., *War and Society in Europe of the Old Regime* (Leicester, 1988).

Boxer, C.R., *The Anglo-Dutch Wars of the 17th Century* (1974).

Boxer, C.R., *The Dutch Seaborne Empire* (1965).

Bruijn, J.R., *The Dutch Navy of the Seventeenth and Eighteenth Centuries* (Columbia, SC, 1993).

Fox, F., *Great Ships: The Battlefleet of Charles II* (Greenwich, 1980).

Fulton, T.W., *The Sovereignty of the Sea* (1911).

Harper, L.A., *The English Navigation Acts* (New York, 1939).

Israel, J.I., *The Dutch Republic: Its Rise, Greatness and Fall 1477–1806* (Oxford, 1995).

Mahan, A.T., *The Influence of Sea Power upon History* (1890).

Oppenheim, M., *A History of the Administration of the Royal Navy 1509–1660* (1896).

Potter, E.B. and C.W. Nimitz, *Sea Power: A Naval History* (1960).

de Wicquefort, A., *Histoire des Provinces-Unies, 1648–1676* (Amsterdam, 1861–74).

Wilson, C., *Profit and Power* (Cambridge, 1957; The Hague, 1978).

De Witt, J. (attributed to), *The True Interest and Political Maxims of the Republic of Holland* (1746), written mainly by P. de la Court.

NAVAL STUDIES

Baumber, M., *General-at-Sea: Robert Blake and the Seventeenth-Century Revolution in Naval Warfare* (1989).

Blok, P.J., *The Life of Admiral De Ruyter* (1933).

Bruijn, J.R., 'Dutch Privateering during the Second and Third Anglo-Dutch Wars', *Acta Historiae Neerlandicae* (The Hague, 1979), xi.

Capp, B., *Cromwell's Navy* (Oxford, 1989).

Davies, J.D., *Gentlemen and Tarpaulins: The Officers and Men of the Restoration Navy* (Oxford, 1991).

Harris, F.R., *The Life of Edward Mountagu, First Earl of Sandwich* (1912).

Lavery, B., *The Ship of the Line* (2 vols; 1983, 1984).

Lewis, M., *The Navy of Britain: A Historical Portrait* (1948).

Ollard, R., *Man of War: Sir Robert Holmes and the Restoration Navy* (1969).

Oudendijk, J.K., *Johan de Witt en de Zeemacht* (Amsterdam, 1944).

Padfield, P., *Tide of Empires: Decisive Naval Campaigns in the Rise of the West, 1481–1654*, vol. i (1979); *1654–1763*, vol. ii (1982).

Rogers, P.G., *The Dutch in the Medway* (1970).

Shomette, D.G. and R.D. Haslach, *Raid on America: The Dutch Naval Campaign of 1672–1674* (Columbia, SC, 1988).

Symcox, G., *The Crisis of French Sea Power, 1688–1697* (The Hague, 1974).

Tedder, A.W., *The Navy of the Restoration* (Cambridge, 1916).

Warnsinck, J.C.M., *Abraham Crijnsen: De verovering van Suriname* (Amsterdam, 1936).

POLITICAL AND ECONOMIC STUDIES

Barbour, V., *Capitalism in Amsterdam in the Seventeenth Century* (Ann Arbor, MI, 1976).

Baxter, S.B., *William III* (1966).

Beresford, J., *The Godfather of Downing Street: Sir George Downing* (1925).

Davies, K.G., *The Royal African Company* (1960).

Davis, R., *The Rise of the English Shipping Industry* (1962).

Ekberg, C.J., *The Failure of Louis XIV's Dutch War* (Chapel Hill, NC, 1979).

Furber, H., *Rival Empires of Trade in the Orient, 1600–1800* (Minneapolis, MN, 1976).

Haley, K.H.D., *William of Orange and the English Opposition* (Oxford, 1953).

Haley, K.H.D., *An English Diplomat in the Low Countries: Sir William Temple and John de Witt* (Oxford, 1986).

Hartmann, C.H., *Clifford of the Cabal* (1937).

Hutton, R., *The Restoration* (Oxford, 1985).

Israel, J.I., *The Dutch Republic and the Hispanic World* (Oxford, 1982).

Israel, J.I., *Dutch Primacy in World Trade, 1585–1740* (Oxford, 1989).

Mousnier, R. (ed.), *Un Nouveau Colbert* (Paris, 1985).

Roorda, D.J., *Partij en Factie* (Groningen, 1978).

Rowe, V.A., *Sir Henry Vane the Younger* (1970).

Rowen, H.H., *The Ambassador Prepares for War* (The Hague, 1957).

Rowen, H.H., *John de Witt: Grand Pensionary of Holland* (Princeton, NJ, 1978).

Sonnino, P., *Louis XIV and the Origins of the Dutch War* (Cambridge, 1988).

Temple, Sir W., *Observations upon the United Provinces of the Netherlands* (ed. Sir G. Clark, Oxford, 1972).

Woolrych, A., *Commonwealth to Protectorate* (Oxford, 1982).

Worden, B., *The Rump Parliament* (Cambridge, 1974).

SOURCE MATERIAL

Anderson, R.C. (ed.), *The Journal of Edward Montagu, first Earl of Sandwich* (1929).

Anderson, R.C. (ed.), *The Journals of Sir Thomas Allin* (1939).

Anderson, R.C. (ed.), *Journals and Narratives of the Third Dutch War* (1946).

Birch, T. (ed.), *A Collection of the State Papers of John Thurloe* (1742).

Christie, W.D. (ed.), *Letters to Sir Joseph Williamson* (1874).

Colenbrander, H.T., *Bescheiden uit Vreemde Archieven omtrent de Groote Nederlandsche Zeeoorlogen* (The Hague, 1919).

Gardiner, S.R. and C.T. Atkinson (eds), *Letters and Papers Relating to the First Dutch War, 1652–1654* (1898–1930).

Grey, A., *Debates of the House of Commons* (1769).

Japikse, N., *De Verwikkelingen tussen de Republiek en Engeland* (The Hague, 1900).

Latham, R. and W. Matthews (eds), *The Diary of Samuel Pepys* (1970–83).

Lister, T.H., *The Life and Administration of Edward, first Earl of Clarendon* vol. iii (1838).

Powell, J.R. and E.K. Timings (eds), *The Rupert and Monck Letter Book, 1666* (1969).

Routledge, F.J. (ed.), *Calendar of the Clarendon State Papers*, vol. v (Oxford, 1970).
Tanner, J.R. (ed.), *Samuel Pepys's Naval Minutes* (1926).

MAPS

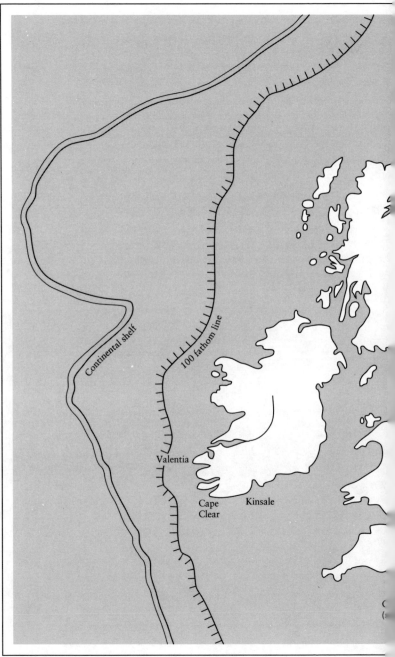

Map 1 **Britain and its seas**

Bergen

Fair Isle

Stavanger

Flekkefjord

The
Skaw

The
Sound

Great
Belt

Copenhagen

ne
(Newcastle)

Dogger
Bank

Little
Belt

Flamborough
Head

Outer
Dowsing

Terschelling

Hamburg

The Dollart
(Ems)

Texel

Leman
Bank

Lowestoft

The Hague

(Southwold) Sole Bay

Goree

the Nore

Schooneveld

ndon

Maas

The Downs

Goodwin
Sands

rtsmouth

Antwerp
(Scheldt)

Calais

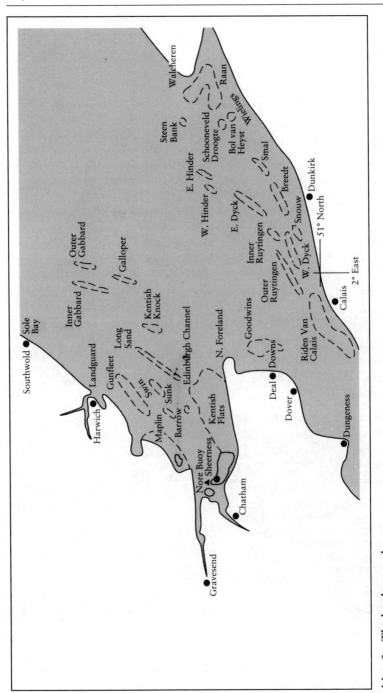

Map 2   The battlegrounds

INDEX

Africa, 12
    Company of Adventurers to, 35–6, 91,
        92, 147, 149–51
Aga, 150
Ahlefeldt, baron, 163
Albemarle, duke of, see Monck
Allin, Sir Thomas, 23, 151, 164
Almirantazgo, 32, 111–12
Amboyna, 34, 142, 147
Ameland, 69
Amersfoort, 188
Amsterdam, 7, 20, 68, 107, 112, 172,
        183, 186, 220
    admiralty, 40, 44–5, 62
    privateers, 27
    ship-building, 40, 46
Andrews, Thomas, 88
Angola, 35
Antigua, 36
Antwerp, 12, 196, 207
Archangel, 23, 69
Arlington, Henry Bennet, earl of, 99, 148,
        166, 170, 195, 212
Arnhem, 188
Articles of War, naval, 50, 122–3
    military, 202
Arton, Willem, 99–100, 198, 199
Asiento, 35
Assessment Bill (1667), 94-5
Ayscue, Sir George, 115–16, 218
Azores, 17

Baltic sea, 23, 26, 93, 119, 219
Barbados, 35
Barebones (or Nominated) Parliament,
        72, 73, 82, 138–41
    anti-Dutch element in, 85
Barrow sand, 19
Batavia, 33
Beaufort, duc de, 169–70, 173
Bergen, 23, 160–3

Bergues bank, 20
Bethel, Slingsby, 85, 143
Beuningen, Conrad van, 195
Beveriningk, H. van, 73, 137, 139, 142
Birch, colonel John, 214
Blackborne, Robert, 49
Blackheath, 202
Blake, Robert, 19, 20, 23, 50, 119, 135
    northern sortie, 27, 115
    in first clash, 114
    poor scouting, 116
    and Kentish Knock, 118
    and Dungeness, 27, 60, 119–22, 123
    in Channel Fight, 125–7
Bol van Heyst, 21
Bol van Knokke, 21
Bordeaux, 31, 141
Boulogne, 173
Bourne, Nehemiah, 118
Brazil, 35, 68, 143
Breda, treaty of, 36
    negotiations at, 174, 178
Breedt bank, 20
Brest, 18, 52, 60, 173, 189
Brille, 195
Brounker, Henry, 158
Buckingham, George Villiers, duke of,
        100, 155, 195, 202

Cabal ministers, 9, 14, 96–7, 100
    aims, 15, 222
    abandoned, 103
Cadiz, 23, 192
Calais, 24, 126–7, 173
Cape Coast Castle, 151
Carlos II, 184–5
Carteret, Sir George, 57
Cats, Jacob, 113
Ceylon, 33, 147
Chaloner, Thomas, 87
Channel Fight, 125–7

Charles I, 7, 12, 84
Charles II, 4, 53, 57, 108, 136, 143–4, 199, 217
  and sovereignty of the seas, 12
  barred from Holland, 73
  De Witt entertains, 143
  instructs Downing, 75
  and the second war, 8–9, 10, 89–90, 145–6, 155, 160
  rejects French mediation, 168
  and the third war, 10–11, 14, 15, 96–7, 98–9, 179–80, 191–2, 197–8
  and French alliance, 193–4, 196, 209, 212
  relations with William, 194, 196–8
  fears subversion, 197–8
  and 1673 campaign, 201, 203–4, 206–7
  denounces Triple Alliance, 211
  and Test Act, 200–1
  Parliament forces to make peace, 101–2, 211, 214–16, 222
  suspected of arbitrary ambitions, 222–3
Chatham, 7, 22, 27, 49, 174
  importance, 62–3
Chimney money, 95
City (of London) interest, 4, 7, 10, 49, 82, 110–11, 141, 145, 149, 151, 192
Clarendon, Edward Hyde, earl of, 57, 75, 93, 145
  principles, 88–9
  on banks, 94–5
  Dungeness exalts, 121–2
Clifford, Sir Thomas, later baron, 91–2, 100
  manages the Commons, 148–9
  and second war, 151, 154, 162–3
  and third war, 96–7, 99
  and Test Act, 200–1
Coevorden, 188
Colbert, J.-B., 14, 31, 79, 169, 223
  and war of 1672, 182–4
Cologne, 186, 187, 188, 207–8
Commons, House of, 8, 56
  and second war, 148–9
  investigates miscarriages, 95–6
  and third war, 200
  passes Test Bill, 200–1
  makes peace inevitable, 215
Commonwealth establishes Council of Trade, 7, 49, 88, 91
  Council of State acts for, 7, 49, 86, 113–14, 119–21, 122–3
Condé, prince, 31, 141

Convoy Acts, 49, 86
Court, Pieter de la, 11, 12, 67, 69, 72, 143, 220
Coventry, Henry, 193
Coventry, Sir William, 51, 55, 63, 91–2, 96, 146, 170
  working methods, 56–8, 90
  on second war, 145, 176
  speeches on third war, 214–15, 222
Crijnssen, Abraham, 36
Crispe, Sir Nicholas, 91
Cromwell, Oliver, 10, 35, 72, 75, 122, 127, 155, 176
  security his main concern, 8, 73–4, 88, 138
  accepts trade as paramount for Holland, 9, 73, 85–6
  and sovereignty of the seas, 12
  as ruler, 85, 222–3
  dissolves Rump, 127
  discards union with Dutch, 86
  makes peace, 138–42
  French alliance, 194
  war against Spain, 32, 90, 143, 211, 221
Curaçao, 35

Danby, Thomas Osborne, earl of, 212
Danzig, 26
Deane, Richard, 122, 130, 135
Declaration of Indulgence (1662), 89
  (1672), 98, 100, 102, 181, 212
Denmark, 26, 142
  toll treaty, 143
  and Bergen attack, 160–3
Dogger Bank, 18, 23
Doleman, lieutenant-colonel, 25, 141, 178
Dollart, 28, 191
Dordrecht, 66, 81, 180
Dover, clash off, 112, 114, 128
  Straits, 22, 113, 173
  secret treaty of, 9, 180, 194, 212, 223–4
Downing, Sir George
  instructions (1663), 75
  intelligence gathering, 24, 76, 156
  intimidatory methods, 8, 68–9, 75–7, 89–90, 148, 153
  sees Dutch as vulnerable, 13, 34, 147
  and VOC, 33, 147
  and De Witt, 76–7, 154
  miscalculations, 145

and second war, 151–4
Treasury reforms, 94–5
contrast with Temple, 152–4
1671 mission, 181
for ending third war, 216
Downs, anchorage, 22, 24, 128, 134
Droogte van Schooneveld, 21
Dungeness, battle off, 25, 27, 39–40, 43, 48, 119–22
Dunkirk, 116, 168, 207
privateers 20, 27, 113, 115
Dyck bank, 20

East India Company, 33–4, 90–1, 92, 151, 154
Elmina, 150
Ems, estuary, 22
Enkhuizen, 71
Estrades, comte d', 66
Estrées, comte d', 189–90
Rupert denounces, 204–5, 208–11
Evertsen, Cornelis, 133
Evertsen, Cornelis (the youngest), 36

Falmouth, Charles Berkeley, earl of, 90, 162
Fighting Instructions, 128–9, 218
Finisterre, 12
Fireships, 41, 44
Flamborough Head, 23
Flanders, 13, 20, 32, 110, 186
Ford, Sir Richard, 151
Four Days Fight (1666), 24, 27, 51, 64, 169–70
France, alliance with, 9, 13, 15, 212–13, 214, 223
trade relations with, 30–1, 112, 223
and second war, 166–70, 172–3, 175
Frederick Henry, 45, 66
Frederick III of Denmark, 160–3
Friesland, 65, 72, 141, 171, 186, 188

Gabbard, sands, 19
battle, 42, 59, 128–30
Galen, Johan van, 32
Galloper sand, 19, 20
Gelderland, 65, 66–7, 69, 185, 186
States of, endorse Perpetual Edict, 78
denounce Commonwealth, 84
oppose peace, 139, 141
Geyl, Pieter, 197
Gibraltar, 23
Glarges, Dutch agent, 24

Godolphin, Sidney, 194
Goree, 156, 196
Gravesend, 176
Great Assembly, 107
Great Ships, 38, 40–2, 51–3, 218
Greenland, 23, 69
Gris Nez, cape, 19, 126
Groningen, 65, 72, 141, 183, 188
Groot, H. de, 79–80, 186
Gunfleet, 19, 206

Haarlem, 71, 183
The Hague, 1653 riot at, 71
Halifax, George Savile, marquis of, 194
Hamburg, 26, 68, 80
Harlingen, 45
Harrison, Thomas, 88, 137
Harwich, 7, 22–3, 24, 60, 61, 176, 178
Hawke, Edward, 4, 220
Heemskirk, Lauris van, 25
Heeswijk, treaty, 196, 212
Heligoland, 28, 34
Helvoetsluis, 24, 197
Holland, province, 7, 65, 69
States of, 7, 71, 80, 109, 183
trade paramount for, 9, 11, 73, 85–6
and Stadtholderate, 65, 77–8, 107
receives Strickland, 82
bars Charles II, 73, 138
passes Seclusion Act, 74, 77, 142
peace moves, 136–7, 139
and William, 186–7
society, 220
Holmes, Sir Robert, 22, 55
his bonfire, 25, 44, 172
African raid, 35, 150
attacks convoy, 188–9
Hoorn, 71, 186
Huygens, Christian, 165

Indonesia, 32–4, 147
Ipswich, 22
Ireland, 84, 109, 169
Catholic Confederates and Holland, 82

James, duke of York, 17, 29, 51, 53, 57, 62, 143, 216
and second war, 8, 89, 90–1, 144, 145–6, 150, 151–2, 155
and third war, 9, 15, 96–7, 175–6
role, 89
and officers, 54–6, 157–8

political principles, 96–7, 100–1, 103,
153, 160, 179, 209
and Pett, 63
strategy, 155–6
Lowestoft victor, 158–9
Sole Bay command, 190–1
and City interests, 193
and Test Act, 200–1
resigns, 203
advises 1673 campaign, 203–4
urges repression, 212
aims suspect, 222–3
Java, 68
Jellicoe, admiral John, 21
Juxon, bishop, 93

Kadzand, 196
Kentish Knock, shoal, 20
battle (1652) 39, 118, 123

Landguard fort, 25, 61, 178
Lawson, Sir John, 54–5, 133, 156, 158
Lee, Sir Thomas, 214
Le Havre, 125
Leiden, 71, 110, 183
Levant Company, 87, 92, 185
Liège, 187
Line, fighting in, 128–9
Lorraine, 186, 187
Louis XIV, 4, 79
despises Dutch, 13
despises House of Commons, 99
enters second war, 166
directs navy, 167
and war of 1672, 14–15, 181–4, 186–7
first campaign, 187–8
demands, 196
and English allies, 194–5, 196, 207–8
vetoes 1673 dissolution, 101, 201
declares war on Spain, 211
opposes Parliament meeting, 212
Catholic policies, 213, 214
undervalues colonies, 36–7
opts for neutralizing England, 102
Louvois, marquis, 99, 182, 195, 210
Lowestoft, battle off (1665), 21, 27, 51,
158–9

Maas, 18, 21, 156
Maastricht, 14, 185, 196, 208
Macassar, 34
Madame, Henrietta d'Orléans, 89, 167–8
Magnus Intercursus, 109

Mahan, A.T., 3
on privateering, 29
Malaga, 17, 192
Martel, marquis, 210–11
Marvell, Andrew, 63
Mary II, 15
Mary of Modena, 15
Maryland, 35
Masulipatam, battle off, 33
Maurice of Nassau, prince, 78
Medway, 19, 52, 96
Mercantilism, 9–10, 29–30, 74
refuted by wars, 221–2, 223–4
Mercantilists, 87, 88, 90–1, 146–7, 153
Cromwell not one, 85, 139–40, 143
Merchant Adventurers, 110, 180
Middleburg, 45
Middle Grounds, 205
Moluccas, 34, 147
Monck, George, 20, 25, 57, 122, 135
as patron, 54–5, 90
at Gabbard, 129–30
imposes blockade, 130–2
Texel victory, 132–3
in Four Days Fight, 169–70
in St James Day Fight, 171
commands during Medway fiasco,
177–8
Montagu, Ralph, 194
Montserrat, 36
Morlaix, 125
Morrice, William, 57
Mun, Thomas, 151
Münster, von Galen, bishop of, 69, 71,
166, 188
Mussert, Anton, 6
Myngs, Christopher, 164

Napoleon I, 4, 173
Narborough, Sir John, 60
Navigation acts, 4, 32, 86
of 1651, 11–12, 49, 74, 85, 87, 110,
111–12, 141
of 1660, 12, 144
Navy Board, 56–8
Nelson, Horatio, 4, 218, 220
Nes, Aert van, 163
New Amsterdam, 51, 147, 150
Newfoundland, 28, 36, 192
New Netherland, 8, 12, 35, 37, 150, 178
New York, 36, 178, 216
Nineteen Propositions (1642), 107
Nominated Parliament, *see* Barebones

Nore, anchorage, 22, 204
North Quarter (of Holland), 45, 69
North Sea, physical characteristics, 16–25
Norway, 12, 18, 22–3
  ports as Dutch shelter, 27

Obdam, Jacob van Wassenaar, 42, 60, 134–5, 149, 156, 165
  his defects, 157–8
Oppenheim, M., 50
Orangist 'party', 71–2, 80–1, 138, 140
  includes traitors, 76
  attacks on St John mission, 83
  attitude to defeats, 135–6
Ormonde, James Butler, duke of, 169
Overijssel, 66, 166, 185, 186
  States of, 69, 141
  endorses Perpetual Edict, 78

Pauw, Adriaen, 72, 114
Penn, Sir William, 55
Pennoyer, William, 88
Pepys, Samuel, 48, 51, 54, 63, 92, 146, 151, 176
  as inspector, 56
  addresses Council, 57–8
Perpetual Edict, 65, 77–8, 80
Peters, Hugh, 141
Pett, Peter, 63, 96
Petty, Sir William, 153
Philip II, 65, 84
Philip IV, 166
Plymouth, 22, 116
Pomponne, marquis de, 182, 184, 208
Portsmouth, 22, 61, 119
Portugal, 35, 143, 152
Powle, Henry, 200
Privateering, 27–30
Prize Money, 123
Providence Island Company, 35
Pulo Run, 34, 92, 154

Raan bank, 21
Ratel bank, 20
Reeves, Sir William, 55
Regent 'party', 65–8, 70–1, 73–6, 79, 85, 167, 214
  splits, 80
Rhine, 18
Roberts, Nicholas, 88
Rotterdam, 42, 44–5, 171, 220
Royal Society, 53

Rump Parliament, 7, 8, 10, 12, 29, 72, 87
  naval programme, 48–9
  administrative reforms, 49–51, 122
  personnel policy, 53–4
  proposes union with Dutch, 82–4, 107–11
  centralizing body, 83–4
  its confidence, 114
Rupert, prince, 17, 19, 25, 53, 73, 146, 156, 159
  as patron, 55, 203
  at Council, 57–8
  and victuallers, 60
  and Four Days Fight, 169–70
  St James Day Fight, 171
  1673 command, 201–11
  reviles French, 205, 208–11
Ruyter, Michiel de, 52, 133, 165, 173, 175
  Channel operation, 115–16
  African operation, 36, 150–1, 159, 162
  St James Day Fight, 171, 218
  Chatham attack, 176–7, 178
  Sole Bay, 190
  fleet weakened, 191–2
  mob hostility to, 193
  defensive success of 1673, 3, 18, 21, 180, 201, 204, 206–7
  offensive sorties, 205, 206
  as inspiration, 6
Ruytingen banks, 20

St Helena, 34, 212
St James Day Fight, 21, 171, 218
St John, Oliver, 72–3, 83, 107–10
St Kitts, 36
St Martin de Ré, 120, 124
St Vincent, John Jervis, earl of, 4
Sandwich, Edward Montagu, earl of, 23, 43, 54–5, 60
  strategy, 156
  Bergen operation, 160–3
  trouble over prizes, 164
  killed at Sole Bay, 190–1
Scheldt, 12, 18
Schomberg, general, 202–3
Schooneveld, 21
  first battle, 205–6
  second, 206
Scilly Isles, 113
Scotland, 84, 108–9, 138, 155, 161
Seclusion, act of, 74, 75, 86

Shaftesbury, Anthony Ashley Cooper, earl
    of, 12, 100
  speeches to Parliament, 198–200, 214,
    222
Sheerness, 22, 61, 176
Shetland Islands, 18, 115
Ships
  Aemilia, 40
  Bonaventure, 121
  Brederode, 39, 130
  Dreadnought, 42
  Garland, 121
  Kruningen, 131
  Little Mary, 172
  Loyal London, 53
  Merlin, 181
  Naseby, 44
  Neptunus, 116
  Prince 190
  Royal Charles, 19, 44, 177, 180
  Royal James, 62, 190
  Royal Katherine, 51, 53
  Royal Oak, 51
  Royal Prince, 20
  Rubis, 173
  St Michael, 190
  Samson, 125
  Sophia Amalia, 131
  Sovereign of the Seas, 124, 131
  Swieten, 131
  Triumph, 125
  Unity, 177
Signalling, in infancy, 128–9
Sluis, 195, 196, 207
Smal bank, 20
Smith, Jeremaiah, 55, 171
Snouw bank, 20
Sole Bay, 22, 23, 156
  battle, 190–1, 197, 218
Southampton, Thomas Wriothesley, earl
    of, 57, 93
Sovereignty of the Seas, 12, 148
Spain, trade with, 32, 111–12
  recognizes Commonwealth, 108
  intervenes in English politics, 101–2,
    213
  Louis XIV goes to war with, 211–12
Spanish Netherlands, 15, 37, 167, 184–5,
    196, 207–8, 213
Spitzbergen, 23, 69
Spragge, Sir Edward, 55, 59, 171, 189,
    192–3, 204, 209

Stadtholderate, 65–6
  'abolished' in Holland, 77
Start Point, engagement off, 114
States General, 18, 68, 72, 74, 82, 94
  permeable, 24, 65, 138
  and constitution, 64–6
  opposes union with Commonwealth,
    73, 107–10
  moves to protect trade, 112–13
  sets out 150 ships, 39–40, 113–14
  pays for new ships, 40–2
  initial strategy, 115–16
  false confidence, 114, 117
  displaces Tromp, 117
  propaganda, 130
  peace moves, 73, 137, 139–40
  divided response to Colbert's tariffs,
    183–4
  and army, 186–7
  ready to submit to Louis, 188
  William addresses, 197
Stop of the Exchequer, 98, 100, 102,
    222
Strickland, Walter, 72–3, 82–3, 107–10
Sumburgh Head, 115
Sunk sand, 19
Surinam, 36–7, 178, 180, 216
Sweden, 160–1, 199, 208

Tangier, 23
Teddiman, Thomas, 162–3
Temple, Lady Dorothy, 181
Temple, Sir William, on Dutch weak-
    nesses, 13
  on Regent class, 6, 11, 67
  on De Witt, 72
  on Dutch government, 222
  contrast with Downing, 152–3
Terschelling, 22, 25, 61, 172
Test Bill and Act, 100–1, 200–1, 203,
    214
Texel, 18, 21, 24, 34, 127, 156
  battle, 64
Thames, 16, 19, 28, 165
Thompson, Maurice, 87
Thompson, William, 87
Thurloe, John, 24, 86, 140
Tirpitz, grand admiral, 3
Tomkins, Sir Thomas, 178
Toulon, 52, 169
Trafalgar, 29
Trier, 208

Treasury, 56, 57–8
  and second war, 93–5
Triple Alliance (1668), 152, 184, 194, 199
  Charles denounces, 211
Tromp, Cornelis ('the younger'), 19, 158–9, 171–2, 205–6, 218
Tromp, Maarten, 19, 20, 21, 60
  English distrust, 113, 139
  orders to, 114, 127
  initial moves, 115
  plans leaked, 24
  northern convoy, 27
  in and out of command, 117–18
  Dungeness victory, 119–21
  Channel Fight, 125–7
  wants great ships, 40–2
  escort duties, 127–8
  Gabbard defeat, 128–30
  killed in Texel battle, 132
  tomb, 48
True Freedom, 65–8
Tsushima, 29
Tuscany, grand duke of, 32
Tyne, coal trade, 16

Union, proposed between Commonwealth and the Dutch, 11, 73–4, 107–10
Utrecht, 188, 213
  Union of, 64, 108, 139
  province, 66–7, 185
  States endorse Perpetual Edict, 77–8
  oppose William becoming captain-general, 138

Vane, Sir Henry, 49
Veilgeld, 45
Vigo, 17
Violet, Thomas, 87, 111
Virginia, 28, 35, 36, 86
Vlie, anchorage, 44, 172
Vlieland, 22, 172, 173
Vlissingen, 21, 160, 192, 195, 207
VOC, 22, 68, 69, 90, 154, 185, 219
  trading system, 32–4, 224
  'actions', 64
  Downing denounces, 76, 147
  and second war, 27, 160–3
  losses, 212

Wadden zee, 69
Wages, seamen's, 47
Walcheren, 196, 201, 203

Warwick, Sir Philip, 93
Werden, Sir John, 203
Wesel, 187
Westerschelling, 172
West India Company, 12, 35–7, 68, 143, 145
  Downing denounces, 76
  and west Africa, 147–8, 149–51
Wielings, anchorage, 20, 21, 24, 132, 191, 205–6
William II, 45, 65, 66, 77, 82–3
William III, 48, 65, 77, 135, 136, 178, 193, 195
  lacks English support, 74–6
  enters Council of State, 78
  and captain-generalship, 186–7
  and defences, 188
  army command, 78–9
  and 1672 alteration, 79–81
  intended as allied puppet, 9, 14
  offers Charles concessions, 14, 194, 196, 197
  English mistaken about, 196
  and sovereignty, 197
  intervenes in English affairs, 102–3, 180, 211, 213–14, 215–16
  model for 1688, 103, 180, 216
William Frederick, 66
Wildt, David and Job de, 46
Wilson, Charles, 9–10
Wirtz, Paulus, 78
With, Witte de, 18, 123
  in command, 117–18
  superseded, 118, 120
  succeeds Tromp, 133
  sortie and gale losses, 134
Witt, Cornelis, 174, 176–7, 190, 193, 220
Witt, Johan de, vital leadership, 6, 11, 47–8, 66, 72, 76–7, 127, 159, 164–5, 170–1
  and trade interests, 12, 69–70, 73, 220
  pressures on, 71, 138, 220
  and True Freedom, 66–7
  and naval affairs, 45–6, 48, 157, 190, 193
  and strategy, 27, 134, 155, 190, 205
  sails with fleet, 13, 21, 163, 164–5, 173–4
  averse to appeasement, 12, 76, 144, 145, 148–9
  and Downing, 74–7, 151–2, 155
  orders African reprisals, 36, 76, 150

initiates Chatham attack, 174–6
and William's pretensions, 142, 186–7
faces French threat, 167, 184–6
neglects army, 78–9
position collapses, 78–81, 187
lynched, 220
Woolwich, 62
Wren, Matthew, 55

Yarmouth, Great, 22, 202–3, 206
York, James duke of, *see* James

Zaandam, 7, 46
Zas, Gerbrand, 99–100, 198, 199

Zeeland, province, 7, 11, 80, 171, 207–8
jealousies, 65
Orangist sympathies, 75
and London embassy, 154
privateers, 27, 36, 192
pensionary denounces Commonwealth,
84
and captain-generalship, 138
and peace (1653–4), 140–1
English plan to invade, 201
Zuyder zee, mini-war on, 191
Zwolle, 188